EUROPE'S LAST SUMMER

EUROPE'S LAST SUMMER

Who Started the Great War in 1914?

DAVID FROMKIN

ALFRED A. KNOPF ✿ NEW YORK 2004

All photographs are reprinted with the kind permission of the Illustrated London News
Library excerpt: "Colonel Edward House" and "Count Graf Berchtold" (Hulton-Deutsch
Collection/Corbis); "German General Erich von Falkenhayn" (Corbis); and "German
Admiral Alfred von Tirpitz" (Bettman/Corbis).

Library of Congress Cataloging-in-Publication Data
Fromkin, David.
Europe's last summer : who started the Great War in 1914? / by David Fromkin.—1st ed.
p. cm.
Includes bibliographical references.
ISBN 0-375-41156-9
1. World War, 1914–1918—Causes.   I. Title: Who started the Great War in 1914?.
II. Title. D511.F746 2004
940.3'11—dc22   2003027391

Manufactured in the United States of America
First Edition

For Alain Silvera—

The peremptory transition from an apparently profound peace to violent general war in a few mid-summer weeks in 1914 continues to defy attempts at explanation.

—JOHN KEEGAN, *The First World War*

CONTENTS

PART SEVEN
COUNTDOWN

PART EIGHT
THE MYSTERY SOLVED

EPILOGUE

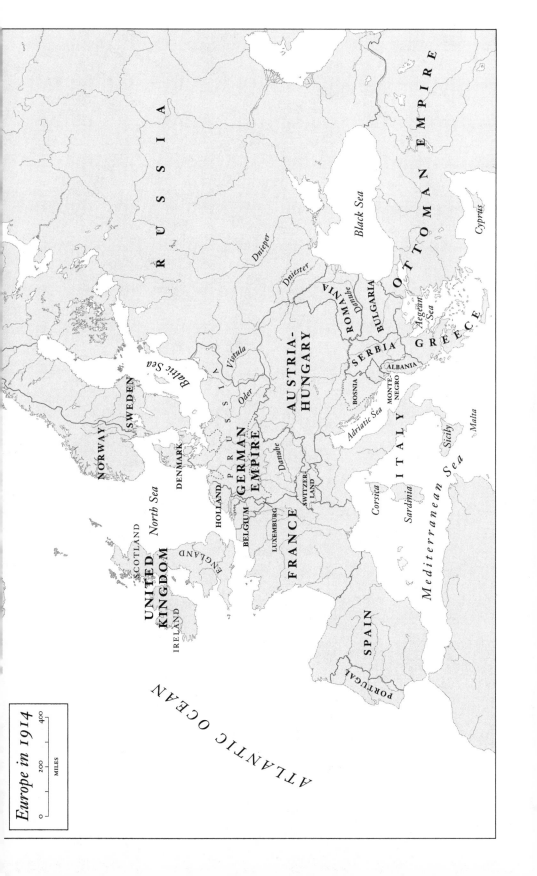

Europe in 1914

MILES
0   200   400

ATLANTIC OCEAN

NORWAY

SWEDEN

UNITED KINGDOM

SCOTLAND

IRELAND

ENGLAND

North Sea

Baltic Sea

DENMARK

HOLLAND

BELGIUM

LUXEMBURG

R U S S I A

P R U S S I A

Vistula

Oder

GERMAN EMPIRE

Danube

FRANCE

SWITZER-
LAND

AUSTRIA-
HUNGARY

Danube

ITALY

Corsica

Sardinia

SPAIN

PORTUGAL

Mediterranean Sea

Sicily

Malta

Adriatic Sea

BOSNIA

MONTE-
NEGRO

ALBANIA

SERBIA

ROMANIA

BULGARIA

Dniester

Dnieper

Black Sea

OTTOMAN EMPIRE

GREECE

Aegean Sea

Cyprus

EUROPE'S LAST SUMMER

PROLOGUE:

(i) *Out of the Blue*

Shortly after eleven o'clock at night on Sunday, December 29, 1997, United Airlines Flight 826, a Boeing 747 carrying 374 passengers and 19 crew, was two hours into its scheduled trip across the Pacific from Tokyo to Honolulu. It had reached its assigned cruising altitude of between 31,000 and 33,000 feet. Meal service was about to be completed. It had been an uneventful trip.

In a terrifying instant everything changed. The plane was struck, without warning, by a force that was invisible. The aircraft abruptly nosed up; then it nosed down into a freefall. Screaming bodies were flung about promiscuously, colliding with ceilings and with serving carts. A thirty-two-year-old Japanese woman was killed and 102 people were injured. Regaining control of the jumbo jet, the captain and cockpit crew guided Flight 826 back to the Japanese airport from which it had taken off hours before.

What was so frightening about this episode was its mysteriousness. Until the moment of impact, the flight had been a normal one. There had been no reason to expect that it would be anything else. There had been no warning: no flash of lightning across the sky. You could not see it coming, whatever "it" may have been. Passengers had no idea what had hit them and airline companies were in no position to assure the public that something similar would not happen again.

Experts quoted by the communications media were of the opinion that Flight 826 had fallen victim to what they called "clear air turbulence." They likened this to a horizontal tornado, but one that you could not see. Some of the experts who were interviewed expressed the hope that within a few years some sort of sensing technology would be developed to detect these invisible storms before they strike. Transparency, the public learned from this episode, signifies little; a pacific sky can rise up in wrath as suddenly as can a pacific ocean.

Something like such an attack of clear air turbulence is supposed by some to have happened to European civilization in 1914 during its passage from the nineteenth to the twentieth century. The world of the 1890s and 1900s had been, not unlike our own age, a time of international congresses, disarmament conferences, globalization of the world economy, and schemes to establish some sort of league of nations to outlaw war. A long stretch of peace and prosperity was expected by the public to go on indefinitely.

Instead, the European world abruptly plunged out of control, crashing and exploding into decades of tyranny, world war, and mass murder. What tornado wrecked civilized Old Europe and the world it then ruled? In retrospect, it may be less of a mystery than some of those who lived through it imagined. The years 1913 and 1914 were ones of dangers and troubles. There were warning signs in the early decades of the twentieth century that catastrophe might well lie ahead; we can see that now, and military and political leaders could see it then.

The sky out of which Europe fell was not empty; on the contrary, it was alive with processes and powers. The forces that were to devastate it—nationalism, socialism, imperialism, and the like—had been in motion for a long time. The European world already was buffeted by high winds. It had been traversing dangerous skies for a long time. The captain and the crew had known it. But the passengers, taken completely by surprise, insistently kept asking: why had they received no warning?

(i i) *The Importance of the Question*

In the summer of 1914 a war broke out in Europe that then spread to Africa, the Middle East, Asia, the Pacific, and the Americas. Known now, somewhat inaccurately, as the First World War, it ended by becoming in many ways the largest conflict that the planet had ever known. It deserved the name by which it was called at the time: the Great War.

To enter the lists, countries of the earth ranged themselves into one or another of two worldwide coalitions. One, led by Great Britain,* France, and Russia, was called the Triple Entente;† the other, led by Germany and Austria-Hungary, was known at first as the Triple Alliance.§ Between them the two coalitions mobilized about 65 million troops. In Germany and France, nations that gambled their entire manhood on the outcome, 80 percent of all males between the ages of fifteen and forty-nine were called to the colors. In the ensuing clashes of arms they were slaughtered.

More than 20 million soldiers and civilians perished in the Great War, and an additional 21 million were wounded. Millions more fell victim to the diseases that the war unleashed: upwards of 20 million people died in the influenza pandemic of 1918–19 alone.

The figures, staggering though they are, fail to tell the whole story or to convey the full impact of the war on the world of 1914. The consequences of the changes wrought by the crisis of European civilization are too many to specify and, in their range and in their depth, made it the turning point in modern history. That would be true even if, as some maintain, the war merely accelerated some of the changes to which it led.

On August 8, 1914, only four days after Great Britain entered the war, the London *Economist* described it as "perhaps the greatest tragedy of human history." That may well remain true. In 1979 the

---

*Beginning in 1801, the official title of Great Britain was the "United Kingdom of Great Britain and Ireland"; for short, the United Kingdom.
†Called "the Allies" during the war.
§With Italy as the third member in peacetime. Called "the Central Powers" during the war.

distinguished American diplomat and historian George Kennan wrote that he had "come to see the First World War, as I think many reasonably thoughtful people have learned to see it, as *the* grand seminal catastrophe of this century."

Fritz Stern, one of the foremost scholars of German affairs, writes of "the first calamity of the twentieth century, the Great War, from which all other calamities sprang."

The military, political, economic, and social earthquakes brought about a redrawing of the map of the world. Empires and dynasties were swept away. New countries took their place. Disintegration of the political structure of the globe continued over the course of the twentieth century. Today the earth is divided into about four times as many independent states as existed when the Europeans went to war in 1914. Many of the new entities—Jordan, Iraq, and Saudi Arabia are examples that come to mind—are countries that never existed before.

The Great War gave birth to terrible forces that would plague the rest of the century. To drive Russia out of the war, the German government financed Lenin's Bolshevik communists, and introduced Lenin himself into Russia in 1917—in Winston Churchill's words, "in the same way that you might send a phial containing a culture of typhoid or of cholera to be poured into the water supply of a great city." Bolshevism was only the first of such war-born furies, followed in years to come by fascism and Nazism.

Yet the war also set in motion two of the great liberation movements of the twentieth century. As Europe tore itself apart, its overlordship of the rest of the planet came undone, and over the course of the century, literally billions of people achieved their independence. Women, too, in parts of the world, broke free from some of the shackles of the past, arguably as a direct consequence of their involvement in war work—jobs in factories and in the armed forces—beginning in 1914.

Another kind of liberation, a wide-ranging freedom from restraint, came out of the Great War and has expanded ever since in behavior, sex life, manners, dress, language, and the arts. Not everybody believes it to be a good thing that so many rules and restrictions have gone by the way. But whether for good or ill, the world has traveled a long way—from the Victorian age to the twenty-first century—along paths that were blasted out for it by the warriors of 1914.

In searching for the origins of any of the great issues that have faced the world during the twentieth century, or that confront it today, it is remarkable how often we come back to the Great War. As George Kennan observed: "all the lines of inquiry, it seems to me, lead back to it." Afterwards the choices narrowed. The United States and even Great Britain had a choice, for example, of whether or not to enter the First World War—indeed disagreement has persisted ever since as to whether they were wise to do so—but, realistically, the two countries had little or no choice at all about whether or not to join battle in the Second.

There was nothing inevitable about the progression from the earlier conflict to the later one. The long fuse could have been cut at many points along the way from 1914 to 1939, but nobody did cut it. So the First World War did in fact lead to the Second, even though it need not have done so, and the Second, whether or not it needed to do so, led to the Cold War. In 1991 historians Steven E. Miller and Sean M. Lynn-Jones maintained: "Most observers describe the present period of international politics as the 'post–Cold War' era but in many ways our age is better defined as the 'post–World War I' era."

From the start, the explosion of 1914 seemed to set off a series of chain reactions, and the serious consequences were soon apparent to contemporaries: In the Introduction to *The Magic Mountain* (1924), Thomas Mann wrote of "the Great War, in the beginning of which so much began that has scarcely yet left off beginning."

Nor has it entirely left off today. On April 21, 2001, the *New York Times* reported from France the return to their homes of thousands of people who had been evacuated temporarily because of a threat from munitions left over from World War I and stored near them. These included shells and mustard gas. The evacuees had been allowed to return home after fifty tons of the more dangerous munitions had been removed. But a hundred tons of the lethal materials remained—and remain. So munitions from the 1914 war may yet explode in the twenty-first century.

Indeed, in a sense they already have. On September 11, 2001, the Muslim fundamentalist suicide attacks on the World Trade Center in New York City destroyed the heart of lower Manhattan and took some three thousand lives. Osama bin Laden, the terrorist chieftain who seemingly conjured up this horror and who threatened more, in his first televised statement afterwards described it as vengeance for what had happened eighty years earlier. By this he presumably meant the intrusion of the Christian European empires into the hitherto Muslim-governed Middle East in the aftermath of—and as a consequence of—the First World War. Bin Laden's sympathizers who hijacked jumbo jets had smashed them into the twin towers in pursuance of a quarrel seemingly rooted in the conflicts of 1914.

Similarly, the Iraq crisis that escalated in 2002–03 drove journalists and broadcast news personalities to their telephones, asking history professors from leading American universities how Iraq had emerged as a state from the embers of the First World War. It was a relevant question, for had there been no world war in 1914, there might well have been no Iraq in 2002.

It was indeed the seminal event of modern times.

What was the First World War about? How did it happen? Who started it? Why did it break out where and when it did? "Millions of deaths, and words, later, historians still have not agreed why," as the "Millennium Special Edition" of *The Economist* (January 1, 1000–December 31, 1999) remarked, adding that "none of it need have happened." From the outset everybody said that the outbreak of war in 1914 was literally triggered by a Bosnian Serb schoolboy when he shot and killed the heir to the Austrian and Hungarian thrones. But practically everybody also agrees that the assassination provided not the cause, but merely the occasion, for first the Balkans, then Europe, and then the rest of the earth to take up arms.

The disproportion between the schoolboy's crime and the conflagration in which the globe was consumed, beginning thirty-seven days later, was too absurd for observers to credit the one as the cause of the other. Tens of millions of people could not be losing their lives, they felt, because one man and his wife—two people of whom many of them had never heard—had lost theirs. It did not seem possible. It could not, everyone said, be true.

Because the Great War was so enormous an event and so fraught with consequences, and because we want to keep anything similar from happening in the future, the inquiry as to how it occurred has become not only the most challenging but also the biggest question in modern history. But it remains elusive; in the words of the historian Laurence Lafore, "the war was many things, not one, and the meanings of the word 'cause' are also many."

. . .

In the 1940s and 1950s scholars tended to believe that they had learned all that there was to be known about the origins of the war, and that all that remained to be disputed was interpretation of the evidence. Beginning in the 1960s, however, sparked by the research of the great German historian Fritz Fischer—of whose views more will be said later—new information has come to light, notably from German, Austrian, and Serbian sources, and hardly a year goes by now without the appearance of new monographs adding considerably to our knowledge. Fischer inspired scholars to comb the archives for what was hidden. What follows in this book is an attempt to look at the old questions in the light of the new knowledge, to summarize the data, and then to draw some conclusions from it.

When and where did the march toward the war of 1914 begin? Recently, in a Boston classroom, I asked university students to pinpoint the first steps—before 1908—along the way. From their responses, the following may illustrate how many roads can be imagined to have led to Sarajevo.

The fourth century A.D.   The decision to divide the Roman Empire between the Latin-speaking West and the Greek-speaking East had lasting consequences. The cultural divide that ramified into two different branches of Christianity, two calendars, and two rival scripts (the Latin and the Cyrillic) persisted. The Roman Catholic Austrians and the Greek Orthodox Serbs, whose quarrel provided the occasion for the 1914 war, were, in that sense, fated to be enemies.

The seventh century.   The Slavs, who were to become Europe's largest ethnic group, moved into the Balkans, where the Teutons already had arrived. The conflict between Slavic and Germanic peoples became a recurring theme of European history, and in the twentieth century pitted Teuton Germans and Austrians against Slavic Russians and Serbs.

The eleventh century.   The formal split between Roman Catholic and Greek Orthodox Christianity generated a conflict of religious faith along the same fault line as those of ethnic group, alphabet, and culture—Roman versus Greek—a fault line that threatened the southeast of Europe and was followed by the political earthquake that struck in 1914.

The fifteenth century.   The conquest of Christian eastern and central Europe by the Muslim Ottoman (or Turkish) Empire deprived the peoples of the Balkans of centuries of experience in self-government. That perhaps contributed to the violence and fractiousness of that area in the years that led up to the 1914 war—and perhaps contributed to bringing it about.

The sixteenth century.   The Protestant Reformation split Western Christendom. It divided the German peoples politically, and led to the curious relationship between Germany and Austria that lay at the heart of the crisis of July 1914.

The seventeenth century.   The beginning of the centuries-long Ottoman retreat from Europe meant that the Turks were abandoning valuable lands that the Christian Great Powers coveted. Desire to seize those lands fed the rivalry between Austria and Russia that set off war in 1914.

1870–71.   The creation of the German Empire and its annexation of French territory in the aftermath of the Franco-Prussian War made another European war likely as soon as France recovered sufficiently to try to take back what it had lost.

1890.   The German emperor dismissed his Chancellor—his prime minister—Prince Otto von Bismarck. The new Chancellor reversed Bismarck's policy of allying with both Austria and Russia to keep the peace between them. Instead, Germany sided with Austria against Russia in the struggle to control the Balkans, which encouraged Austria to follow a dangerously bellicose policy that seemed likely to provoke an eventual Russian response.

1890s.   Rebuffed by Germany, and seeing no other alternative, reactionary, monarchical Russia was drawn into an alliance with republican France. This convinced Germany's leaders that war was inevitable sooner or later, and that Germany stood a better chance of winning if it were waged sooner rather than later.

1900s.   Germany's attempt to rival Britain as a naval power was seen in London as a vital threat.

1903.   In a bloody coup d'état in Serbia, army officers belonging to a secret society butchered their pro-Austrian king and queen and replaced them with a rival dynasty that was pro-Russian. Austrian leaders reacted by planning to punish Serbia—a plan that if carried out threatened to lead to a dangerously wider conflict.

1905.   The First Moroccan Crisis was a complicated affair. It will be described in Chapter 12. In it Germany's aggressive diplomacy had the unintended effect of unifying the other countries against it. Britain moved from mere friendship with France—the Entente Cordiale—to something closer to informal alliance, including conversations between the two governments and military staff talks, and later to agreement and conversation with France's ally Russia. There was a hardening of European alignments into rival and potentially enemy blocs: France, Britain, and Russia on one side, and an isolated Germany—with only halfhearted support from Austria-Hungary and Italy—on the other.

To some extent all of these were right answers. Other dates—among them 1908, which is discussed in the pages that follow—also served as the starting points of fuse lines that led to the explosions of 1914. All of them can be said to have contributed something to the coming of war.

Yet, in a sense all of them are wrong answers, too, to the question of why the conflict came. Thirty-seven days before the Great War the European world was comfortably at peace. Europe's leaders were starting their summer vacations and none of them expected to be disturbed while away. What went wrong?

All of the fuse lines identified by my students had been as dangerous to the peace of Europe in 1910 and 1912 as they were in 1914. Since they had not led to war in 1910 or 1912, why did they in 1914? The question is not only why war came, but why war came in the European summer of 1914; not why war? but—why *this* war?

Why did things happen as they did and not otherwise is a question that historians have been asking ever since Herodotus and Thucydides, Greeks of the fifth century B.C., started to do so more than twenty-five hundred years ago. Whether such questions can be answered with any accuracy remains debatable; often so many tributaries flow into the stream that it is difficult to say which is its real source.

In its magnitude and many dimensions, the First World War is perhaps a supreme example of the complexity that challenges and baffles historians. Arthur Balfour, a prewar British Prime Minister, longtime Conservative statesman, philosopher, and named sponsor of the Jewish state in Palestine, is quoted somewhere as having said the war was too big to be comprehended.

, Not merely, therefore, is the explanation of the war the biggest question in modern history; it is an exemplary question, compelling us to reexamine what we mean by such words as "cause." There were causes—many of them—for Europe's Great Powers to be disposed to go to war with one another. There were other causes—immediate ones, with which this book is concerned—for them to have gone to war when and where and how they did.

(i i i) *A Summer to Remember*

To the man or woman in the streets of the Western world—someone who was alive in the vibrant early years of the twentieth century— nothing would have seemed further away than war. In those years men who dreamed of battlefield adventure had been hard pressed to find a war in which they could participate. In the year 1901, and in the thirteen years that followed, the peoples of western Europe and the English-speaking Americas were becoming consumers rather than warriors. They looked forward to more: more progress, more prosperity, more peace. The United States at that time (commented an English observer) "sailed upon a summer sea," but so did Great Britain, France, and others. There had been no war among the Great Powers for nearly half a century, and the globalization of the world economy suggested that war had become a thing of the past. The culmination of those years in the hot, sun-drenched, gorgeous summer of 1914, the most beautiful within living memory, was remembered by many Europeans as a kind of Eden. Stefan Zweig spoke for many when he wrote that he had rarely experienced a summer "more luxuriant, more beautiful, and, I am tempted to say, more summery."

Middle- and upper-class Britons in particular saw themselves as living in an idyllic world in which economic realities would keep Europe's Great Powers from waging war on one another. For those with a comfortable income, the world in their time was more free than it is today. According to the historian A. J. P. Taylor, "until August 1914 a sensible, law-abiding Englishman could pass through life and hardly notice the existence of the state." You could live anywhere you liked and as you liked. You could go to practically anywhere in the world without anyone's permission. For the most part, you needed no passports, and many had none. The French geographer André Siegfried traveled all around the world with no identification other than his visiting card: not even a business card, but a personal one.

John Maynard Keynes remembered it, with wonder, as an era without exchange controls or customs barriers. You could bring anything you liked into Britain or send anything out. You could take any amount of currency with you when you traveled, or send (or bring back) any amount of currency; your bank did not report it to the government, as it does today. And if you decided to invest any amount of money in almost any country abroad, there was nobody whose permission had to be asked, nor was permission needed to withdraw that investment and any profits it may have earned when you wanted to do so.

Even more than today, it was a time of free capital flows and free movements of people and goods. An outstanding current study of the world as of 2000 tells us that there was more globalization before the 1914 war than there is now: "much of the final quarter of the twentieth century was spent merely recovering ground lost in the previous seventy-five years."

Economic and financial intermingling and interdependence were among the powerful trends that made it seem that warfare among the major European powers had become impractical—and, indeed, obsolete.

One could easily feel safe in that world. Americans felt it at least as much if not more than Europeans. The historian and diplomat George Kennan remembers that before the 1914 war Americans felt a sense of security "such as I suppose no people had ever had since the days of the Roman Empire." They felt little need for government. Until 1913, when an appropriate amendment to the Constitution was ratified, the Congress was deemed to lack even the power to enact taxes on income.

Stefan Zweig, the Austrian-Jewish author, remembering those antebellum years decades later, remarked that "When I attempt to find a simple formula for the period in which I grew up, prior to the First World War, I hope that I convey its fullness by calling it the Golden Age of Security. Everything in our almost thousand-year-old Austrian monarchy seemed based on permanency."

In the Western world, it was by and large true that ordinary people felt no apprehension. As will be seen, there were leaders who worried, but in the winter and spring of 1914 not even they expected war to break out in the summer.

France, it is true, would have liked to recover territories taken away by Germany decades before, but those well placed to judge were certain that France would not start a war to get them back. Russia, as France's ally, was well informed on French official thinking; and the Russian Prime Minister reported to the Czar on December 13, 1913, that "All French statesmen want quiet and peace. They are willing to work with Germany." These feelings seemed to be reciprocated by the Germans. John Keiger, a leading scholar of the politics of those years, has argued: "There is no doubt that at the end of 1913 Franco-German relations were on a better footing than for years." Germany feared an eventual war with Russia, but in 1913, Berlin recognized that Russia was in no condition to wage a war, and would not be able to do so for years to come. It was axiomatic that Britain wanted peace. So, as Professor Keiger writes, "the spring and summer of 1914 were marked in Europe by a period of exceptional calm." None of the European Great Powers believed that any one of the others was about to launch a war of aggression against it—at least not in the immediate future.

Like airline passengers on United Airlines Flight 826, Europeans and Americans in the glorious last days of June 1914 cruised ahead above a summer sea and beneath a cloudless sky—until they were hit by a bolt that they wrongly believed came from out of the blue.

PART ONE

EUROPE'S TENSIONS

CHAPTER 1: **EMPIRES CLASH**

A t the start of the twentieth century Europe was at the peak of human accomplishment. In industry, technology, and science it had advanced beyond all previous societies. In wealth, knowledge, and power it exceeded any civilization that ever had existed.

Europe is almost the smallest of the continents: 3 or 4 million square miles in extent, depending on how you define its eastern frontiers. By contrast, the largest continent, Asia, has 17 million square miles. Indeed, some geographers viewed Europe as a mere peninsula of Asia.

Yet, by the beginning of the 1900s, the Great Powers of Europe—a mere handful of countries—had come to rule most of the earth. Between them, Austria-Hungary, France, Germany, Great Britain, Italy, and Russia dominated Europe, Africa, Asia, the Pacific, and even substantial parts of the Western Hemisphere. Of what little remained, much belonged to less powerful European states: Belgium,

Holland, Portugal, and Spain. When all of its empires were added together, Europe spanned the globe.

But the European empires were of greatly unequal size and strength, an imbalance that led to instability; and as they were rivals, their leaders were continuously matching them against one another in their minds, trying to guess who would defeat whom in case of war and with whom, therefore, it would be best to ally. Military prowess was seen as a supreme value in an age that mistakenly believed Charles Darwin's survival of the fittest to refer to the most murderous rather than (as we now understand it) to the best adapted.

The British Empire was the wealthiest, most powerful, and largest of the Great Powers. It controlled over a quarter of the land surface and a quarter of the population of the globe, and its navy dominated the world ocean that occupies more than 70 percent of the planet. Germany, a newly created confederation led by militarist Prussia, commanded the most powerful land army. Russia, the world's largest country, a backward giant that sprawled across two continents, remained an enigma; enfeebled by a war it lost to Japan in 1904–05, and by the revolution of 1905, it turned itself around by industrializing and arming with financial backing from France. France, despite exploiting a large empire, no longer was a match for Germany and therefore backed Russia as a counterweight to Teutonic power. The Dual Monarchy of Austria-Hungary ruled a variety of nationalities who were restless and often in conflict. Italy, a new state, as a latecomer aspiring to take its place among the powers, hungered to be treated as an equal.

It was commonly believed at the time that the road to wealth and greatness for European powers was through the acquisition of more colonies. The problem was that the Great Powers already controlled so much of the world that there was little left for others to take. Repeatedly, in going forward, the European powers ran up against one another. Time and again, war threatened, and only skilled diplomacy and self-restraint enabled them to pull back from the brink. The decades before 1914 were punctuated by crises, almost any one of which might have led to war.

It was no accident that some of the more conspicuous of these crises resulted from moves by Germany. It was because Germany's emperor—the Kaiser, or Caesar—in changing his Chancellor in 1890 also changed his government's policy. Otto von Bismarck, the iron-willed leader who had created Germany in 1870–71, was skeptical of imperialism.* Far from believing that overseas colonies bring additional wealth and power, he apparently viewed them as a drain on both. In order to distract France from thoughts of recovering territories in Europe that Germany had seized—in Alsace-Lorraine—Bismarck encouraged and supported France in seeking new acquisitions in North Africa and Asia. As such a policy would bring France into frequent collisions with imperial England and Russia, thus dividing Germany's potential rivals, it suited all of Bismarck's purposes.

Post-Bismarck Germany coveted the overseas territories that the Iron Chancellor had regarded as mere fool's gold. It positioned itself to take part in the coming partition of China. But the rulers in Berlin had come to the game too late. Germany no longer could win an empire on a scale proportioned to its position as the greatest military power in Europe. There was not world enough. No more continents were there for the taking: no more Africas, no more Americas. Nonetheless—heedlessly—Wilhelmine Germany displayed an interest in overseas land.

As France moved deeper into Morocco at the beginning of the twentieth century to round out its North African empire, Germany, instead of offering encouragement and support, as Bismarck would have done, stepped in to oppose. These German moves misfired and sparked two of the more high-profile international crises of those years: the Morocco crises of 1905–06 and of 1911. To the German government these maneuvers may have been mere probes, but they caused genuine alarm in Europe.

In retrospect, it is clear the problem was that Germany's post-1890 hunger for empire could no longer be satisfied except by taking overseas territories away from the other European countries. This was not something likely to be accomplished by peaceful means. Could Germany therefore content itself with remaining the leading military and industrial power on the Continent but with African and Asian empires smaller than those of England or France? Germans themselves disagreed, of course, about what the answer to that question ought to be, and the climate of opinion was changing. Germany in

---

*For reasons not entirely clear, Bismarck briefly departed from this policy in the early 1880s, when Germany acquired a small number of colonies.

1914 was the only country on the Continent with more industrial than farm workers, and the growing strength of its socialist and working-class masses suggested that the nation might be compelled to focus its attention on solving problems at home rather than on adventures abroad. Alternatively, it suggested that Germany's leaders would have to pursue an aggressive foreign policy in order to distract attention from problems at home that remained unsolved.

CHAPTER 2: **CLASSES STRUGGLE**

Nor was Germany alone in being divided against itself. Europe before the war was in the grip of social and economic upheavals that were reshaping its structure and its politics. The Industrial Revolution that had begun in eighteenth-century France and England continued, at an accelerated pace, to effect radical changes in those two countries, as well as in Germany, and was making similar changes in others. Agrarian Europe, in part still feudal, and smokestack Europe, bringing modernity, lived literally at the same time but figuratively centuries apart. Some still were living as though in the fourteenth century, with their pack animals and their slow, almost unchanging village rhythms, while others inhabited the crowded, sprawling cities of the twentieth century, driven by the newly invented internal combustion machine and informed by the telegraph.

At the same time, the growth of an urban factory-working population in the Industrial Revolution brought conflict between that population and factory owners over wages and working conditions. It also pitted both workers and manufacturers, on the one hand, who could expand their exports only in a free-trade world, against farmers, who needed protection, and the cash-poor landed gentry on the other. Class became a line of division and loyalty—the chief line according to many. Domestic strife threatened all the countries of Western Europe.

In Britain, the Labour party was formed to speak for a working class no longer content to be represented by the Liberal party, which sympathized with wage-earners but spoke as the voice of the professional classes and even some of the well-born. On the Continent, labor also turned to socialism, with growing success at the polls: in the German elections of 1912, the Social Democrats emerged as the largest single party in the Reichstag. It should have been some consolation to German and British conservatives that workers in their countries usually expressed their socialism peacefully by voting rather than (as Syndicalists did in France, Spain, and Italy) by strikes, riots, and terrorist attacks. But governments, in these times of frequent war crises, worried that their peoples might not support them if war broke out. The issue had another side to it: foreign adventures could distract from class and social conflict and bring the people instead to rally around the flag. Which would it be? Would class and social clashes divide, or would international conflicts unite?

CHAPTER 3: **NATIONS QUARREL**

To socialist internationalism, the rival was nationalism, a passion that increasingly was taking priority over all else in the minds and hearts of Europeans as the nineteenth century departed and the twentieth arrived. Even Britain contracted the fever. Ireland—or at any rate its Roman Catholic majority—agitated violently for autonomy or independence, and clashed with the Protestants of Ulster who prepared to take up arms to defend the union with Great Britain.

Edwardian England already was a surprisingly violent country, torn by such issues as industrial wages and working conditions and also by the cause of woman suffrage. It was rocked, too, by a constitutional crisis that was also a class crisis. The crisis focused on two interrelated issues: the budget, and the power of the hereditary House of Lords to veto legislation enacted by the popularly elected House of Commons. Between them these conflicts eroded the sense of national solidarity.

Now that the country also was polarized on the question of home rule for Ireland, large sections of the army and of the Unionist-Conservative party seemed prepared to defy law and government in order to hold on to the union with Ireland. The precedent set by the United States in 1861 was troubling. Would there be a British civil war?

On the continent of Europe the flames of nationalism threatened to burn down even structures that had endured for centuries. Hapsburg-ruled Austria, a holdover from the Middle Ages that until recently had been headed by the so-called Holy Roman Empire, remained, as it had been in the nineteenth century, the principal enemy of European nationalism. The two great new nations of Germany and Italy had been carved out of domains that the Hapsburgs once had dominated. At universities, coffeehouses, and in the dimly lit hiding places of secret societies and terrorists, in the Balkans and Central Europe in the early years of the twentieth century, plans were being hatched by ethnic groups that aspired to achieve something similar. The nationalists were in contact with one another and with nihilists, anarchists, socialists, and others who lived and conspired in the obscurity of the political underground. It was there that Serbs, Croats, Czechs, and others plotted to disrupt and destroy the Austrian Empire.

The Hapsburgs were a dynasty that over the course of a thousand years had come to rule a motley collection of territories and peoples—a multinational empire that held no prospect of ever becoming a homogeneous national state. Centered in German-speaking Vienna, Austria-Hungary encompassed a variety of languages, ethnic groups, and climates. Its 50 million people comprised perhaps eleven or so nations or parts thereof. Many of its lands originally had been dowries that had come with marriage to territorial heiresses: whatever else you might say about them, the Hapsburg family wedded well. At its height in the sixteenth century, when it included Spain and much of the New World, the Hapsburg family holdings comprised the largest empire in the world. Hapsburg roots went back to Christmas Day 800, when Charlemagne the Frank was crowned emperor of the Roman Empire in the West by the pope. As Holy Roman Emperor, a post to which a Hapsburg was almost always elected from the fifteenth century until it was abolished in the early nineteenth century, the Hapsburgs dominated Central Europe, including its many German- and Italian-speaking political entities.

In the aftermath of the 1848 revolutions, they lost their Italian possessions to the newly unified Italy, and they were excluded from Prussian-organized, newly unified Germany in 1870–71. Once the leader of Europe's Germans and Italians, the Hapsburg emperor was left as the odd man out.

Left alone with a German core—of Austria's 28 million inhabitants, only 10 million were German—and a restive empire of Central European and Balkan peoples, mostly Slavs, the Hapsburg ruler Franz Joseph found himself presiding over a political entity that arguably was not viable. The solution that he found in 1867 was a compact between Austria and a Hungary that was ruled by its Magyar minority, in which Franz Joseph served both as emperor of Austria and king of Hungary. The Dual Monarchy, as it was called, was a state in which Austria and Hungary each had its own parliament and its own Prime Minister, but there was only one foreign minister, one war minister, one finance minister—and, of course, only one monarch of both the Austrian empire and the Hungarian kingdom. The peoples who ruled were the minority Germans of Austria and the Magyar minority in Hungary. What they attempted to rule, in the words of one Hapsburg statesman, was "eight nations, seventeen countries, twenty parliamentary groups, twenty-seven parties"—and a spectrum of peoples and religions.

Europe was rapidly becoming a continent of nation-states. As it entered the twentieth century, a chief weakness of Austria-Hungary was that it was on what looked to be the wrong side of history. But what was threatening to bring it down was a force that was not entirely progressive either; nationalism had its atavistic aspects.

Whether considered to be a political philosophy or its contrary, a type of mass delirium, nationalism was ambivalent. It was the democratic belief that each nation had the right to become independent and to rule itself. But it also was the illiberal insistence that nonmembers of the nation should assimilate, be denied civic rights, be expelled, or even be killed. Nationalism was hating some as an expression of loving others. To add to the murkiness, there was no agreement on what constitutes a nationality. The 1911 edition of the *Encyclopaedia Britannica* calls it a "vague term" and remarked that "a 'nationality' . . . represents a common feeling and an organized claim rather than distinct attributes which can be comprised in a strict definition." So there was no general agreement on which groups were nations and which were not. It was one more issue for Europe to fight about. Some thought—some still think—that it was the main thing that Europe had to fight about.

In the absence of scientific measurement of public opinion through polls, historians are unable to tell us with any certainty what the people of Europe thought or felt in the pre-1914 age. This leaves a gap in our knowledge. It is not so great a gap as it would be today, for a century ago the public played little role in the formation of foreign policy. But public opinion was of some significance, in that decision-makers presumably did take it into account—to the extent that they knew what it was.

Evidence suggests that the most widespread feeling in Europe at the time was xenophobia: a great deal of hostility toward one another. The ethnic groups of the Balkans provided a conspicuous example of mutual hatred, but countries far more advanced exhibited such tendencies too.

England is a case in point. It had been in conflict or at war with France on and off since the eleventh century—in other words, for about a thousand years. Anti-French feeling remained high well into the twentieth century. Even during the First World War, in which the two countries were allies, British and French officers schemed and maneuvered against one another to take control of the postwar Arab Middle East.

Britain came into collision with Russia much later than it did with France, but once they did clash it was all across the board. The two countries opposed each other on one point after another, economically, politically, militarily, and ideologically, until Britons grew to object to Russians not merely for what they did but for who they were. The story is recounted at length in a classic: *The Genesis of Russophobia in Great Britain* by John Howes Gleason.

Germany came into existence as a state only in 1871, and seemed to be a possible ally—the idea was discussed at the highest levels more than once—but the British became suspicious of Germany and then antagonistic. This was for a variety of reasons, thoroughly discussed in Paul Kennedy's definitive account, *The Rise of the Anglo-German Antagonism.*

So the British, though they believed themselves to be open-minded, detested the peoples of the next three ranking Great Powers: the French, the Russians, and the Germans.

The questions that European statesmen attempted to resolve at the dawn of the twentieth century therefore were being faced against a background of peoples who harbored hostile, sometimes warlike, sentiments.

The rise of independent mass-circulation newspapers in the nineteenth century in such European countries as England and France brought to bear upon decision-making yet another powerful influence impossible to calculate precisely. Appealing to popular fears and prejudices in order to win circulation, the press seems to have exacerbated hatred and divisions among Europeans. Of the anti-German British press and the anti-British German press, the German emperor wrote to the King of England in 1901: "The Press is awful on both sides."

CHAPTER 4: **COUNTRIES ARM**

Nationalism, as preached by Giuseppe Mazzini and his disciples in nineteenth-century Europe, was supposed to bring peace. Instead it brought war. So it was with an even more profound development of the time: the energy revolution that was made possible when Michael Faraday learned how to generate electricity.

Practically limitless power was the new thing that made almost all else possible. Henry Adams, historian and prophet, the American Janus who saw both behind and ahead, identified it. Marveling at the dynamos he saw at the Chicago (1893) and Paris (1900) world fairs, he speculated that they might render all past human history obsolete. It would "upset schoolmasters," he observed, but "professorial necks" had been "broken" a few times before since Europe began, and of these few times, "the nearest approach to the revolution of 1900 was that of 310, when Constantine set up the Cross." Indeed the rays of electricity were something that Adams found almost supernatural: an "energy like that of the Cross."

It was natural that Adams should be optimistic; he was a child of the century that believed history was the story of progress. Before the nineteenth century began men had looked *backward* to a golden age. Now they looked forward to it.

Europeans and Americans were fascinated by speculations about the future. A new genre of fantasy fictions catered to their tastes. Jules Verne and H. G. Wells were the pioneers in creating tales of scientific and technological marvels: of flying machines, life below the oceans, and interplanetary travel.

The focus on all the wonders that the future held in store for an empowered humanity may have been somewhat unbalanced. Only a few saw that the dark side of the otherwise Promethean story was that the human race made use of its amazing possibilities by calling forth explosive new powers of destruction.

In an often-quoted letter written when war came in 1914, Henry James, the famous American novelist resident in England, wrote: "The plunge of civilization into this abyss of blood and darkness . . . is a thing that so gives away the whole long age during which we have supposed the world to be, with whatever abatement, gradually bettering, that to have to take it all now for what the treacherous years were all the while really making for and *meaning* is too tragic for any words." Science had not made human beings more peaceful and civilized; it had betrayed such hopes and instead had made it possible for armies to be more savagely destructive than warriors of earlier times could have dreamed of being.

What Europe was building up toward was not a better world, but a giant smashup, as, in the first twentieth-century war among modern industrial societies, the accumulated explosive power that advanced science had developed was concentrated on the goal of mass destruction.

Why did contemporaries believe that they were headed for a more peaceful world? How could they dismiss the possibility of a war among European powers from their fears and their minds? Why were they taken by surprise by the outbreak of war? Did they never look to see what their leading industry was manufacturing?

Looking back, perhaps the most remarkable feature of the prewar international landscape was the accelerating arms race. The German armaments firm Krupp was the largest single business in Europe. Its giant rivals—Skoda, Creusot, Schneider, and Vickers-Maxim—also were enormous. In large part, in the new industrial age, Europe's business had become the business of preparing to fight a war. In retrospect the intense arms race was the most visible feature of Europe's political landscape in those antebellum years. It is odd that the man in the street did not see this with equal clarity at the time.

The European war economy had become immense in scale, but it did not bring security. A technological breakthrough such as Britain's development of the *Dreadnought,* rendering all existing battleships obsolete, not merely forced a country to write off its previous efforts and investments, but risked leaving it naked before its enemies during the years required to catch up.

Each adjusted its military manpower requirements—its blend of regular army, conscripts, and reserves of one sort or another—to at least match the levels of its potential adversaries. The unrelenting competitiveness achieved the opposite of what was intended. The buildup in the armed forces was intended to achieve national security, but instead undermined it: the arms race, driven by mutual fears, ended by making all the Great Powers of Europe radically insecure.

All the Great Powers—even Russia, after the 1905 revolution—were relatively open societies in which the appropriation of funds by parliaments for military purposes could be scrutinized by rival states, whose analyses were not infrequently colored by alarmism. As military programs mandated by legislation embodied schedules, countries were aware of one another's production timetables for armaments and therefore could be tempted to launch a preemptive strike.

An innovation dating from the nineteenth century was that the armed forces of the respective countries now routinely prepared contingency plans for making war on their rivals should hostilities break out. These, of course, were secret, although governments usually had at least an idea of what each other's overall strategy would be.

There was no great mystery as to who potential enemies were likely to be. France and Russia, despite major ideological differences, were known to be allies, driven together by Germany's threat to both of them. Germany was closely bound up with Austria-Hungary, and also was allied with the unreliable Italians, even though the Italians still harbored territorial claims against Austria. Great Britain, though preferring to remain neutral, was being impelled by the growth of German ambitions to draw closer to France and—for France's sake—to Russia.

The various war crises of the early twentieth century jolted the Great Powers into initiating joint staff talks with the armed forces of their allies. Secret army and navy discussions between Britain and France in 1905–06 and 1911 dealt with how to meet an attack by Germany. In 1908–09 similar talks were begun by the chiefs of the German and Austro-Hungarian general staffs and were focused on a possible war with Russia. Secret naval talks between Britain and Russia were authorized by the British cabinet in May 1914 and, when Berlin learned of them, terrified Germany. Such joint talks did not commit the European governments in a formal sense, yet in transforming theory into practice Europe's governments somehow took a further giant step on the road that led to 1914. And as it happened, they did define the war to come. They produced a script that in fact was to be followed. They provided a good indication of who would stay with which coalition: Germany and Austria would stick together, while Britain would decide to back France and Russia.

Whether or not their accelerating arms race made conflict inevitable, as British Foreign Secretary Sir Edward Grey claimed, the Great Powers of Europe somehow brought the event closer by engaging in what were essentially dress rehearsals for war—and not just for any war, but for the opening stages of the very war they were indeed about to wage.

Was it fear of one another, driven by the arms race, and feeding on itself, that was pushing Europe to the brink? Or was it inborn aggression, pent up during the unnaturally long four decades of peace among the Great Powers, that now threatened to explode? Or were governments, as many were to say, deliberately maneuvering their countries toward war in order to distract attention from domestic problems that looked to be insoluble? Or were some governments pursuing aggressive or dangerous policies they should have known that other countries would be obliged to resist by force of arms? Whatever the reasons, as Helmuth von Moltke, chief of Germany's general staff, told the civilian Chancellor in a memorandum dated December 2, 1912: "All sides are preparing for European War, which all sides expect sooner or later."

War plans were criticized and changed in the light of experience gained in war games. They were updated in response to changing circumstances and to new information about enemy plans gleaned from espionage by the intelligence services. France was exceptional in that, on the eve of war, it modified its war plans in the light of a fashionable philosophy. The new French doctrine was that morale was the key to victory. It was a view derived from the teachings of military officers Ardant du Picq (1821–70)* and Ferdinand Foch (1851–1929). That it was the moral rather than the material that ought to be emphasized seemed to be confirmed by the philosophy of Henri Bergson (1859–1941), who saw in the *élan vital*—the life force—the energy that propelled evolution. These views lent themselves to the glorification of the attack—at the expense, perhaps, of prudence—and that manifested themselves in the bias toward the offensive that many were to criticize later in Plan XVII, the organizational and strategic plan adopted by France in May 1913.

Of all the strategies explored in advance by the military chiefs of the European powers, the one that was to figure most largely in later thinking about the war was the scheme named after Count Alfred von Schlieffen, the German general to whom the design was attributed. Schlieffen (1833–1913) served as chief of Germany's Great General Staff from 1891 to 1906. The general staff of the Prussian army had been called "Great" since 1871, to distinguish it from the general staffs of other states in the German confederation: Bavaria, Saxony, and Württemberg. An elite body of about 650 officers, the Great General Staff served as the brains and nerve center of the army.

In its first hypothetical war plan after German unification in 1871, the Great General Staff imagined a conflict in which the enemy consisted of a coalition of France, Austria-Hungary, and Russia. This, the most dangerous of possibilities, corresponded to the German nightmare of being surrounded: the "Slav East and the Latin West against the center of Europe," in the words of Helmuth von Moltke—known as Moltke "the elder"—then chief of the general staff. From 1879 on, following the alliance agreement with Austria-Hungary, Germany's planning always made provision for a war against France and Russia: an unlikely combination on ideological grounds, for France was an advanced democracy and Russia was a backward tyranny. Driven together—against the odds—by the Ger-

---

*Some sources give his date of birth as 1831.

man threat, in 1894 France and Russia did indeed enter into an alliance, and Germany's war plans stopped being hypothetical. Successive chiefs of the Great General Staff asked not whether such a war would occur, but when. The difficult challenge that they faced—how to fight a two-front war successfully—had arisen because of the ineptness of their country's leaders in foreign policy.

Moltke the Elder and his successor, Count Alfred von Waldersee, planned to fight Russia in a limited war that would compel the Czar to make peace quickly, while at about the same time battling France with the objective of negotiating peace on favorable terms. It was a moderate strategy, defensive in spirit, aimed at coming out ahead. But it did mean splitting forces in order to fight both enemies at the same time.

Count von Schlieffen took over as chief of the general staff on February 7, 1891. He was appointed despite his lack of combat experience. Lonely since the death of his wife, he was a solitary figure with narrow professional interests. He was a sarcastic officer whose twisted monocle made him look like the caricature of a Prussian.

Schlieffen conducted what was almost a university for the officers under his command. He put them to work testing and reworking deployment plans annually in the light of what was learned in frequent war games and in horseback rides to study the terrain. Under his supervision staff officers prepared forty-nine different overall strategic plans for the European war they believed was coming: sixteen against France alone, fourteen against Russia alone, and nineteen against them together.

In the event of a two-front war, Germany essentially had three choices. One of them—fighting France and Russia at the same time—seemed a risky strategy for an outnumbered Germany. Dealing with Russia first seemed impractical; the Russians, even if defeated, could retreat into the almost endless interior of their vast country: they could not be dealt a quick knockout blow. Moreover, the Russians were arming and building armies and railroads at a rapid pace; they were becoming more formidable opponents all the time. On the other hand, Schlieffen, as of 1905, held a low opinion of Russian military capabilities.

A number of factors pointed to a strategy of engaging France first, and to the military mind, the only practical way for Germany to attack France was through neutral Belgium. Some officers in the French high command understood this. In Britain, Winston Churchill knew it; he had learned it at a confidential briefing of Britain's Committee of Imperial Defence in 1911. The reasons for it had been explained to the committee by Major General Sir Henry Wilson, Director of Military Operations at the War Office.

At the end of Schlieffen's tenure as chief of staff, he composed an informal memorandum outlining for his successor how such an invasion of France through Belgium might be done. The memorandum assumed that Germany had at its disposal for the hypothetical attack ninety divisions—at a time when only seventy were available. Does this mean that the memo was not really a proposal? Does it mean that it really was only a demonstration on paper that Germany needed a larger army than the war ministry was willing to raise? Was it a document meant to persuade the war ministry to change its mind? Whatever else it may have been, it served as a scenario and probably is best viewed as such.

The Schlieffen memoranda of 1905–06 remain subjects of intense controversy. After the First World War came to an end, German generals who survived the war claimed that it had been lost only because dead colleagues had failed to follow to the letter an alleged secret Schlieffen plan that would have proved a guide to victory.

Their claim was in large part accepted. The plan supposedly called for almost the entire German army to constitute a right arm—a right flank—that would drive to the Dutch and Belgian coasts, and then sweep down to envelop western France, then turn and scoop up Paris on the way to a decisive victory east of Paris: a victory over a French army that at that point would be completely surrounded. France would be destroyed forever as a Great Power. It all would have taken a matter of weeks, and the German army would then have been transferred east to deal with Russia.

Throughout the twentieth century, and now into the twenty-first, historians have debated the consequences of the so-called Schlieffen plan. Its rigid timetable supposedly forced Germany to initiate the war when and as it did. The course of events in the summer of 1914 often is pictured as an example of automation, as though the government of Berlin were caught up in the grip of its own unchangeable secret plan. We now can see that any such account is a distorted one.

We have scholarly resources not available generations ago. Schlieffen's papers, carried off by Americans, were discovered in Washington, D.C., in 1953 in the National Archives. After the pioneering research of Gerhard Ritter in the 1950s, lucidly seconded in 2001 by John Keegan, it became clear that, whatever else it might have been, the Schlieffen memorandum of 1905, with its 1906 supplement, was not a plan. It was not operational. It did not go into details or issue orders. It can be viewed in context by reading a selection of Schlieffen's military writings, which has just appeared in English translation by Robert T. Foley.

A further challenge—mounted as this is being written—is the publication of *Inventing the Schlieffen Plan* by Terence Zuber. Based on archival material that he tells us has not been used before, Zuber argues that even the memoranda we speak of as embodying the Schlieffen strategy proposal do not express his actually proposed strategies and his war plans and ideas.

Of course Germany did invade France through Belgium, as Schlieffen's memorandum imagined it would do. But that was pursuant to what with more accuracy should be called the Moltke plan, for it was during Moltke's tenure of office that the operational document—the actual plan for invading France—was promulgated.

Reviewing the Schlieffen memoranda some five years later, in 1911, Moltke indicated in his notes that he agreed that France should be invaded through Belgium. The decision exercised a sort of multiplier effect on Germany's quarrels. In the context of Germany's post-1890 foreign policy, it created the very encircling coalition Germans professed to fear. It also automatically transformed a German war into a European war that as a result would become a world war. If Germany attacked Russia, Germany would start by invading Belgium, Luxemburg, and France, thereby bringing them, too, into the war, thus also bringing Great Britain into the war, bringing in, in addition, India, Australia, New Zealand, South Africa, Canada, and others too, possibly including Britain's Pacific ally, Japan.

All of this rousing up of additional enemies was undertaken in pursuance of a strategy that even in the words of a scholar who believes in the existence of the Schlieffen scheme, "never achieved the final, perfected form that is sometimes imputed to it."

Schlieffen envisaged violating the neutrality of Luxemburg, Belgium, and Holland in invading France. Moltke decided instead to leave

Holland alone. In the first place, Dutch armed resistance might tip the scales against the invaders; in the second, if a war of attrition developed, Germany would need a neutral Netherlands as a conduit for supplies. These were both good reasons for respecting Dutch neutrality.

One of the consequences of doing so, however, was to narrow the invasion route through which the German forces were to move. It would be a corridor twelve miles wide. It could be dominated by the Belgian fortifications at Liège. So, relying on total surprise and a sprinter's speed, German forces would have to seize Liège before the enemy even knew that war was upon them. All this would be possible only if there was complete secrecy. Moltke therefore did not allow even Germany's other military leaders—let alone the civilian ones—to share this information.

One other point later—in the summer of 1914—assumed great importance. The increased speed of Russia's mobilization ability, and the strengthening of its armed forces, meant that in the event of war, Germany on its own might not have the ability to ward off Russia's first blow. It would have to call on Austria-Hungary to help. That was to prove a key to understanding the crisis of July 1914.

In the unified German federation that Prussia had organized into a single power in the wars of the 1860s and 1870s, the armed forces played a disproportionately large role and—through it—so did the King of Prussia, who served not only as German emperor but also as military chief. As Chancellor—Germany's civilian leader—Otto von Bismarck wore a military uniform, seeking to identify himself with the military service and thereby indicating where he, who had created the new state and was the author of its constitution, believed that power rested.

Vested in the Kaiser were almost dictatorial powers in the great matters of war and peace: almost, but not quite. His was the power to declare war or to make peace—so long as he could obtain the countersignature of the Chancellor. But as the Chancellor was appointed by the Kaiser and served at his pleasure, this did not provide much of a check on the monarch's power.

In the Imperial German army, the Kaiser served as supreme warlord. Immediately below him were three distinct bodies that sometimes competed with one another: the Prussian War Ministry, the

War Cabinet, and the Great General Staff. Their functions were separate but sometimes overlapping. They, too, were appointed by the Kaiser.

It often was said, after he was made chief of the Great General Staff in 1906, that the younger Moltke had been chosen because Wilhelm liked him. Moltke's biographer, Annika Mombauer, in a recently published work based in part on previously unknown primary sources, tells us that he "had been the Kaiser's friend as well as his long-term adjutant," that as a young man he was "a tall dashing military figure," and that "his pleasant manners and varied cultural pursuits made him an appealing candidate."

Born in East Prussia, Moltke came of the right stock. His candidacy cannot have been hurt by the fact that he was a nephew of the great Moltke—Moltke the Elder, as he was known subsequently— the commander of Bismarck's armies who, in defeating Denmark, Austria, and then France, had been the general whose victories created modern Germany. The nephew knew what he owed to his uncle's name. On the occasion of his general staff appointment, he asked Wilhelm: "Does Your Majesty really believe that you will win the first prize twice in the same lottery?"

Big and heavy, he was fifty-eight years old at the time of his appointment. Although he painted, played the cello, and took an interest in spiritualist matters, he held conventional military and political views. Goethe's *Faust* is said to have been "his constant companion"; but it would have taken much more than his rather ordinary intellect to suspect that *Faust* might bear some relevance to the bid for total power that Prussia was mounting in his time.

Appreciating that Austria was of vital importance to his plans, Moltke worked with his Austrian counterpart, Franz Conrad von Hötzendorf, to strengthen the Austro-German alliance. He succeeded in restoring warmth to a relationship that had been strained. Both chiefs of staff, it transpired nonetheless, held back and failed to give their entire confidence to one another. Moltke did not reveal the extent of his need for Austrian assistance in meeting the initial Russian attack that he expected. Conrad, in turn, did not admit that Austria was going to focus on destroying Serbia and would hope Germany—by itself—would assume full responsibility for dealing with the Czar's armies.

Until recently, the common view among scholars, especially in Germany, has been that Moltke was inadequate, weak, and of less than major importance. The appearance of Mombauer's biography should change that view. Moltke was a figure of considerable significance both for what he did and for what he did not do.

As a favorite of the Kaiser's who therefore was in a position to get a hearing for his views, Moltke took the lead in advancing two propositions: first, that the alliance with Austria was absolutely central to Germany and had to be given top priority; and second, that war against the Triple Entente—Britain, France, and Russia, three countries that had pledged mutual friendship—was bound to break out not much later than 1916 or 1917, and that Germany would lose the war unless it launched a preventive attack immediately. Certain that war would come, Moltke wanted it sooner rather than later. He wanted it even though, like many of his colleagues, he feared that it would bring European civilization to an end.

CHAPTER 5: ZARATHUSTRA PROPHESIES

The greatest arms race the world had known was not only waged among mutually hostile nations, busily planning to destroy one another, but took place in a civilization in which it was widely believed that only destruction could bring regeneration. The prophet of the age was the powerfully eloquent, though unsystematic philosopher Friedrich Nietzsche (1844–1900). Nietzsche preached the values of the irrational. Though he was German, his message struck a chord in many countries. He was a European figure, not a parochial German one. Fittingly, he made his home in Switzerland and Italy.

The French Revolution of 1789 had ushered in a century of revolutions that had failed to achieve the dreams they embodied. Unfulfilled revolutions and revolutions betrayed had left Europe frustrated, and in a mood—following Nietzsche—to smash things. Rejecting Europe's inherited values, Nietzsche had proclaimed in *Thus Spake Zarathustra* that "God is dead!"

The debut of the Stravinsky-Nijinsky ballet *Le Sacre du Printemps* on May 29, 1913, at the Théatre des Champs-Elysées in Paris, is often taken as the symbol of the Nietzschean rebellion in all the arts. Crowds hating the ballet—a pagan celebration with deafening dissonances—screamed their protests against what they regarded as savagery exalted in the place of civilization. Hysteria and frenzy seemed to be the order of the day.

It may well be that the European sense of frustration—the sense of stalemate in life, art, and politics—led to a violent sense of abandon, of letting go: a sense that the world ought to be blown up, and let the consequences be what they may. Europe's Nietzschean mood seemed to play some sort of role in making the Great War possible.

As A. J. P. Taylor writes: "Men's minds seem to have been on edge in the last two or three years before the war in a way they had not been before, as though they had become unconsciously weary of peace and security. You can see it in things remote from international politics—in the artistic movement called Futurism, in the militant suffragettes. . . , in the working-class trend toward Syndicalism. Men wanted violence for its own sake; they welcomed war as a relief from materialism. European civilization was, in fact, breaking down even before war destroyed it."

In the opening years of the twentieth century, Europeans glorified violence, and certain groups among them, at least, felt a need for radical change. Across the whole spectrum of existence, change was overcoming Europe at a pace faster than ever before—and far faster than Europe knew how to cope with. A panoramic view of Europe in the years 1900 to 1914 would show prominently that the Continent was racing ahead in a scientific, technological, and industrial revolution, powered by almost limitless energy, that was transforming almost everything; that violence was endemic in the service of social, economic, political, class, ethnic, and national strife; that Europe focused its activities largely on an escalating, dizzying arms race on a scale that the world never had seen before; and that, in the center of the Continent's affairs, powerful, dynamic Germany had made strategic arrangements such that, if it went to war, it would bring almost all Europe and much of the rest of the planet into the war for or against it.

Given these conditions, does not the question "How could war have broken out in such a peaceful world?" rather answer itself?

Would it not have been more to the point to ask how statesmen could have continued to avoid war much longer? How had they managed to keep the peace for so long? Which is not to say that war could *not* have been averted, but merely that, by 1914, it might have taken extraordinary skill to keep on averting it.

Today, we take it for granted that governments hope to keep the peace. It is our often unarticulated assumption. Since the development of weapons of mass destruction, everybody would lose, we say, if war were to break out among the Great Powers. The human race, we are told, might not survive such a conflict. Our principal international institution, the United Nations, is described as a peacekeeping organization because preventing war is the primary reason that the countries of the earth have joined together.

It would be a mistake, however, to assume that a century ago world leaders would have shared such a view. Their thinking at the time was well expressed in what has been called "the first great speech" in the political career of Theodore Roosevelt, newly appointed assistant secretary of the navy in the incoming administration of U.S. President William McKinley. Addressing the Naval War College in 1897, Roosevelt claimed: "No triumph of peace is quite so great as the supreme triumphs of war." War, he declared, was a fine and healthy thing. "All the great masterful races have been fighting races; and the minute that a race loses the hard fighting virtues, then . . . it has lost its proud right to stand as the equal of the best." He argued: "Cowardice in a race, as in an individual, is the unpardonable sin." Someday circumstances might be different, he said, but until they were, war would continue to be needed. "As yet no nation can hold its place in the world, or can do any work really worth doing unless it stands ready to guard its rights with an armed hand."

The speech was reprinted in full in all major American newspapers, and the chorus of approval from the press all around the United States made it clear that Roosevelt was not speaking for himself alone. He lived in a world in which war was considered desirable—even necessary.

Franz Conrad von Hötzendorf, chief of staff of the Dual Monarchy's armed forces, was another leader who frequently expressed his opinion that war was "the basic principle behind all the events on this earth." It also, as he saw it, was the key to personal success. He was carrying on a love affair with a married woman, and was of the view that if he could come back from the battlefield as a war hero, his mistress could be persuaded to leave her wealthy husband.

The pursuit of "honor" was a frequent theme of the times. In Conrad's personal vision, a warrior's nobility wins him the love of women and the acclaim of men. Heads of state and government in the conflicts of 1914 were to argue that their country's honor *compelled* them to join in the fray; U.S. President Woodrow Wilson used the concept in his address to Congress in 1917 asking for a declaration of war against Germany. Some—Conrad was one, and his octogenarian emperor Franz Joseph was another—at times felt that they had to lead their country into a war because of their code of honor, even if they were likely to lose.

These views—held by warriors and aristocrats on the one hand, and by many artists and intellectuals on the other—were not necessarily shared by the masses, including workers, farmers, and the peace-loving commercial and middle classes. But the public played no role in the war-and-peace decisions: decisions that they did not even know were being made behind closed doors.

The several dozen leaders who did discuss and decide these matters lived in a world of their own, and it was a world in which war and warriors were glorified.

CHAPTER 6: **DIPLOMATS ALIGN**

Among the Great Powers of Europe, peace had prevailed from 1871 to 1914. It was a long run. It is at least arguable that what had made that achievement possible was not only the skill but also the character and the outlook of Europe's statesmen. In large part they were a sort of extended family: monarchs and aristocrats whom the French Revolution had failed to sweep away. Shaped by the tolerance and the values of the eighteenth century, they had kept their positions and their system throughout the nineteenth. They were bound together by ties of education, of culture, and, in many cases, of blood. The conduct of foreign affairs was their shared vocation. Cosmopolitan and disinclined to prejudices, they tended at times to put the welfare of Europe as a whole ahead of that of their own country. Indeed, it was not unusual for a diplomat to take service with a foreign country: for a German or a Corsican, for example, to serve as foreign minister of Russia. Once—a long time before, it is true—an Austrian, the Count of Stainville, had been Vienna's envoy to Paris at the same time that his son was Paris's envoy to Vienna.

Hans Morgenthau (1904–80), the great twentieth-century theorist of international relations, describes the way it used to be in terms that exude nostalgia:

> In the seventeenth and eighteenth centuries, and to a lessening degree up to the First World War, international morality was the concern of a personal sovereign—that is, a certain individual prince and his successors—and of a relatively small, cohesive, and homogeneous group of aristocratic rulers. The prince and the aristocratic rulers of a particular nation were in constant, intimate contact with the princes and aristocratic rulers of other nations. They were joined together by family ties, a common language (French), common cultural values, a common style of life, and common moral convictions about what a gentleman was and was not allowed to do in his relations with another gentleman, whether of his own or of a foreign nation.

In other words, they played the game of world politics as though it had rules. The loss of aristocratic values and the weakening of ties were what made the behavior of some of the statesmen in July 1914 possible.

In our democratic age, we tend to forget how great a role continued to be played by kings and emperors and by the hereditary aristocracy as recently as a century ago, not merely by their values and their codes of conduct, but by themselves. We have been reminded of it by a study that has just been published, *Royalty and Diplomacy in Europe, 1890–1914,* by Roderick R. McLean. Personal friendships among monarchs could help to bring countries together. The reverse could also be true. Both possibilities could be seen at work in the ambivalent relationship between the two most powerful Continental emperors, Nicholas II of Russia and Wilhelm II of Germany. Each could exercise almost absolute powers within his country in matters of war and peace.

Czar Nicholas II succeeded to the Russian throne at the end of 1894 and was crowned the following year. Deferential and inexperienced, he had been described only shortly before by his father as inadequate: "He is nothing but a boy, whose judgments are childish."

Kaiser Wilhelm II undertook to guide his young relative through the jungles of world politics. There was nearly a decade's age difference between the two. Moreover, Nicholas was hesitant where Wilhelm was assertive. The young Czar was so polite that the Kaiser believed he was hearing agreement even when he was not. Wilhelm initiated a secret correspondence with him that lasted for nearly two decades. At first Nicholas welcomed the letters.

In 1896 the two emperors met for a conference in Breslau, in what now is Poland. Agreements between them were reached easily. But Wilhelm's desire to tutor and dominate turned Nicholas against him. From then on, the Czar regarded the Kaiser with a dislike bordering on hostility. Nicholas decided that he wanted to break off their correspondence. Ignoring Nicholas's desires, Wilhelm continued to write to him for a further eighteen years. On occasion the two rulers did hold meetings. After one such, in 1902, Nicholas commented: "He's raving mad!"

From time to time the Kaiser did seem to exert some influence; he may have played a part in persuading the Czar to involve his empire in a war against Japan (1904–05), a war that proved to be a disaster. Mostly, however, Nicholas preferred neither to see nor to hear from his tiresome relative. In this he was not alone.

Queen Victoria, the Kaiser's grandmother, warned Nicholas against Wilhelm's "mischievous and unstraight-forward proceedings." To her prime minister, Victoria described Wilhelm as "a hot-headed, conceited, and wrong-headed young man." She did not invite Wilhelm to her Diamond Jubilee (1897) or to her eightieth birthday celebration (1899). In his own version of history, the Kaiser described himself as Victoria's favorite grandson.

For all of the German emperor's failings, he was a blood relative and was treated as such. This solidarity among cousins was a sentiment that made for peace and stability between the Czar and the Kaiser. McLean tells us: "Until at least 1908, both monarchs remained convinced that neither would undertake a hostile act against the other."

These personal relationships played their role in the story of how Europe managed *not* to have a war among the Great Powers in the opening years of the twentieth century. But ultimately family ties did not succeed in relaxing the tensions that arose among the powers. Indeed it would have taken statesmanship of a high order to guide the countries of Europe through the explosive issues with which they had to deal. It was like walking through minefields.

PART TWO

WALKING THROUGH MINEFIELDS

CHAPTER 7: THE EASTERN QUESTION

Ever since the beginning of the nineteenth century, the statesmen of Europe—the handful of prime ministers, foreign secretaries, and chancellery officials who dealt with arcane issues of foreign policy—remained convinced that they knew how (though not when) their world would be brought to an end. The war among the advanced industrial Great Powers, they believed, would be occasioned by the breakup of the Ottoman Empire, as its vast and valuable territories excited the predatory instincts of the rival expansionist European empires. There had been a time, centuries before, when the Turks had ruled not just the Middle East but much of North Africa and Balkan Europe as well—all the way to the gates of Vienna. Now the Sultan's backward and demoralized forces were in full, if slow, retreat before the Christians. Which European powers would take, in particular, southeastern Europe for themselves—"the Eastern Question"—was commonly seen as the most explosive long-range issue in international politics. "One day the great European

War will come out of some damned foolish thing in the Balkans," Bismarck was quoted as saying at the end of his life.

Fearing the cataclysm, with its incalculable consequences, Great Britain traditionally tried to postpone facing the issue by propping up the decaying Turkish empire. On the opposite side, Austria, later joined by Russia, pursued expansionist policies at the Sultan's expense, looking toward an eventual partition of the Ottoman domains.

As so often happens when the political world focuses on a particular threat, the threat in question failed to materialize; the danger was averted. Over the course of the nineteenth century, one Christian people after another in southeastern Europe threw off the shackles of Ottoman rule without then being absorbed by a Great Power. By the first decade of the twentieth century Romania, Bulgaria, Serbia, Montenegro, and Greece all had become at least de facto free countries. They were quarrelsome nations; some at times were aggressive rivals; and each set its own course in world affairs. They coveted the territories remaining to the Turks in Europe. By the beginning of the twentieth century Constantinople mostly had to fear these local states rather than the Great Powers. The greatest of the Great Powers—Britain, France, Germany, and even Russia—now preferred the Ottoman frontier to remain where it was. In April 1897, Russia and Austria-Hungary agreed to preserve the status quo in what remained of the Ottoman Balkans.

In this respect, the chancelleries of Europe could breathe a sigh of relief. For a century they had been walking through a minefield, and they had emerged from it not merely alive but relatively unscathed.

CHAPTER 8: A CHALLENGE
FOR THE ARCHDUKE

The Hapsburgs had served as a ruling dynasty in Europe for so long that it could easily be forgotten that the country they ruled in 1914—Austria-Hungary, or the Dual Monarchy—was of quite recent origin. It was so new that the man who created it—the emperor Franz Joseph—was still alive and ruled. In 1914, Austria-Hungary was forty-seven years old; Franz Joseph, eighty-four.

The Dual Monarchy was an improvisation. There had been an urgent need of it in the 1860s when the Germans of Austria, expelled from the world that Prussia consolidated, found themselves cut off from other Germans and unable to stand on their own. A permanent alliance with the Magyar rulers of Hungary was Franz Joseph's solution in 1867. The economic provisions of the agreement were not permanent; they came up for renewal every ten years.

But Austria and Hungary had interests and ambitions that sometimes were antithetical. Archduke Franz Ferdinand, Franz Joseph's nephew and heir presumptive, had devoted much thought to the question of how he would reconstitute the Hapsburg lands when he ascended the throne. One plan ascribed to him was to create a triple monarchy, joining Slavs to Germans and Magyars as a governing people of the empire, enabling Austro-Germans to play the Slavs off against the Magyars. He seems to have dropped that scheme in favor of others, all aimed at restoring Austrian greatness.

Franz Ferdinand deplored the consequences of his country's Hungarian connection. His feelings in this respect were both known and reciprocated. It was not unreasonable to predict that when Franz Joseph died and Franz Ferdinand ascended the throne with radical constitutional changes in mind, disturbances would ensue.

Austria-Hungary was a ramshackle structure, then, only with difficulty holding itself together, and maintaining its formal ranking as a Great Power in part by courtesy of the others. So in retrospect the Eastern Question—the issue of what to do with the European possessions of a collapsing Turkish empire—overlapped an emerging Austrian question: what to do with the shaky Dual Monarchy. There were those who asserted that, after the Sultan of Turkey, the Hapsburg emperor was the new Sick Man of Europe. In the deadly game of world politics, Austria-Hungary continued to hunt, but also was being hunted. The Eastern Question had been turned upside down and stood on its head. The Hapsburgs had coveted Balkan lands; now Balkan peoples coveted Hapsburg lands.

Austria-Hungary was in area one of the largest states in Europe. Two of its perhaps eleven nationalities, Germans and Magyars, exercised most of the political power. In Austria the one-third of its population that was German tended to dominate the two-thirds that was not; in Hungary, the 40 percent that was Magyar ruled the 60 percent that was not.

Nationalism had been sweeping Europe since the days of the French Revolution. It inspired a literature in which a repressive Austria was singled out as a villain. Thus, sinister and unbending, and an implacable enemy of the liberties of mankind, Hapsburg Austria casts a dark shadow over Europe in such works as Stendhal's *Charterhouse of Parma*. Some, and maybe most, of the leading ardent nationalities' movements in Europe—those of the Czechs, for example, and a number of ethnicities in the Balkans—aimed at breaking up the Hapsburg Empire, or at least decentralizing it.

One of Austria-Hungary's weak spots was that it ruled so many Slavic peoples—members of the largest ethnic group in Europe—and that Slavic Russia, it was feared, could exert a pull on their loyalties by sponsoring pan-Slavism.

Historians tell us that the Austrian army was strong, although it had an astonishing record, going back more than a century, of losing battles and wars.

The generals of the Dual Monarchy knew that they could not fight, on their own, on equal terms against Russia, with its vast expanses and enormous population. In order to stand a chance Austria-Hungary would require the protection of Germany.

CHAPTER 9: **EXPLOSIVE GERMANY**

As it entered the twentieth century, the German state was still in its infancy. Yet in many ways it already had become—or perhaps had been from the start—out of date in its political structure. In the thirty years of its existence, Germany had stopped being an essentially agricultural country and had surged ahead to become the Continent's most dynamic commercial and industrial power. One result was that the country was now divided against itself.

As noted before, farming interests still demanded protective tariffs in order to survive, while industry now pushed for the free trade it needed in order to thrive. This was but one of the many contradictions that made Kaiser Wilhelm II's Reich so difficult to fathom—and to govern. At the cutting edge of the modern world in some respects, Germany was obsolete in politics, and therefore unable to reconcile the diverse trends to which modernism gave rise.

According to Volker R. Berghahn, "the salient feature of German domestic politics before 1914 was . . . an almost total impasse." He quotes Gustav Schmidt to explain: "The notion of several groups blocking each other and hence blocking a way out of the deadlock offers 'the key to an understanding of German politics in the last years before the war.' " Some, under the spell of Nietzsche, believed that the solution was to dynamite society. It was not easy to identify an alternative that did not involve violence.

Until the nineteenth century the German peoples of Europe had been fragmented. In the former Holy Roman Empire alone, they dwelt in hundreds of principalities, cities, and other quasi-sovereignties. Napoleon restructured them. The Allies who defeated Napoleon tried their hand at restructuring too. In the end, unification came from within the German-speaking world.

The country we know today as Germany derives from the German Empire, which was created through a series of wars culminating in 1870–71 by militarist, Protestant Prussia, led by Otto von Bismarck. Bismarck's new unified Germany contained less than half the German peoples of Europe. It consisted of the kingdom of Prussia, three other kingdoms, eighteen duchies, and three free cities. But Bismarck deliberately excluded Austria, which had led the German states of Europe. He did so, of course, in order to secure Prussia's own leadership in German Europe. This also had the effect of ensuring a Protestant majority in the German federation. A later Chancellor of Germany, Prince Bernhard von Bülow, reminded his government's representatives abroad in 1906 that if the German-speaking Austrians were to be incorporated into Germany, "We shall thereby receive an increase of about fifteen million Catholics so that the Protestants would become a minority . . . the proportion of strength between the Protestants and the Catholics would become similar to that which at the time led to the Thirty Years War, i.e., a virtual dissolution of the German empire." In Germany, Bismarck had chosen to bring into the political world a smaller country that he and his fellow Prussians could control rather than a larger one that they could not, and that continued to be Berlin's preference.

Yet it became Germany's belief that, in case of war, Austria would be indispensable as an ally, even though Austria was weaker than Germany. The continued existence of the Hapsburg Empire was viewed in Berlin as a vital German interest, indeed, perhaps as Germany's main vital interest in international politics.

Prussia, undemocratic and militaristic in its culture, was controlled by its army and the largely impoverished landowning Junker class that led its officer corps. In turn, Prussia exerted considerable control, and in time of war almost total control, over the rest of Germany. Germany, by industrializing rapidly, made itself into the economic leader of the Continent, but in doing so necessarily converted much of its population into an industrial proletariat. The workers could not be admitted into the officer corps of the army without diluting the aristocratic Prussian character of the corps—and the regime it supported. So Germany, despite harboring ambitions to dominate Europe and perhaps even the world, deliberately chose not to increase the size of its army to the extent that would be required to realize such expansionist dreams.

Admiral Alfred Tirpitz explained in 1896 that in the end the armed forces existed "to suppress internal revolutions." The very industrial revolution that was making Germany the greatest country on the Continent was at the same time generating forces that were threatening the regime. It was only one of the many contradictions in Germany's policies.

Driving Germany's industrial growth was the country's educational system. Here, too, was a contradiction. The best-educated general public in Europe was unlikely in the long run to tolerate an archaic government structure or a leadership drawn exclusively from a narrow pool.

Long after the Great War, sympathetic foreign observers were to make the argument that Germany's increasing greatness should have been peacefully accommodated by the other powers: that they should have appeased Berlin. Put this way, the responsibility for the outbreak of war falls on the shoulders of the main countries—Britain, France, Russia, and the United States—that eventually stood in the way of Germany's rise to world power. They gave Germany, the argument runs, no way to assert itself other than through war. As the French historian Elie Halévy understandingly put it in the 1930s: "But suppose that, presently, one nation is found to have gained immensely in military or economic strength at the expense of one or many of the others . . . for such a disturbance of equilibrium man has not yet discovered any method of peaceful adjustment. . . . it can be rectified only by an outburst of violence—a war."

Again, however, one arrives at a contradiction. As will be shown presently, the Kaiser and other German leaders in 1912 and 1913 believed that their country was becoming weaker, not stronger, relative to the other powers. As will be seen, the chief of the general staff felt that Germany ought to launch a war as soon as possible precisely because the chances of winning it would be less every year. War was necessary, in other words, not to accommodate German strength, but to accommodate German weakness.

For a time, the arms race seemed to offer a way out. Germany, in the process of overtaking Britain as Europe's leading economy, ought therefore to have been able to outspend its rivals for military purposes. But an archaic constitutional structure and the consequent lack of a progressive tax system kept Germany from translating a growing economy into growing government revenues. By the start of the twentieth century Germany had reached the limits, spending all that it could, and more than it should, on the military. In his authoritative study of pre–World War I Germany, Berghahn writes: "German armaments policy was almost exclusively responsible for the Reich's financial plight. Over the years a relatively constant figure of about *90 per cent* of the Reich budget had been spent on the Army and Navy" (emphasis added).

A leader like Franklin D. Roosevelt might have lifted the eyes of Germans to some higher vision, and brought people together through sheer charisma. Germany's Kaiser Wilhelm II seemed to aspire to play such a role. He wore glittering uniforms and mounted noble chargers, and, at times, uttered dramatic pronouncements. But he fell short: he had no aptitude for the role.

Through the many years of his reign his support dwindled among the German people, and plunged during several public scandals of which more will be said later. It is curious that in foreign countries he was taken as the embodiment of the Prussian Junker military tradition, when his popularity was so low among Prussian military Junkers.

Kaiser Wilhelm II was half English; his mother was Queen Victoria's daughter. He exhibited strange attitudes toward England—a kaleidoscope of love, hate, envy, admiration, and a desire to be accepted as at least an equal—and these contradictions are explained by many biographers on the basis of his feelings for either his mother or his grandmother.

At birth he was found to be in a breech position in his mother's body. The attending physicians were not fully capable of dealing with this: at the time less than 2 percent of breech babies were born alive. Wilhelm survived—barely—but with permanent injuries.

It seems likely that Wilhelm II was emotionally unbalanced because of the various injuries suffered in childbirth. It remains an open and controversial question whether he suffered brain damage. His left arm remained permanently paralyzed, and the reactions of others to his withered limb may have affected him in one way or another. John Röhl, the leading student of his life and times, has concluded, on the basis of considerable medical evidence, that Wilhelm was deprived of oxygen during childbirth and suffered all his life from the results: personality defects such as a lack of objectivity and excessive sensitivity. This, in Röhl's view, was aggravated by the rigors of his childhood, including the treatments of his twisted neck by such methods as the use of a "headstretching machine" and the treatment of his arm by inserting it into a freshly slaughtered hare. His love of military uniforms, his devotion to hunting, and his identification with Achilles suggest that he yearned for a martial glory that he could never achieve.

In 1888, Wilhelm ascended the throne as King of Prussia and German Emperor. By 1913, at the age of fifty-four, he therefore had reigned for a quarter century. During that time he had presided over affairs in a number of international crises that had threatened to bring about a European war, and in all of them war had been avoided, with Wilhelm himself in each case eventually coming down on the side of peace. The decision was his to make. The constitution of the German federation gave him the power to declare war. He often toyed with the idea of doing so.

His was a disturbing influence. He was nervous, high-strung, and mercurial. Caught up in the excitement of the moment, he would threaten and posture, playing the warlord who would lead his nation into battle; later he would take it all back. Military and civilian officials who worked with him learned never to rely on the decisions he announced off the cuff; there had been too many false alarms.

The accounts left to us by his associates show an undisciplined and inconsistent figure, on the childish side, emotionally taut, often on the verge of breakdown, broadly ignorant but with no hesitation about making unqualified announcements about any number of matters about which he knew nothing. Egotistical and inclined to mega-lomania, he often spoke and even acted as though he were an absolute ruler. This was particularly true in foreign affairs. To Britain's Prince of Wales he once boasted: "I am the sole master of German policy and my country must follow me wherever I go." He might have exercised more influence over policy had he not been so capricious and unpredictable, and had he not reversed himself so often. As it was, ministers learned to disregard what the Kaiser told them much of the time, and, as one does with a child, to "manage" him. This was made easier because he was so rarely around; most of the time he was away hunting or yacht-cruising. He was in residence in Berlin only from January to May of a normal year.

Until Wilhelm II became the Kaiser, German policy was set largely by the Chancellor, Otto von Bismarck. Wilhelm, an untried young monarch, felt uncomfortable with the elderly veteran and his policies. He disagreed with Bismarck on such matters as how to deal with industrial strife: at the time Wilhelm sided with striking factory workers, Bismarck with factory owners. In 1890, Wilhelm asserted his authority by dismissing the Iron Chancellor.

In 1890, after Bismarck had been dismissed, the Kaiser's new ministers allowed the Reinsurance Treaty, a Bismarck creation, to lapse. It had been an essential element in German policy, affirming German friendship with Russia after already having affirmed friendship with Austria-Hungary. In Bismarck's vision, it bound the three empires together in such a way as to keep the rivalry in the Balkans between Russia and Austria under control. Germany would throw its weight against whichever of its two allies threatened to upset the delicate balance between them. Berlin would keep both of them as allies, providing Germany with security on its eastern front. The treaties were kept secret: Russia did not know of Germany's treaty with Austria; Austria did not know of Germany's treaty with Russia.

For a century historians have blamed the Kaiser for allowing the Reinsurance Treaty to lapse. Scholars now have shown that the responsibility was not entirely his. On March 21, 1890, Wilhelm assured the Russian ambassador that he planned to renew the treaty. On March 27, told that his foreign policy advisers were opposed to it, he said, "then it cannot be done. I am extremely sorry." It was typical of him, while claiming to be an absolute monarch, to allow himself to be overruled.

From Bismarck, power passed within the German government to those who looked east: who perhaps dreamed of expanding territory, influence, or markets via the Balkans and perhaps Russia into the Middle East and on to China.

Behind this policy vision lay their dark historical vision of a fated clash between Teutonic peoples, on the one side, and the peoples of the East, Slavs and Orientals, in which the Easterners, if defeated, were to become servants or slaves. It was the counterpart of the pan-Slav ambitions animating some of the policymakers in St. Petersburg.

A question still debated is whether Wilhelm II played a great part in formulating policy. One area in which his judgment *did* have a considerable determining influence was in the shift of emphasis in grand strategy in the late 1890s: Germany's new focus on naval policy.

The main figure with whom that strategy was associated was the state secretary of the Naval Office, the newly ennobled Admiral Alfred von Tirpitz. Tirpitz represented, in a sense, the rising middle classes. His plan seemed to solve several problems at once. It called for the creation of a major battleship fleet. Building it might bring high employment and prosperity, and thus buy off, as it were, a section of the hitherto socialist working class.

This naval program consumed more and more money, and was made possible only by the peculiar order of priorities of the army ministry. According to Berghahn, "From the mid-1890s onwards, naval expenditure increased enormously while, at the same time, the expansion of the Army came to a virtual standstill. . . . There followed two decades of stagnation." The funds were available to expand the navy only because the army chose not to expand; "it was the leadership of the Army itself that had called a halt to expansion." The generals had done so in order to avoid opening the ranks of the officer corps to what they regarded as unreliable elements: persons lacking a Junker Prussian background.

As Berghahn writes, a function of the officer corps was "guaranteeing absolute loyalty to the existing order and its supreme military commander, the monarch." Rather than enlarge, the better to combat enemies abroad, the ministry of war chose to remain at current force levels in order to combat enemies at home.

The naval expansion launched by Tirpitz supposedly would enable Germany to compete against the other powers for colonies. It would allow Germany to extend its reach anywhere in the world and not just in and around Europe. Germany would engage in world politics, not merely in continental politics. By its very nature the program posed a challenge to Great Britain, against whom, in fact, it was directed. In building a major navy, in attempting to obtain a colonial empire, and in trying to play a role on the global stage, Germany was setting out either to rival England or to take England's place.

In retrospect, this was a self-defeating policy. Germany, along with its Austrian ally, is situated in the center of Europe. It has neighbors on all sides. Geographically it is encircled. The German nightmare has always been that of being encircled by a combination of hostile powers. It was Wilhelmine Germany itself that translated that nightmare into a reality, with its aggressive foreign policy and its unwise alliance decisions.

To the west there was France, estranged by the loss of Alsace and parts of Lorraine to Germany in the war of 1870–71. Bismarck, in his day, distracted the French by backing their quest for empire; under Wilhelm II, Germany instead deepened the rift by opposing French imperialism, notably during the Moroccan crises of 1906 and 1911.

To the east was Russia, which Berlin deliberately estranged by letting the Reinsurance Treaty lapse. Germany made the fateful choice to back Austria against Russia. Thus it had enemies on both sides, east and west, conjuring up the very two-front war that haunted its generals.

To the south, Italy had territorial assertions against Austria that made it likely that Rome would rally to the other side. The German-Austrian alliance might well have to fight on a southern front, too.

Now, in the early 1900s, the Tirpitz program estranged Great Britain as well. England, France, and Russia, which were in many ways natural enemies of one another, and had been in conflict for more than a century as rivals for empire in Asia and elsewhere, were given no choice but to band together. So the hostile encirclement that Germany so much feared was achieved by Germany itself. But the Kaiser and his entourage, including the country's military leaders, chose instead to blame everyone else.

Insofar as he remained steady in support of any policy, the Kaiser consistently backed Tirpitz and his naval policy. This brought the monarch into alignment with a broad segment of the middle class favoring expansion of trade, creation of a fleet to back up the drive for trade, and recognition by foreign powers of Germany's growing greatness. It was a policy that aroused fear in Germany's neighbors. On the other hand, it did not lead Germans to feel more secure.

Given the relative consistency with which he pushed navalism, the Kaiser might well have been convicted of responsibility for the 1914 war if it had come about as a result of the naval challenge that he mounted against Great Britain. But it did not. Germany dropped out of the naval arms race several years before the war began; navalism then lost its relevance as a German world strategy.

It was the other and rival military party, the Prussian-led army, that eventually led Germany along the road it took in 1914. To be seen clearly, German militarism at that time has to be understood not as a single phenomenon with two aspects but as two rival programs: that of the navy and that of the army. Paradoxically—a word that, along with "oddly," has to be used often in discussing Wilhelmine Germany—Tirpitz and Wilhelm, whether they knew it or not, headed the party of peace. This was because the navy, in the Tirpitz grand plan, would take years to be ready for any possible confrontation with England. And the navy did not want to fight until it was ready. So Tirpitz was for peace now and war so much later as to have little relevance to the politics of his time. To the navy, the enemy was the British Empire; to the army, it was Russia.

The army was less than enthusiastic about the Kaiser. His backing of the navy threatened Junker control of the German Empire; among other things, it opened up paths for advancement to new men from the professional and middle classes. Moreover, his tendency to retreat from international confrontation whenever there appeared to be a real risk of war was seen as cowardly through army eyes.

Gloom brought about by the Kaiser's inadequacies fed into a larger worldview pessimism characteristic of pre-1914 Germany and affecting such leaders as the younger Moltke. This pervasive gloom was due, Fritz Fischer tells us, to devotion to the ideals of a vanishing pre-capitalist world and its values, which could never be restored.

No portrait of Germany as it was a century ago would be complete without mention of its cultural and academic preeminence. "Einstein's Germany," as Fritz Stern has called it, was poised to lead the world in learning and in the sciences. It produced great literature and great music. German was the language of scholarship. Those who hoped to pursue a serious career in classical studies, philosophy, sociology, or the natural sciences were well advised to enter German universities. Germans, arguably, were the most accomplished people in the world.

An advanced country inside a backward governmental structure, broadly humanist yet narrowly militarist, Germany was a land of paradoxes. Outside observers saw it as the coming country, the land of the future, while its own leaders believed that its time was running out. It was dazzlingly successful but profoundly troubled, powerful but fearful to the point of paranoia. It was symbolized by its ruler, who was both physically and emotionally unbalanced. Located in the heart of Europe, Germany was at the heart of Europe's problems.

In retrospect, it seems odd that observers—the observers who were surprised by the outbreak of war in 1914—did not see that many of Germany's leaders were spoiling for a fight, and sooner or later—if they could get around the Kaiser—might well have their way. An American, Edward House, saw it, but many Europeans did not.*

If House were to be believed, everything pointed to a war in which Europe would go up in flames. The difficulty was in predicting when and where the first step would be taken. In retrospect, a strong case can be made for the proposition that the first step was taken in Ottoman Turkey in 1908.

*For House, see p. 104.

PART THREE

DRIFTING TOWARD WAR

CHAPTER 10: MACEDONIA – OUT OF CONTROL

The most difficult, complicated, and long-lived problem faced by . . . [the Turkish Sultan] was the Macedonian Question. . . . From the Congress of Berlin until World War I the issue occupied Ottoman and European statesmen alike more than any other single diplomatic problem.

—Shaw and Shaw, *History of the
Ottoman Empire and Modern Turkey*

It looks very much as though the drift toward war began, insofar as any movement in history *has* a beginning, in the old imperial city of Constantinople: yesterday's Byzantium and today's Istanbul. Dominating the straits that separate Europe from Asia, it occupies a site that has been at the center of world politics since the fabled, and perhaps fabulous, Agamemnon, Ulysses, and Achilles embarked for nearby Troy. For more than a thousand years after the fourth century A.D., Constantinople had served as the capital of the Eastern Roman Empire. For five hundred years afterwards it was the capital of the Ottoman (or Turkish) Empire. It had outlived two civilizations and in the early 1900s seemed poised to outlive a third.

It was, however, at a low point in its fortunes. Its glory was faded, as was its beauty. It had not kept up with the times. Most of its streets remained unpaved; the shoes and boots of its million inhabitants were covered with mud when it rained and with dust when it did not. Electricity had not yet been introduced. The city was known for its powerful winds, blowing sometimes from one direction, sometimes from another. That the winds of change would blow its empire away sometime soon was a view commonly held, but it was less easy to predict from which quarter the winds would blow.

It was in Macedonia, a Turkish territory in the center of the turbulent Balkans coveted by Greece, Serbia, and Bulgaria alike, that the disruptive forces were unloosed. Macedonia was frontier country, lawless and out of control; it resisted efforts to police it. It was a prey to brigandage, guerrilla warfare, blood feuds, terrorism, assassinations, massacres, reprisals, uprisings, and almost every form of violence and bloodshed known to humankind. The Ottoman Third Army, charged with the duty of pacifying it, was infiltrated by members of one of Turkey's many subversive secret societies: the Committee of Union and Progress (C.U.P.), known as the Young Turkey party. The Young Turks advocated modernization. Their goal was to reform the empire in order to stop Europe from taking any more Ottoman territory.

For Bulgaria, too, which regarded Macedonia as its southern half, the fighting was an experience that gave rise to clandestine and murderous ultra-nationalist military societies. Much later—in the 1920s and 1930s—they would ally with Italian fascism and leave a bloodstained trail through Balkan history.

Macedonia played much the same role for Serbia, another claimant to the province. Serbian officers and other volunteers underwent the same experience of guerrilla fighting and dirty warfare. In Serbia, too, one result of the turmoil was the creation of secret societies by ultra-nationalist army officers. As will be seen later, it was such a group in Serbia, the Black Hand, that often has been blamed for starting the First World War. Macedonia was the school that shaped the Serbian ultra-nationalists. Emerging from a past that was incendiary, they played a direct role in setting their world on fire. Like the Bulgarians, the Serbs took to assassination to achieve their ends, and, like the Bulgarians, they turned on their own governments and politicians. The Turkish, Bulgarian, and Serbian secret military societies were similar to one another except that each wanted Macedonia for its own. And it was the Young Turks who surfaced first to achieve their aims.

The Young Turks were spurred to act by the news, in June 1908, of a proposal by Russia and Britain to restore order in Macedonia by sending in European officers to serve as a police force. If implemented, which, in retrospect at least, seems to have been highly unlikely, this would have meant that Turkey might well lose one more province.

The Young Turks, surfacing briefly, contacted the European powers to protest against the proposal. Amidst great confusion, the Sultan sent officials to arrest various C.U.P. leaders, but the Young Turks evaded arrest and went on to spark a rebellion. Responding to the mounting disorder, the Sultan, on July 24, 1908, decreed restoration of the constitution, which was the main Young Turk demand. The next year the Sultan abdicated in favor of his brother.

A new phase had opened up in Ottoman politics. It was not clear who would lead or in which direction the leaders would go. Not until 1913 did the Young Turks find themselves securely in control of the Ottoman Empire. But Europeans were on notice that change might finally be in the air.

To Alois Lexa von Aehrenthal, the foreign minister of Austria-Hungary, it seemed possible that the Young Turk rebellion might represent a genuine revolution in Ottoman affairs. It might mean that the reform and modernization that the Young Turks advocated might actually be attempted—and might endanger Hapsburg interests in the Balkans.

Viewed in that way, a signal had been sounded. Now, it could be argued, was the moment to act—or never. Time was running out. Either the Young Turks would reinvigorate their empire and put a stop to further annexations by European powers or the Ottoman state would continue to disintegrate. The accession to power of the Young Turkey party seems to have conveyed a message to Vienna: to strike immediately while Turkey was still weak and before some other European power struck first.

CHAPTER 11: AUSTRIA — FIRST OFF THE MARK

As of 1908 the Dual Monarchy of Austria-Hungary administered the dual Balkan provinces of Bosnia-Herzegovina, whose nominal ruler continued to be the Ottoman Sultan. Turkey had been in the process of losing the provinces in the 1870s to a native rebellion and then a war with Russia when the other Great Powers of Europe stepped in to settle matters and preserve the balance of power among themselves.

At the Congress of Berlin in 1878, the powers had split the ownership of the provinces in two: legal title to remain with Turkey, but with the actual right to occupy—provisionally—being awarded to the Dual Monarchy. The settlement did not, in fact, settle matters. The Hapsburg Empire was obliged to send in an army of between 200,000 and 300,000 troops to quell the local fighters for independence. The provinces were coveted by many; indeed each of the partners in the Dual Monarchy, Austria and Hungary, wanted them for itself, so a decision had to be postponed indefinitely in order to preserve the Dual Monarchy's domestic balance of power. A decision as

to who eventually would replace the Ottoman Sultan as legal ruler
had to be similarly postponed to preserve the even more fragile balance of power among the states of Europe. Meanwhile the largely
Slavic inhabitants of the provinces cherished ambitions of their own
for national independence, while their fellow Slavs, in neighboring
Serbia, across the river, dreamed of annexing them.

Baron von Aehrenthal, foreign minister of the Dual Monarchy
(1906–12), elevated from Baron to Count in 1909, gloried in his reputation as the most highly esteemed foreign secretary of his time. At
the foreign office, he surrounded himself with a staff of aristocratic
young aides who became his disciples. Admirers thought him clever;
detractors, *too* clever.

Aehrenthal saw in the Young Turk rebellion an opportunity to
score a dazzling success in the continuing rivalry among imperial
Great Powers. Whether taking the Balkan provinces proved to provide the first—or the last—chance to dismember the Ottoman
Empire hardly mattered; in either event Austria-Hungary would
move ahead of the other powers by striking first. It was a propitious
moment: Russia, formerly Austria's chief rival in the Balkans, was so
weakened by losing the war against Japan (1904–05) and by the revolution of 1905 as to be practically *hors de combat*.

On October 6, 1908, the Dual Monarchy announced its annexation of Bosnia-Herzegovina. To distract attention from the proclamation, Aehrenthal encouraged Bulgaria, which nominally had
remained until then under Turkish sovereignty, to proclaim legal
independence the day before. Further throwing dust into the eyes of
Europe's other foreign ministers, he also proposed to withdraw
Hapsburg troops that he regarded as useless from the neighboring
Turkish district of Novibazar. Aehrenthal, who kept his own
monarch, Franz Joseph, in the dark about these maneuvers, lied
repeatedly to other European governments about what he was doing
and what he was pushing Bulgaria to do. It was an example of the ero-
sion of the aristocratic code of conduct that formerly had typified
European leaders.

The most violent reaction came from the small but vigorous
Balkan monarchy of Serbia, champion of South Slav rights. Serbia
long had regarded Bosnia-Herzegovina as part of its heartland. Many
elements in the government, in the military, and in the population
thought immediately of mobilization against Austria or of going to

war. Narodna Odbrana, a Serbian nationalist paramilitary organization, sprang up to champion the Serbian cause.

Even the Kaiser was appalled, terming the annexation "fearful stupidity" and lamenting, "Thus my Turkish policy, so carefully built up over twenty years, is thrown away." He learned of the Austrian move only from the newspapers and expressed himself as "deeply offended in my feelings as an ally" by Aehrenthal's secrecy; to which Germany's Chancellor responded: "Our problem could be stated as follows: we must not risk the loss of Austria—with her fifty million inhabitants, her strong and efficient army, but still less must we let ourselves be dragged by her into the midst of an armed conflict which . . . might lead to a general war, in which we certainly had nothing to gain."

Alexander Izvolsky, the foreign secretary of Russia, which was Austria's main rival in the region, initially made no objection to the Austrian grab. He believed that Aehrenthal had promised him that the Hapsburg Empire would help secure compensation for the Czar: free passage for Russia through Constantinople and the Straits. Indeed, Izvolsky believed that he had a definite promise from Aehrenthal in this regard and felt cheated that it was not kept. But a bullying note in undiplomatic language from Berlin dissuaded the Czar from championing the Serbian cause. Germany's acting foreign minister, the aggressive Alfred von Kiderlen-Wächter, on Bülow's behalf used menacing language—that of ultimatums—in communicating with Izvolsky: "we expect a definite answer: yes or no; any evasive, involved, or vague answer would have to be regarded by us as a refusal." Russia, reeling from defeat and revolution in 1905, had little choice but to submit. It was all the more humiliating to Izvolsky because other leading figures in his government who did not share his goals at the Straits were astonished that he had let Aehrenthal get away with taking Bosnia.

Austria's annexation of Bosnia-Herzegovina upset the fragile balance of power in the Balkans. Izvolsky, whether to hit back at Aehrenthal or for some other reason, sent Nicolai Hartwig as minister to Serbia (1909–14). Hartwig was a pan-Slav militant with a following of his own in Russia. He set out to bring Balkan states into a common front to take some or all of the lands still occupied by the Ottoman Empire in Europe. This was a difficult task—getting the quarrelsome rival states of the Christian Balkans to agree on anything seemed hopeless at times—but, as Hartwig showed, it was not impossible.

Hartwig began by forging an alliance between Serbia and Bulgaria, and then joining that alliance to an accord with Russia. Arrangements with Greece and Montenegro followed.

Chancellor von Bülow had approved the use of humiliating language in dealing with Russia. Perhaps it was because he wanted to score an evident triumph. He needed one.

Bülow had been appointed to his position largely through the influence of Philipp Eulenburg, the Kaiser's best friend. Following a series of homosexual scandals and prosecutions, Eulenburg had been obliged to retreat into exile. Tales of transvestite follies and decadent parties seemed to implicate the Kaiser himself.

As Chancellor, Bülow had been obliged to recognize that Germany could not keep up the naval arms race with Britain, a contest that had been central to the Tirpitz policy that he and the Kaiser had embraced. He himself realized the difficulty of supporting the budget and saw no way of raising the taxes that were needed to do so.

As the Bosnian crisis was playing itself out, Bülow faced another scandal: a controversial newspaper interview given by the Kaiser that had been cleared in advance by the Chancellor.

The interview had been granted by Wilhelm to a British friend, who worked up his notes into an article that was published by the London *Daily Telegraph* in October 1908. The article meant to show that the Kaiser was pro-British and that England therefore had nothing to fear from Germany. Wilhelm claimed that during the recent Boer War in South Africa (in which German interests and sympathies lay with the Boers and against England) he personally had prevented other European powers from combining against Britain. Even more, the Kaiser claimed to have devised and delivered strategic plans for Britain that had enabled Britain to win the war. The British were enraged, and in this they were not alone.

The German people, the German parliament, and all German parties denounced Wilhelm. There was a question as to whether the Kaiser might be forced to abdicate. Of course he had not, as he claimed, provided the British generals with their campaign plans. But Bülow, who had failed to adequately vet the indiscreet remarks of his monarch, now failed to defend him. To save himself he lied and did not admit that he had cleared the interview. In 1909, Bülow resigned. A new Chancellor took office, Theobald von Bethmann Hollweg, a civil servant, but of an old and wealthy Rhineland family. Bethmann knew he was not Wilhelm's preferred choice for the office, and his willingness to stand up to the Kaiser was questioned then and is questioned still. Bethmann was an outsider—not Prussian, not military— who did not have, nor did he ever develop, personal relationships with the leaders of the armed forces or with the emperor.

For the Prussian military, demoralized by the discrediting of Wilhelm, it seemed evident that the only way to save the monarchy and therefore their way of life was to go to war. The chief of the Military Cabinet, General Moritz von Lyncker, claimed that war was needed in order to get Germany "out of the internal and external difficulties." But he added that the Kaiser probably would not have the nerve to adopt this solution.

Moltke, chief of the Great General Staff, believed that war was inevitable, and the sooner the better. He was disappointed that the Bosnian crisis was resolved peacefully; such an opportunity of war, he warned, "will not come so soon again under such propitious circumstances."

Having completed the annexation of Bosnia-Herzegovina, Aehrenthal set out to preserve the new status quo in the Balkans. He wanted no further changes. He tried to persuade the powers that Austria did not intend to take Macedonia next. But Russia viewed what he had done as aggressive and therefore believed that Austria-Hungary had become expansionist. To counter that expansionism, Russia felt impelled to organize pro-Russian, anti-Austrian sentiment in the Balkans. In turn, the Dual Monarchy saw this as Russian expansionism, requiring defensive measures of its own.

The treaty of 1879 between Germany and Austria had been a defensive alliance: if either country were attacked—but *only* if it were the country that was attacked—the other was bound to come to its aid. But in January 1909, at the climax of the Bosnia-Herzegovina crisis, Conrad, Austria's chief of staff, had asked Moltke, his German counterpart, what Germany would do if Austria invaded Serbia and thereby provoked Russia into intervening. Moltke replied that Germany would protect Austria anyway, even though Austria would have started it. Moreover, Germany would go to war not only against Russia, but also against France, since France was Russia's ally.

In his history of Germany, Gordon Craig notes that Austria thereafter relied upon Moltke's pledge as a binding commitment: "In effect, Moltke had changed the treaty of 1879 from a defensive to an offensive treaty and placed his country at the mercy of the adventurers in Vienna." It should be added that Moltke's pledge was backed by the Chancellor.

CHAPTER 12: FRANCE AND GERMANY MAKE THEIR PLAY

For a long time France had been eyeing Morocco. It was the last territory in North Africa that remained independent, and it would nicely complement the nation's holdings in Algeria and Tunisia. France was moving to assert a presence in Morocco when, in 1905, Germany unexpectedly intervened. The Kaiser, albeit reluctantly, was sent by his government on a trip—by ship, through a Force 8 gale—to champion Moroccan independence. On Germany's part this was a pretext aimed at disrupting the newly formed Entente of Britain with France. But the German maneuver failed: Britain sided with France. An international conference convened and sympathized with France, too. The conference awarded France the leading role in Moroccan affairs by a treaty signed at Algeciras in 1906. At Germany's insistence the treaty pledged the Europeans to uphold the rule of the Sultan, not to undermine Morocco's independence, as France (or at least its colonialist party) actually aimed to do and in fact went ahead to do.

In March 1911, according to French authorities, rebel tribes brought disorder to the interior of Morocco and threatened one of the capital cities, Fez. The Sultan of Morocco appealed to France to send troops and to restore order. In Berlin it was believed that the tribal uprising had been fomented by the French in order to provide them with an excuse for occupying the country. Even if the uprising were genuine, it was safe to assume that once French troops were installed in Morocco, they would remain. The new German foreign secretary, Alfred von Kiderlen-Wächter, decided to spring a trap. Until the French acted he did nothing but remind them that to do so would abrogate existing treaty arrangements and lead to negotiations to replace them. His aim was to force France to offer Germany substantial compensation: enormous tracts in Africa. In turn, such a diplomatic triumph would shore up the Berlin government's position in the forthcoming parliamentary elections of 1912, where prospects otherwise were quite bleak.

French troops occupied Fez on May 21, 1911. Without consulting even such key members of his own government as the armed forces chiefs, Kiderlen sent a naval cruiser, the *Panther*, to anchor in the harbor of Agadir on Morocco's Atlantic coast. He then asserted Germany's claims on July 1. Apparently he assumed that England, as France's longstanding imperialist rival, would stay out of the conflict. So would Russia, unwilling to risk war for a country as far away and unimportant as Morocco. Austria-Hungary was an ally and so, at least in theory, was Italy.

Kiderlen's calculation was that an isolated France would give way. But it turned out that France was not isolated. Great Britain rallied to its support: Chancellor of the Exchequer David Lloyd George, though of radical, pacifist-leaning, anti-imperialist political origins, made that clear in a rousing speech at a Mansion House banquet on July 21. Russia, too, with some ambiguity, seemed to sympathize with France, while Austria-Hungary refused to extend even diplomatic support for Germany. Italy was of no help.

The Kaiser and his political friends, reluctant from the start to let the foreign secretary play out his risky hand, weighed in on the side of peace. Germany backed down. Austria had gotten away with annexing Bosnia-Herzegovina due to German support, so France had gotten away with taking Morocco due to Britain's aid. France, which already held Algeria and Tunisia, now received Germany's recognition of its protectorate over Morocco too. In return, Germany was awarded compensation in Africa that it deemed to be inadequate. All was agreed November 4, 1911.

Everything seemed to fall into place in the wake of the Agadir crisis. The outlines of a future war, although not its cause, became increasingly clear. Germany had been put on notice that Great Britain might well come in on France's side, and that Russia would do so too if what was at stake was France's survival rather than a mere colonial issue.

Germany could not rely on Italy, a nominal ally, nor even on the Dual Monarchy. Regarding the Austrian alliance as vital, Germany learned at Agadir that it was a one-way affair: Berlin would help to pursue Vienna's interests, but Vienna would not help to pursue Berlin's. Chancellor Theobald von Bethmann Hollweg had known it even before the crisis; he had told the Kaiser: "If it comes to a war, we must hope that Austria is attacked so that she needs our help and not that we are attacked so that it would depend on Austria's decision whether she will remain faithful to the alliance." In other words, a conflict would have to be Austria's in the first instance or else Vienna would sit out the war.

The Agadir crisis alerted Germany to another danger: financial vulnerability. It decided to collect all the cash that was owing to it. Beginning in mid-summer 1911, Germany's central bank, the Reichsbank, systematically called in foreign debts, a program that if continued would have been completed within five years and would have turned Germany into a total debtor. By 1916, Berlin would have repatriated all of its own money. But it also would be holding hoards of cash that it had borrowed from other European powers, and that now would finance a war against them.

German deeds and words in the summer of 1911—the dispatch of the *Panther* to Morocco and the language used in communicating with the Great Powers—alarmed Europe and brought about a sharp reaction. There is irony in this because they were the work neither of the Kaiser nor of the Chancellor, but of a somewhat out-of-control foreign secretary who died at the end of the year after downing six cognacs.

David Lloyd George, Chancellor of the Exchequer in Britain's Liberal government, was one of those former anti-imperialists whose mind was changed by and about the Germans. Hence the Mansion

House speech in which he pledged to spend whatever it took to maintain England's supremacy. His young political protégé Winston Churchill, home secretary and a leading friend of Germany's as late as the spring of 1911, reversed his position too and foresaw the coming world war.

Churchill later recalled that on the afternoon of July 24, 1911, as he walked with Lloyd George by the fountains of Buckingham Palace, a messenger caught up with them to bring the Chancellor in all urgency to see the foreign secretary, Sir Edward Grey. In his room at the House of Commons, Grey told them: "I have just received a communication from the German Ambassador so stiff that the Fleet might be attacked at any moment." And indeed, the Royal Navy was put on alert immediately.

Grey, Lloyd George, Churchill, and other interested ministers met irregularly during the summer as the crisis in Morocco played itself out. Under the pressure of events, government leaders became aware that Britain was unprepared for war. Secret staff talks with Belgium and France in 1905–06, renewed from time to time along with some exchanges of information, and discussions within the armed services and within government committees, had arrived at contrasting and inconclusive results.

A whole-day top-level conference of the Committee of Imperial Defence convened August 23, on the initiative of Director of Military Operations Major General Henry Wilson. It seems that this was the only time before 1914 that the two armed services, army and navy, outlined their respective and competing strategies for waging war. At the conference a decision was made between the two: Britain would not merely fight the war at sea; it would also send an army—an expeditionary force—to fight a land war on the continent of Europe alongside France and against Germany.

Participants were shocked to discover two great failings on the part of the Royal Navy. The fleet was not prepared to transport the expeditionary force from Britain to the Continent, and it refused to create the equivalent of the army's general staff. To ride roughshod over the entrenched admirals, it would be necessary to find a new civilian head of the Admiralty: someone dynamic. In October, Prime Minister Asquith appointed controversial, energetic young Winston Churchill a month before his thirty-seventh birthday. Churchill, in a memorandum that he prepared and circulated, already had discerned the main outlines of the coming world war and threw himself into a frenzy of activity as he prepared to win it.

In Britain's war plans, Germany was the enemy. The ally was France.

To tell of France in the world politics of 1914 is to speak of its leader, Raymond Poincaré. His policy was—and remains—widely misunderstood. It was and is assumed that he aimed at reversing the results of the Franco-Prussian War: that he sought to lead a crusade to recover the lost territories, above all, territories in the land of his birthplace, Lorraine. This was not so, according to his most recent biographer, John Keiger. Rather, he was a moderate centrist who preferred peaceful accommodations.

Remarkably little was known of his conduct of affairs until quite recently. As late as the 1980s, his two biographers in France were unaware that Poincaré's private papers existed; indeed, the more recent of the two claimed in 1984 that the French statesman had destroyed his papers. It remained for Poincaré's first English-language biographer, Keiger, whose work was published in 1997, to study and make use of these materials.

Raymond Poincaré, born in the town of Bar-le-Duc in western Lorraine on August 20, 1860, a person of formidable weight and solidity, grew to be the dominant public figure in the French politics of his time. On his father's side, he came from a family of professionals distinguished in the sciences and in education for more than a century. His mother's ancestors were judges and politicians. His cousin Henri became one of the leading mathematicians of the twentieth century.

Virtuous, cautious, abstemious, middle-of-the-road, and essentially nonpartisan, he nonetheless was driven by a fierce competitiveness: by an ambition to win all of life's contests. At the age of twenty he became the youngest barrister in France. At twenty-six he was elected the youngest member of parliament. At fifty-two, on January 17, 1913, he was the youngest person ever elected to be President, a seven-year position. He also was the first to be elected directly from the office of Prime Minister to that of President. As President, he was a dominating figure. By the summer of 1914, he had taken almost full control of French foreign policy. With regard to Germany, he stood in a typically middle position among the center-left forces, between his pro-German colleague Joseph Caillaux and the lone wolf German-hating Georges Clemenceau. But an observer at the time might have discerned a tilt in favor of Berlin. On January 20, 1914, Poincaré dined at the German embassy—the first time a President of France had done so since 1870.

Keiger suggests that Poincaré's increased friendship with Germany was the product of confidence, stemming in part from the results of the First Balkan War, in which the Balkan forces, trained and armed by France, defeated the Ottoman armies, trained and armed by Germany. Moreover, Poincaré took up the cause of the French colonialist alliance, the Comité de l'Orient, which sought control of Syria, Lebanon, and Palestine should the Turkish empire collapse—an objective which might well pit France against its allies England and Russia.

Yet it transpired that as France set about rounding off its colonial designs, Britain, its traditional rival, offered not opposition, but support. And Germany, which once had encouraged France's imperial ambitions, now stood in the way. New alliances and alignments were in the process of formation. Change was in the air.

Germany, having once again alienated the other powers in the *Panther* episode, now took measures to defend against the hostility it had aroused. In the words of David G. Herrmann, an authority on the pre-1914 arms race, "The most significant military consequence of the second Moroccan crisis remained the German decision to embark on an extraordinary program of land armament in the expectation of a future war. . . . The resulting German army law started an international spiral of land-armaments construction. The Germans regarded themselves as responding to a threat from all sides, but . . . they took the plunge in full expectation that their rivals would react" in the same way, by a massive new arms buildup "and that war would only be a matter of time. In due course, the prophecy fulfilled itself."

As the Moroccan crisis drew to a close, another European power staked out a claim to parts of the Muslim world: Italy, the peninsula that stretches from central Europe to the middle of the Mediterranean Sea. It had never been unified since the fall of Rome nearly

1,500 years before. Its more than 30 million people now were searching for a role in world affairs.

Italy was a geographical entity that had become a country only recently, in the war of 1859. It had acquired its capital city of Rome in the early 1870s. It claimed to rank as a Great Power and felt the need to win colonies, such as older, more established countries possessed. Italians harbored even more ambitious goals: they dreamed of their ancestors in ancient Rome and hoped to win similar glory. Austria-Hungary's move in the Balkans followed by France's in North Africa jolted the Italians into pursuing such aims.

CHAPTER 13: **ITALY GRASPS; THEN THE BALKANS DO TOO**

The territory of Tripolitania, now part of Libya, was Italy's first target. Under the indolent sway of the Ottoman government, Tripolitania, along with adjoining Cyrenaica, was ruled minimally and defended inadequately. For years, Italian diplomats had been clearing the way for a future takeover. In 1900, France had waived any objections it might have had in return for Italy's similar waiver in regard to France's hoped-for annexation of Morocco.

Later the Italians made similar arrangements with the Austrians in regard to Bosnia-Herzegovina and with the Russians in respect to the Straits of the Dardanelles. To keep Italy as an ally, Germany agreed to the Tripoli venture; Britain concurred in hopes of detaching Italy from that alliance.

So once Austria had moved on Bosnia, and France on Morocco, the Italian press and public urged their leaders to go ahead before it became too late. In a leisurely fashion more Mediterranean than modern, the Italian government then gave the other powers notice of its intention to go to war—some two months in advance.

As a young Italian diplomat later remembered it, "I . . . expected that the communication itself would create a stir. Nothing of the kind! Nobody took the slightest notice. . . . People thought that we were bluffing."

On September 29, 1911, Italy declared war, accusing Turkey of injuring Italian interests. Italy occupied the Libyan coastline quickly, but then was bogged down in the interior. Fighting continued for about a year. A cease-fire took effect October 15, 1912, followed by a peace that left Italy in possession not only of Libya but also of Rhodes and other Dodecanese islands off the shore of Turkey in the eastern Mediterranean.

The Italian war was a signal to Hartwig's Russian-inspired Balkan alliance that their time had come to strike—and to preempt Austria. The pace of conflict was accelerating; the clashes began to overlap. The Italo-Turkish war started before the Second Moroccan Crisis was resolved, and now out of the embers of countless local blood feuds, the First Balkan War caught fire in 1912 before the Italian colonial war was concluded. Indeed, the main reason that the Turkish government accepted Italy's terms for concluding hostilities was its need to focus on southeastern Europe. There was a revolt in Albania, a border conflict with Montenegro, continuing guerrilla warfare in Macedonia, and, above all, turmoil in Constantinople, where opponents of the Young Turks briefly had come to power.

As seen earlier, on March 13, 1912, Bulgaria and Serbia had been brought together by the pan-Slav Russian Nicolai Hartwig, who inspired them to take advantage of the Italian war to press their own claims against a distracted Turkey. Greece joined later. So, by verbal agreement, did Montenegro. Russia did not, at first, apprise France of what was afoot; even later Russia did not keep France informed fully. But even St. Petersburg may not have been kept advised: Hartwig was running something close to a rogue operation. Izvolsky and other leaders of the Russian government "denounced the dangers of Hartwig's 'incurable Austrophobia' " and what the historian Dominic Lieven has recently called "his disloyalty to overall Russian foreign policy."

The Balkan peoples harbored murderous hatreds against one another, and asserted rival claims to territories and frontiers, but they acted together in order to strike at Turkey before it could make peace with Italy. Mounting a crusade to free all that remained of the Ottoman Empire in Christian southeastern Europe, Montenegro declared war on Turkey on October 8, 1912, followed by its allies Bulgaria, Serbia, and Greece on October 17. Turkey immediately brought the war with Italy to an end.

The Ottoman forces were, to everyone's surprise, quickly and utterly defeated. They were driven from almost all of Turkey-in-Europe. In a month of lightning warfare, the Balkan states had practically brought the Eastern Question to a close. This was a role that the Great Powers had always imagined that they themselves would play. Now they scrambled to make sure that whatever settlement was reached—by others—would not threaten their vital interests. Their task was complicated by a change of personnel: the foreign secretaries of Germany and Austria died, the foreign secretary of Russia resigned, and their replacements did not carry the same weight.

In December 1912 a conference of ambassadors convened in London. Sixty-three sittings ensued. Macedonia was partitioned. Bulgaria felt cheated of its share by Serbia and Greece. A peace treaty was signed May 30, 1913, but did not last. A month later, on the night of June 29–30, Bulgaria turned against its former allies, Serbia and Greece, in a surprise attack ordered by King Ferdinand I without consulting even his own government. It led to the so-called Second Balkan War, in which Bulgaria was defeated by Serbia, Greece, Turkey, and Romania.

The Treaty of Bucharest, signed on August 10, and negotiated by the local states rather than by the Great Powers, brought the First and Second Balkan Wars to an end. Austria-Hungary was taken by surprise. It had wanted to see Serbia crushed—hoping and believing that Turkey would win the first war and Bulgaria the second—and might well have intervened to dictate different results had there been time. As it was, the Hapsburg Empire feared for its future. The fears centered on victorious Serbia and its sponsor, Russia.

Austrian fears were not unjustified. During the Balkan wars, Russia's new foreign minister, Serge Sazonov, told the Serbian ambassador in St. Petersburg that "we shall shake Austria to the foundations," and that in winning as much as possible in the peace negotiations "we must be content with what we shall receive, regarding it as an installment, for the future belongs to us."

It was Austria-Hungary itself, having annexed Bosnia-

Herzegovina, that had provoked Russia and Serbia to seek revenge. It was possible that Serbia, which had doubled in size, and its allies Russia and the forces of pan-Slavism would continue their advance. Aehrenthal had upset the Balkan balance of power in 1908 in Austria's favor. Now Hartwig had upset the balance in Russia's favor. In turn, would the Dual Monarchy riposte? Or would Germandom continue to retreat before Slavdom?

CHAPTER 14: **THE SLAVIC TIDE**

Times had changed. In the nineteenth century, when foreign policy alignments and readjustments tended to focus on ideology, Russia and the Germanic states of Austria and Prussia had been the closest of allies. In 1912 they still shared the same outlook, the same reactionary politics, and the same values. But their solidarity, based on common beliefs, gave way to a life-or-death conflict based on a clash of interests and a power rivalry.

The clash of interests was in the Balkans, where it was believed that Austria, in order to survive, would have to put down all challenges by Slavic peoples. In turn, Austria's survival as a Great Power was a vital German interest. Moreover, the sheer size of Russia, and its startlingly rapid growth in power as it industrialized with French financial backing, turned the czarist empire into Germany's potential rival for supremacy on the Continent. The Teuton versus Slav aspect of that potential contest reflected race hatred. Moreover in seeing Germany's future in terms of penetration and exploitation of the

Middle East and Far East, the Kaiser imagined yet another goal that could be achieved only by overcoming the Slavic world.

Inconsistent as he so often was, the Kaiser also was a latecomer to these views. In the early days of the Balkan wars he found it unobjectionable that the Ottoman Empire should be defeated. Its Young Turks, he decided, deserved to be "flung out of Europe" for having overthrown "my friend the Sultan." The future of the Balkans should be determined by its peoples, he believed, and for the Great Powers to intervene to "keep the peace" would only backfire: the peoples would turn against the powers. Instead the powers should form a "ring" within which the local forces could fight it out. "Let these people get on with it," he wrote in his irresponsible, thoughtless, and typically ambiguous marginal notes (which lend themselves therefore to various readings). "Either they will take some blows or they will deal some out. . . . The Eastern Question must be solved with blood and iron." Decisions would be made on the battlefield. Blood would be spilled; that was inevitable. But only after that could negotiation play a role. "Afterwards there will be time to talk." But this process— the Balkan ethnic wars, followed by a peace conference at which terms were dictated largely by the local victors—in order to produce an outcome acceptable to the German powers must occur "at the right time for us! And that is now!"—while France and Russia remained unprepared for war.

Shortly after scribbling these marginal notes, the Kaiser ordered his foreign office not to "hinder the Bulgars, Serbs, and Greeks in their legitimate quest for victory." In a marginal note he foresaw the possible creation of a "United States of the Balkans" that might serve politically as a buffer between Austria and Russia, thus solving that problem. It also might provide an important market for German exports.

As crisis loomed ahead in the final months of the First Balkan War, with victorious Serbia and Montenegro seeking an outlet to the sea— Scutari, on the Adriatic in formerly Ottoman Albania—and with Austria opposing that claim, the Kaiser wrote to his foreign secretary: "I see absolutely no danger for Austria's existence, or prestige, in a Serbian harbor on the Adriatic" and "I think it unadvisable needlessly to oppose the Serbian wish." He denied that the terms of the Triple Alliance (Germany, Austria, and Italy) required his country to do so; the alliance only "was intended to guarantee the integrity of current territorial possessions." He added that "to be sure, some of the changes wrought in the Balkans by the war are inconvenient and unwelcome for Vienna, but none [is] so important that we ought on that account to expose ourselves to a military involvement. I could not carry the responsibility for that before my conscience or my people."

He restated his position often: he would "under no circumstances be prepared to march against Paris and Moscow on account of Albania." In a memorandum to the foreign office he called it absurd to risk an "existential struggle with three Great Powers, in which Germany may possibly perish" simply because "Austria doesn't want to have the Serbs in Albania."

Among many other messages, Wilhelm cabled his foreign secretary on November 9, 1912: "have spoken in detail to the Reich Chancellor along the lines of my instruction to you and have emphasized that *under no circumstances will I march against Paris and Moscow on account of Albania.*"

The Kaiser wanted to make clear to Austria that only if Russia attacked—and if Austria had not provoked the attack—would Berlin back Vienna. He was dissuaded. Chancellor von Bethmann Hollweg, perhaps stiffened by the view of Admiral George Alexander von Müller, the Kaiser's naval aide, apparently argued that Austria would lose faith in the German guarantee if such a message were sent to Vienna and that the German public would be furious. Instead, the government should urge Austria to demonstrate moderation so as to make a German intervention "comprehensible to the German people." (But if public opinion would be furious if Austria were abandoned, was not the Austrian case already "comprehensible"?)

In the last half of November, having met with service officers and civilian officials, the Kaiser was satisfied. Public opinion, he decided, now regarded Austria as the provoked party; "the position which I wanted has been reached."

On November 21 the Kaiser's great friend Archduke Franz Ferdinand, heir to the Hapsburg throne, arrived in Berlin and received from Wilhelm and from Moltke assurances that Germany would back Austria "in all circumstances" even at the risk of war with Britain, France, and Russia. The Kaiser apparently was persuaded that Austria now *was* the provoked party and that England and France would not intervene. These may have been his conditions, albeit unspoken. And German foreign office opinion was that "today both Italy and England are on our side": the risk was far less than might appear. Whether for that reason or another, the German leaders made their secret commitment public. The foreign minister told the parliament on November 28: "If Austria is forced, *for whatever reason*, to fight for its position as a Great Power, then we must stand by her side" (emphasis added). In London the British foreign secretary was startled: did Germany, he asked, really mean to give Austria "a blank cheque," and to support Vienna in whatever it did, even if it were in the wrong, and even in a war of aggression that it had started? Sir Edward Grey told the German ambassador that "the consequences of such a policy" would be "incalculable."

Grey acted to make sure that the Kaiser did not misunderstand England's position. If Germany would not let Austria disappear as a Great Power, neither would England let France disappear as such. Grey apparently spoke to R. B. Haldane, the Lord Chancellor, who as war minister had remade the British army, and the result was a message from London that sparked a fresh crisis.

The date was December 8, 1912. On short notice, the Kaiser convened a meeting in his Berlin quarters with a number of his military leaders: four, according to one account, and six according to another. They met at 11 a.m. to consider the import of the telegram from London. In addition to Wilhelm the participants included Admiral Müller, chief of the Kaiser's Naval Cabinet; Admiral von Tirpitz, the naval leader; General von Moltke, the army chief of staff; Vice Admiral August von Heeringen, head of the admiralty staff, and perhaps also his brother General Josias von Heeringen, Prussian minister of war, and the chief of the Military Cabinet, Moritz Freiherr von Lyncker. Not present were the civilian leaders: Chancellor von Bethmann Hollweg and the foreign secretary, Gottlieb von Jagow.

This secret conference was drawn to the world's attention only a half century later, when the historian Fritz Fischer showed that it could have been evidence of a deliberate plan by the Kaiser and his military chiefs to bring about a European war in June 1914. The interpretation of the 1912 conference remains an open question, although most leading historians today tend not to accept Fischer's views without at least some qualification. John Röhl, perhaps the closest in his views to Fischer, makes the persuasive point that we now have additional documentation in unusual abundance to help us understand the notes by Admiral Müller that, in an earlier garbled version, had been our only source.

The Kaiser called the conference because Germany's Anglophile ambassador in London, Prince Karl Max von Lichnowsky, had cabled him with news of a conversation he had just held with Lord Haldane, Britain's Germanophile former minister of war. According to the Kaiser, Haldane apparently spoke for Sir Edward Grey. Given the channel of communication chosen—Lichnowsky and Haldane, two men devoted to the cause of improving relations between England and Germany—it would have been safe to infer that Grey was supplying medicine that, despite its apparent bitterness, was prescribed for the patient's own good. The message from Grey brought to the Kaiser's attention something that any student of international relations ought to have known: that it was in Britain's vital interest to maintain the balance of power in Europe. If Germany were to attack France, Britain would intervene on France's side, for preserving the independence and Great Power status of France was one of England's vital interests. Implied in the cable was the message that London did not object if Germany increased its lead as the wealthiest and most militarily powerful country on the Continent so long as other powers, especially those of Western Europe, were allowed to retain their independence. In his angry marginal notes on the text of the telegram, Wilhelm described the English principle of the balance of power as an "idiocy" which would make England "eternally into our enemy."

The Kaiser, according to one secondhand version, was "in a most agitated state" and "in an openly war-like mood." In Admiral von Müller's firsthand account, Wilhelm welcomed Haldane's message as providing "a desirable clarification" of Britain's intentions, showing those among Germany's planners who had wanted to allow for the possibility of England's neutrality the error of their ways. In the light of Haldane's message, Germany, if it went to war, should plan on fighting Britain as well, and to that end, the navy should speed up such measures as building its U-boat fleet.

According to the Kaiser, speaking in December, in the middle of the Balkan wars, Austria "must deal energetically" with Serbia; and "if Russia supports the Serbs, which she evidently does . . . then war would be unavoidable for us, too." Moltke said, "I believe a war is unavoidable and the sooner the better." But—and it was to prove a significant "but"—Moltke added that "we ought to do more through the press" to build up popular support for a war against Russia.

The Kaiser and Moltke urged immediate war. Tirpitz, speaking for the navy, agreed in part but asked "postponement of the great fight for one and a half years." The fleet needed time to complete widening and deepening the Kiel Canal and work on the base at Heligoland. Moltke objected that the navy would not be ready even then, and that the army, which was running out of money, would be in a worse position.

The meeting seems to have disbanded in a show of pro-war sentiment but without arriving at an agreed decision. A target date had been mentioned but had not been firmly set. A disappointed Admiral von Müller noted in his diary: "The result" of the conference "amounted to almost o." Müller wrote to the Chancellor that afternoon, reporting what had been said and decided at what became known as the "war council." Müller transmitted the Kaiser's order to use the press to prepare the people for a future war with Russia. In the week or so following the conference, the Kaiser spoke often of the coming war in excited terms, repeatedly describing it as a racial conflict.

Ever since Fritz Fischer publicized evidence of the council, historians have wondered whether it could be a coincidence that one and a half years later the war did in fact break out. (Shortly after the council ended, Wilhelm told the Swiss minister that the racial struggle "will probably take place in one or two years.")

In the nearly two years that followed the war council, Germans started a new and more frantic arms race, but it had been decided upon and set in motion long before. According to a leading student of the arms race, David Herrmann, it had been undertaken, in part, in an act of interservice rivalry, in which the army made a preemptive strike against the navy, seeking a rise in funding large enough so that an increase for the fleet too would be out of the question. Another reason was that both the public and the army had been jolted by the Moroccan crisis of 1911 into an awareness that Germany would face real challenges in a war against a European coalition.

But the First Balkan War, ending in December 1912 at the time of the war council, "had an even more galvanizing effect," we are told by Herrmann, that "transformed the atmosphere of tension into one of emergency." The Slavs seemingly were moving ahead, and

Austria-Hungary, in a paralysis of policy and power, was doing nothing to stop them. German party leaders spoke openly of the possibility of a world war.

The war ministry persevered in trying to limit the army's numbers in order to preserve Prussian Junker control of it, while the alarmed Moltke proposed a nearly 50 percent rise in its size. The army bill of 1912 was large, but that of 1913 was the largest in German history. The German peacetime military machine was running at full capacity; the increases could not be fully digested until 1916.

As the German leaders were aware, their frantic arms buildup would inspire other countries to try to match it. But they had arrived at some kind of limit. As Germany was then constituted, it probably was not possible to expand any further. The political organization was too ramshackle; the taxation system too archaic and unprogressive. Germany could not afford to continue its military expansion for much longer. The only thing that could justify military expenditures at their 1913 level was to go to war in the immediate future. But German public opinion was not ready for it. Moltke wrote to Conrad, chief of the Austrian General Staff, in February 1913 that it would be hard to find a rallying cry that would persuade the German public to go to war—yet.

CHAPTER 15: EUROPE GOES TO THE BRINK

Between 1908 and 1913 the Young Turk revolt had been followed by one European intervention after another in lands that once had been or still were Ottoman. The uprising in Turkey had led to Austria's annexation of Bosnia-Herzegovina. France then had made its move in Morocco, inspiring Italy to strike at the Ottoman Empire in Libya and the Aegean, while Serbia, Montenegro, Greece, and Bulgaria attacked it in the Balkans. In those five years the Great Powers had managed to steer clear of one another, averting one clash after another, while at the same time moving ever closer to ultimate collision. Total arms spending by the six Great Powers between 1908 and 1913 went up by 50 percent.

Taken together the events of those years worked a change in the face of European politics.

- Britain, in the Agadir crisis, indicated that it would abandon its traditional isolation in order to stand by France if France were threatened by Germany—even if it were France's fault.

- France, in the Balkan wars, showed that it would go beyond its purely defensive treaty to back Russia in a conflict with Germany started by Russia.
- Germany, isolated in the Agadir crisis despite its defensive treaty with the Dual Monarchy, moved in the direction of supporting the Hapsburg Empire—supporting it (as Moltke pledged to Conrad in the Bosnia-Herzegovina crisis) even in an act of aggression—rather than be isolated again.
- Italy, unpredictable militarily even against the slow-moving Ottoman Empire, was not to be relied upon.
- Turkey-in-Europe, liberated by the Balkan peoples themselves rather than (as had been expected) by the Great Powers, fell prey therefore to the volatile violence and passions of its rival ethnic groups, rather than enjoying the stability that Great Power balance of power might have brought.
- Serbia, exulting in its lightning victories in two Balkan wars, looked forward to expanding.
- Austria, mortally afraid of Serbian designs, came to believe that striking first might be its only hope. Austria, regarding the Balkan states as potentially a single bloc—and, as such, the equivalent of a new Great Power—worried that it might become a Slav and Greek Orthodox entity, aligned with Russia, which therefore might fundamentally shift the balance of forces in Europe in favor of France/Russia.
- The Kaiser, for a time, saw the shift in the balance of power as creating a buffer that might solve the problem of Austro-Russian rivalry, while allowing Christians to unite in expanding eastward against Islam.

On October 23, 1913, Wilhelm described the outcome of the Balkan wars to the Austro-Hungarian foreign minister by saying: "What was taking place was an historic process to be classed in the same category as the great migrations of people, the present case was a powerful forward surge of the Slavs. War between East and West was in the long run inevitable." He continued by saying: "The Slavs are born not to rule but to obey." His bizarre conception at the time was that Serbia could be persuaded to accept Austria's leadership and save the West. Under Teutonic leadership, Christianity would look eastward for expansion as once the tide of Islam had flowed westward.

Of all the shifts in inclination and perception that took place in European international politics during the years before the war, perhaps the one most at odds with our perceptions today was the belief, widely held in Berlin, that Germany was growing weaker. In retrospect, what strikes us is that, to the contrary, Germany was surging ahead industrially and militarily; it was growing stronger. The industrial and other figures are there to prove it, and at the time such astute British politicians and businessmen as Joseph Chamberlain saw British decline vis-à-vis Germany as a reality. But Moltke spoke for many in seats of power in Germany who regarded an eventual war as unavoidable—and who were convinced that it could be won only if fought sooner rather than later. If Austria needed a war today, Germany needed one, in Moltke's view, no later than tomorrow.

Although, as the Kaiser's new perspective indicated, Europe was pulling back from the brink, the brink remained close. Between 1908 and 1913, Europeans had moved the line permanently closer to it. Earlier, the powers were bound by secret treaties of alliance that pledged them to help each other in case of an attack. Now the alliances no longer were defensive. France would fight for Russia, and Britain might well fight for France, right or wrong, as would Germany for Austria. The question that the war would settle would be: which of the Great Powers would remain a Great Power? As of 1914, only one of them felt its status—and existence—immediately threatened unless it took prompt action, and that power was Austria-Hungary.

Encirclement was Germany's nightmare, and Germany had brought it upon itself. Located in the heart of Europe, the country had so effectively terrified its neighbors that they had banded together in self-defense. In turn, what its neighbors had been driven to do had further reinforced Germany's paranoia. What had started as a dark fantasy was converted by Germany's own actions into a reality. France, England, and Russia had no intention of attacking Germany, but they were making contingency plans for combining against the Kaiser's empire if and when it attacked them.

Culturally, in every way the most and best educated population in Europe—that of Germany—was telling itself that it was being suffocated by a European civilization that was pressing in on it from all sides. It was not evident then nor is it now why the Germans felt that way, but it is clear that they did.

Such sentiments were certainly apparent in military and political matters. Historians believe there was an easing of tensions between England and Germany in 1914 as they settled such conflicts as those relating to the German plan to build a Berlin-to-Baghdad railway and to appoint a German general officer, Otto Liman von Sanders, to reorganize the Ottoman army. But when Germany's Anglophile ambassador in London sent home a message urging Germany and Britain to stick together, a high Berlin foreign policy official could only imagine that the ambassador had been duped by the British: "again put into swaddling clothes" (June 27, 1914). When a Russian newspaper urged Entente preparedness, "Against us" was the Kaiser's marginal note; "they are working on high pressure for an early war with us." To the newspaper's assertion that "Russia and France want no war," the Kaiser scribbled "Twaddle!"

CHAPTER 16: **MORE BALKAN TREMORS**

In the turbulent Balkans of the early twentieth century, peace treaties seemed to be no more than temporary truces during which the parties schemed at realignment for the next round of fighting. So it was in mid-June 1914, as Kaiser Wilhelm II held discussions with his friend Archduke Franz Ferdinand. These talks were followed by a far-ranging conversation between Franz Ferdinand and Count Berchtold, foreign minister of the Dual Monarchy. These, in turn, led to the drafting by several hands within the Hapsburg foreign ministry of a memorandum outlining a grand strategy for Austria-Hungary.

Wilhelm and Franz Ferdinand met at the Archduke's country estate, Konopischt, in Bohemia (today's Czech Republic). No transcript survives, but there is evidence that Franz Ferdinand had been asked by his emperor, Franz Joseph, to obtain from Wilhelm a commitment to continue to back Austria unconditionally, such as he had given in November 1912, and that Wilhelm had avoided providing such a statement. The Austrian government believed that Serbia posed a mortal danger, but the Kaiser disagreed.

The political relationship between Wilhelm and Franz Ferdinand was far more complex than it appeared on the surface. For the Kaiser, it was, at least in part, a friendship of convenience. He had set out to form a bond with the Hapsburg heir apparent. In some respects that was easy to do because of their shared tastes, including a passion for hunting. Wilhelm made a point of treating Sophie, Franz Ferdinand's wife, as an Archduchess, a position denied to her in her own country. He dealt with the Archduke as though he were the political partner that, upon the death of elderly Franz Joseph, he might well become. He worked at making a friend of Franz Ferdinand, but Franz Ferdinand may not have been entirely fond of Wilhelm. There were tensions within the Austro-German alliance.

Both were men of autocratic temperament. They were impatient and held strong biases. But Franz Ferdinand was Roman Catholic while Wilhelm was Lutheran. And the Archduke deeply resented the descent of the Hapsburg Empire from its first place among the powers of Europe to its position in 1914 as a junior partner to Wilhelm's Germany. He detested Hungary, and deplored the weakness that drove Austria to make the Magyars a partner in government. Wilhelm, on the contrary, spoke highly of Count István Tisza, the Hungarian Prime Minister, but failed to convince Franz Ferdinand.

Both men entertained hopes of an eventual détente with Russia, whose Czar shared their belief in royal absolutism. But just as Wilhelm allowed his anti-Slav racism to overcome his monarchist ideology, Nicholas subordinated his ideology to his country's national interest. And it should be noted that the Kaiser had a paranoid fear that Russia was planning a war against Germany.

Time and again, during the frequent war crises that were so conspicuous a feature of their time, both men chose peace, and were distrusted by the military in their respective countries for having done so. Both men were intemperate in their use of language: Franz Ferdinand in dealing with people, Wilhelm in dealing with politics.

Though in theory they were closest allies, the Kaiser's Germany pursued ambitious economic plans in Asia, and even in the Balkans from which Franz Ferdinand's Dual Monarchy was excluded. Austria-Hungary would not back Germany in Morocco; Germany would not support Austria-Hungary in Albania. Regarding the belligerents in the Second Balkan War, Germany was for Greece and Austria was for Bulgaria. Austrians could not understand how Germany could fail to see why Serbia, which had just doubled in size, terrified them. Serbia exercised a powerful magnetic pull on the substantial Slavic population of the Hapsburg Empire.

In policy planning in June 1914, the question for the two empires was which country should be their main Balkan ally: Romania or Bulgaria? Germany chose Romania while Austria chose, once again, Bulgaria. But on this issue Franz Ferdinand parted company with his government; he, like the Kaiser, was for Romania.

Here they were in counsel together, two of the most disliked men in European public life, yet, within the ranks of their own governments, perhaps the only ones of consequence who again and again favored pulling back from the brink of war. They were misunderstood by the outside world. The Kaiser, who loved to talk tough, often ranted and raved like a belligerent adolescent trying to impress his peers, but while his tirades were bellicose, his decisions—when the time to act arrived—by and large were not. There was no reason to misunderstand Franz Ferdinand, however; he spoke as well as worked to achieve peace.

General Conrad, sometime Austrian chief of staff, recalled Franz Ferdinand's aide-de-camp as saying in 1913, "The Archduke has sounded the retreat all along the line, he will on no account have war with Russia, he will not allow it. He wants not a plum tree, not a sheep from Serbia." Berchtold, Austria's foreign minister, said to Conrad, "The Heir Apparent is all on the side of peace." Reportedly Franz Ferdinand told dinner guests that Austria had nothing to gain from conquering Serbia; going to war would be "a bit of nonsense."

On March 16, 1914, Conrad spoke, as he so often did, of going to war as soon as possible against Russia. He was speaking to the German ambassador in Vienna, who explained why it could not happen: "Two important people are against it, your Archduke Franz Ferdinand and my Kaiser."

A secret truth about the politics of 1914—something of which the outside world had no suspicion—was that if these two men continued to work together in pursuit of their common policy goals, the Great

Powers of Europe might well have remained at peace. The wars of 1914 would not have taken place.

Count Berchtold had come to Konopischt the day after Wilhelm left. It was Sunday, June 14, two weeks before Franz Ferdinand's scheduled trip to Sarajevo. The two men and their wives spent the day together. Afterwards Berchtold put his foreign ministry officials to work on questions that were at issue. It was not really *his* staff. It consisted of a clique of talented firebrands he had inherited from Aehrenthal, who had known how to control their high spirits. Now Berchtold was giving them their head. His aim was to summarize Austria's current thinking on world affairs: where the Dual Monarchy was and where it hoped to go.

One concern was Albania, a country created by the European powers as a buffer to contain Serbian expansionism. The assumption had been that it would be Austro-German in orientation; indeed, Albania had been provided with a German monarch. Yet Italy—nominally the ally of Austria and Germany in the Triple Alliance—was maneuvering to achieve hegemony in the newly created country. Italy was becoming a rival and perhaps an enemy.

Was Russia a concern? Wilhelm and Franz Ferdinand tended to think not, and favored a thaw in relations with the Czar. However, some in the foreign office in Vienna feared that, as in 1912, pan-Slav Russians would be able to unite all the Balkan countries—only this time against Germany and Austria instead of against Turkey.

Wilhelm thought that the Balkan states would remain disunited. The trick was to back the right combination of them. Romania was at the top of his list. Its monarch had secretly pledged—personally—to support the Triple Alliance. That did not bind his country. Wilhelm and Franz Ferdinand hoped for a public and secure commitment.

A problem was that Austria was bound to Hungary in the Dual Monarchy, and Hungary and Romania had an apparently irreconcilable conflict—one that endures today. Franz Ferdinand was fiercely anti-Hungarian, and wanted to ally with Romania at Hungary's expense. The Kaiser would not face the issue; he admired Hungary's premier, Count István Tisza, and felt that the Hungary-Romania conflict could somehow be made to go away. He also wanted to bring in Greece as an ally, but lacked convincing evidence that Greece would wish to do so. Finally, he hoped to reconcile Serbia and Austria—much to the disgust of the Austrians, who tried in vain to convince him that Serbia was a menace that somehow had to be eliminated. In effect, the Kaiser was proposing to re-create the victorious alliance of the Second Balkan War, but this time have it led by Germany and the Dual Monarchy. He argued for going with what had been the winning side.

Berchtold saw things the other way around. The Dual Monarchy's foreign minister did not believe that Romania would be an ally of Austria's; it would not back Austria-Hungary because of the Hungarian conflict, and the Dual Monarchy would therefore have to ally with Romania's enemy, Bulgaria. Bulgaria had ties with Turkey, so Greece would have to be thrown on the other side. Therefore Berchtold would essentially reconstitute the alliance pattern of the Second Balkan War too, but he would take over what had been not the winning, but the losing side.

On the eve of the world crisis, there was no agreement in Berlin or Vienna as to who was the enemy or what was the quarrel in the troublesome Balkans.

As regards Europe as a whole, the two empires were reasonably clear as to who was on what side: they themselves, maybe joined by Italy, on one side; Russia and France, maybe with England, on the other. Moreover, the two chiefs of the general staff, Helmuth von Moltke in Germany and Franz Conrad von Hötzendorf in Austria-Hungary, were in close touch with one another and sometimes discussed their respective war plans. Both generals often urged launching preventive war.

Indeed, in the words of Hew Strachan, "Conrad first proposed preventive war against Serbia in 1906, and he did so again in 1908–9, in 1912–13, in October 1913, and May 1914: between 1 January 1913 and 1 January 1914 he proposed a Serbian war twenty-five times."

But the generals were subordinated to monarchs who opted for peace. And in Germany, Moltke also was opposed by Tirpitz, who wanted a cold war—at least for many years to come—rather than a hot one, and whose focus was on a conflict with England rather than with the land powers of France and Russia. Then, too, lobbying against Moltke was the ministry of war, which wanted to keep the officer corps small enough to ensure Prussian control of Germany—which was a level too low to win a war.

Even Moltke, in the circumstances of 1913, had cautioned against launching a war because it was the wrong time to do so. He continued to believe "that a European war is bound to come sooner or later, in which the issue will be one of a struggle between Germandom and Slavdom." But, in his view, a war should not be initiated until public opinion could be rallied around the cause. In Moltke's words: "When starting a world war one has to think very carefully."

As the twentieth century dawned, Europeans were richer and more powerful than anybody ever had been before. They should also have felt more secure than anybody had felt before. But they did not. They—or at least their governments—were in the grip of fear. They sensed the tremors. Where or when, they did not know, but they were convinced an earthquake was going to strike.

Across the ocean, at least one American statesman was sufficiently attuned to European realities to feel the same thing. His name was Edward House. He could speak for the President, and he decided to try his hand at preventing the cataclysm that threatened.

CHAPTER 17: **AN AMERICAN TRIES TO STOP IT**

New York City, May 16, 1914. An immense crowd gathered at the docks to witness the departures of passengers on the transatlantic ocean liner *Imperator* bound for Europe. Among those who could be observed boarding the vessel was Edward House: Colonel House, to give him his honorary Texas title.

House, aged fifty-five, was described by the *New York Sun* as "a slender, middle-aged man with a gray, close-cropped moustache, well dressed, calm-looking" who walked quietly but firmly. He spoke quietly too, at times in tones that seemed silken.

He was a lifelong insider in politics, although he was never a candidate for public office. He was someone to whom others confided their secrets. He may have been the best listener of his time. Those who spoke with him came away with the conviction that he had understood them, which usually was true, and that he fully sympathized with them, which often was not.

A man of independent wealth, on familiar terms with the great figures of Wall Street, he lived in Manhattan while maintaining a residence and his political power base in his home state of Texas. When needed, he commuted by train to Washington, D.C., to meet at the White House with his best friend and closest associate, the first-term, reform-minded American chief executive Woodrow Wilson, whom House had helped elect to the presidency in the freak election of 1912. In that election the two Republican candidates, former President Theodore Roosevelt, running as a Progressive, and incumbent President William Howard Taft, had split the Republican majority between them, allowing Wilson—the candidate of the minority party, the Democrats—to slip through to victory with less than 50 percent of the popular vote, though far more than half of the electoral college.

Woodrow Wilson was one of the oddest men ever elected to the presidency. A recluse who felt at ease only with women and children, he lacked a taste for politics or a liking for politicians, finding deals and compromises distasteful, and political ambition—except his own—sordid.

Serendipity brought Wilson together with House in the 1912 election. House became his alter ego. Once Wilson was elected, to a large extent House took charge of the political aspects of the presidency: the chores that Wilson either could not or would not do for himself. House often interviewed those who wanted jobs or favors from the new administration. If there were deals to be made or trades to be transacted, he did them. Scholars continue to dispute the respective contributions of the two men to the positive accomplishments of the Wilson administration, but House played a key role in such important matters as the establishment of the Federal Reserve Bank, tariff reform, and the institution of the income tax.

In the field of foreign affairs, at least in the opening two years of the Wilson presidency, it was House, a gifted student of international politics, who took an interest in European developments, while Wilson, who had no background in the field, did not.

House noted, in the spring of 1914: "the President had given very little thought to the existing situation in Europe." He himself was quite concerned by what he saw and foresaw. House apparently was almost alone among American statesmen in understanding the implications of the Balkan wars, in sensing that they could end by threatening the peace and stability of the world.

To head off the dangers that he perceived ahead, House proposed to go to Europe to negotiate the creation of a new international structure that would bring a lasting peace among all the Great Powers. Wilson gave his full and admiring support to the endeavor. House's own private name for the mission on which he was to embark was "the great adventure."

House's effectiveness, and his value to the President, were due in large part to his discretion. Secrets were confided to him because it was believed that he could be trusted not to reveal them. Of course, this aroused widespread popular curiosity. Picturing House as a man of mystery, a newspaper editor told one of his reporters: "House sees nobody. He can't be reached. Nobody knows his address, and his telephone number is private." But that was an exaggeration; House made himself available, as good politicians do. Thus aboard the *Imperator*, and although preoccupied by thoughts of his secret mission, he found time to deal with a cable from a woman asking that her husband, a U.S. consular official, be promoted from a posting in Rio to one in London. "Even at sea there is no rest from the office seekers" was House's comment.

The mission with which House had entrusted himself was to persuade Germany and Britain to join with the United States in an alliance to keep the peace. It was a long-held idea of his that the chief powers of Europe had accumulated so much power in their hands that, together with America, they could prevent major wars.

It was an idea that was, so to speak, in the air. Theodore Roosevelt at one time had envisaged the creation of a cartel of perhaps five Great Powers to keep the world at peace. Ideas for a league of nations also surfaced from time to time in Great Britain's Liberal administration.

Andrew Carnegie, the steel magnate who had become one of the world's wealthiest men, had pursued a project not unlike House's a few years earlier. Aiming at an alliance of "Teutonic nations," Carnegie asked rhetorically, "Why should these Teutonic nations ever quarrel?" He imagined that he had lined up the support of the British government, notably of Prime Minister Herbert Asquith and Foreign Secretary Sir Edward Grey, for his plan. For it to come into existence, Carnegie believed all that was required was that Kaiser Wilhelm II should take the lead.

"It lies today in the power of one man to found this league of peace," Carnegie explained in 1907. "It is in the hands of the German emperor alone of all men, that the power to abolish war seems to rest." For reasons not entirely clear, Carnegie thought his plans were ruined by the death of England's King Edward VII in 1910.

Like Carnegie, House believed that he had the support of the British government for his scheme and that the key to its viability was to gain the support of the Kaiser. In the spring of 1914, immediately upon disembarking in Europe, House therefore made his way to Germany. Aboard ship and on arriving in Germany, House sounded out opinion among well-placed and well-informed Germans and what he heard boded ill for the cause of peace. From Berlin he wrote to the President on May 29 that what he had learned thus far "tended to confirm the opinion as to the nearly impossible chance of bettering conditions." Indeed, he wrote, "the situation is extraordinary. It is jingoism run stark mad." House predicted "an awful cataclysm" unless he or Wilson took a hand in events because "No one in Europe can do it. There is too much hatred, too many jealousies."

In Russia there was a violent press campaign against Austria. In Austria there was a violent press campaign against Russia. The Pan-German League, a well-connected pressure group in Germany, announced (April 19, 1914) that "France and Russia are preparing for the decisive struggle with Germany and Austria-Hungary and they intend to strike at the first opportunity." A newspaper headline (March 11, 1914) warned Germans that "a war, the like of which history has never seen, is approaching."

In House's analysis Russia and France would "close in" on Germany and its ally Austria-Hungary if Britain gave the word. But Britain hesitated to do so: if Germany were crushed, who would be left to restrain Russia? Still, if Germany continued to threaten English naval supremacy, London would have no choice but to meet Berlin's challenge.

Hence, House's peace plan: an agreement between Britain and Germany to limit the size of their respective navies, the agreement to be brokered by the United States. This could bring about the essentially peaceful world that America desired, but—always the realist—House cautioned that there might be "some disadvantage to us" in Britain and Germany getting together.

Tirpitz pointed to a different flaw in House's plan. "He disclaimed any desire for conquest, and insisted that it was peace that Germany wanted, but the way to maintain it was to put fear into the hearts of her enemies." House wanted Germany to stop expanding its navy, but Tirpitz desired instead "to increase its expansion."

House's main goal was to set up a meeting with Germany's ruler, and he achieved it. On June 1, in the course of a day-long festival that included religious ceremonies, parades, and the awarding of medals, House was accorded a private personal meeting with the Kaiser that lasted a half hour.

House's diary entry indicates that the two men discussed "the European situation as it affected the Anglo-Saxon race." In the Kaiser's expressed view, England, Germany, and the United States represented Christian civilization. Latins and Slavs were semi-barbarous, he believed, and also unreliable, so England was wrong to ally with France and Russia. On the other hand, the Teutonic core—Germany, Britain, America—should ally with all the other Euro-peans in defense of Western civilization "as against the Oriental races."

House tried to persuade the Kaiser that Germany should abandon its challenge to British naval power. Britain then would no longer have to ally itself with Russia. It was only the threat posed by Germany that drove Britain into Russia's arms. Russia was, if anything, Britain's natural enemy. In other words, it was within the Kaiser's power to accomplish what he claimed to want: England to detach itself from the alliance with Russia and France, and instead to ally itself with Germany.

House "spoke of the community of interests between England, Germany and the United States and thought that if they stood together the peace of the world could be maintained. . . . However, in my opinion, there could be no understanding between Germany and England so long as he continued to increase his navy." The Kaiser responded that he needed a strong navy, but that when his current enlargement program terminated he would stop.

House said that his idea was that an American—he or the President—might be in a better position than a European to bring the European powers together. The Kaiser agreed. House said he had wanted to see the Kaiser first, and now would go directly to London to try to secure Britain's agreement, too, to an initiative by the United States along these lines.

House left Germany hopefully. From Paris he reported on June 3 to the President that he had spoken with almost every German of consequence at his meetings and that "I am glad to tell you that I have been as successful as anticipated and have ample material to open negotiations in London." The German emperor had "seemed pleased that I had undertaken to start the work" and "concurred also in my suggestion that whatever program America, England, and Germany agreed to would be successful."

The heart of the matter, as House saw it, was that "both England and Germany have one feeling in common and that is fear of one another." His task, he believed, was to dispel these fears by bringing together the leaders of the two countries and encouraging them to get to know and to trust one another. House believed in face-to-face resolution of problems at the top. He considered it "essential that principals should get together" to iron out misunderstandings. He felt that he was "in a fair way to a beginning of the great task that I have undertaken."

House traveled to London on June 9. He noted in his diary that Walter Hines Page, the U.S. ambassador to Britain, "was kind enough to say that he considered my work in Germany the most important done in this generation." Page arranged for House to meet with Sir Edward Grey. It was not easy. House explained to Wilson: "I find here everything cluttered up with social affairs and it is impossible to work quickly. Here they have thoughts on Ascot, garden parties, etc., etc."

On June 27 the meeting with Grey finally took place over lunch. Although others were present, House and Grey did almost all the talking. They had a wide-ranging discussion of the troubled European political situation. They agreed that France's leaders had given up all thought of recovering the territories in Alsace and Lorraine, or of taking revenge on Germany. The French people still harbored such a dream, but statesmen in France recognized that the continuing growth of the German population vis-à-vis France made that goal an ever more remote possibility.

As to Russia and Britain, Grey remarked that the two came into contact with each other at so many points around the world that it was important to keep on the best of terms. Grey claimed to understand Germany's felt need to build a large fleet. It was House who warned Grey—and not Grey who warned House—"of the militant war spirit in Germany and of the high tension of the people. . . . I thought Germany would strike quickly when she moved. That there would be no parley or discussion. That when she felt that a difficulty could not be overcome by peaceful negotiations, she would take no chances, but would strike. I thought the Kaiser himself and most of his immediate advisors did not want war because they wished Germany to expand commercially and grow in wealth, but the army was military and aggressive and ready for war at any time."

Yet the two men agreed—less than twenty-four hours before Archduke Franz Ferdinand was assassinated—that "Neither England, Germany, Russia, nor France desire war." Looking presciently to a less visible but more long-term threat to global stability, House urged the four European powers to enter into an agreement with the United States whereby, acting together, they could provide credit at lower interest notes to "the undeveloped countries of the earth."

As the month of June drew to a close House continued to meet with European leaders in pursuit of his American dream for the world.

A decade later, Grey wrote: "House had just come from Berlin, and he had spoken with grave feeling of the impression he had received there; how the air seemed full of the clash of arms, of readiness to strike. This might have been discounted as the impression which would naturally have been produced on an American seeing at close quarters a continental military system for the first time. It was alien to our temperament as to his, but it was familiar to us. We had lived beside it for years; we had known and watched its growth ever since 1870. But House was a man of exceptional knowledge and cool judgment. What if this militarism had now taken control of policy?"

In the spring of 1914, as House pursued his mission, the chiefs of staff of Germany and Austria, Moltke and Conrad, took the baths together at Carlsbad in Bohemia. They discussed war plans. Moltke also held talks that spring with Gottlieb von Jagow, Germany's foreign minister. Jagow noted that Moltke told him that in two or three years the "military superiority of our enemies would . . . be so great that he did not know how he could overcome them. Today we would still be a match for them. In his opinion there was no alternative to making preventive war in order to defeat the enemy while there was still a chance of victory. The Chief of the General Staff therefore proposed that I should conduct a policy with the aim of provoking a war in the near future."

PART FOUR

MURDER!

CHAPTER 18: **THE LAST WALTZ**

Although Franz Ferdinand von Osterreich-Este, nephew of the elderly emperor Franz Joseph and heir apparent to the Hapsburg thrones of Austria and Hungary, was neither consistent nor coherent in his vision of his empire's future, the pieces of his thinking did to some extent fall into place. They took on the hue of a historical mission of *restoration*, for, if all his political preferences and desires were gratified, it would have amounted to that. Deeply Roman Catholic and anti-Italian, he wanted to undo the unification of Italy that had been achieved under secular auspices a half century earlier; he would have broken up the Italian state and restored papal and Austrian rule. He would have liked the Hapsburg Empire to return to its position in the front row and rank at least equally with Germany in the European power equation. He would revoke Hungary's equal partnership in the Dual Monarchy, and instead would have returned to a central power structure in which all the other nationalities (or at least the numerous Slavs) exercised an equal limited autonomy. Finally, he would have repaired the breach with Russia that dated from the last half of the nineteenth century and would once again combine with the Czar and the King of Prussia to promote the cause of monarchism and traditional values in European and world affairs, as they had, for example, in 1815 as the Holy Alliance.

In the spring of 1914 the heir apparent was fifty years old. He appeared to have recovered from the illnesses that had plagued him in earlier years. He was of medium height and on the heavy side. His fierce black upturned handlebar mustache was thicker than that of the Kaiser, but it turned up a few degrees less sharply.

Franz Ferdinand maintained his own para-governmental military chancellery, with the consent of the emperor: Franz Joseph had extended official recognition to it in 1908. With the aid of this personal staff, Franz Ferdinand, in the words of a recent historian, "came to enjoy influence, even power, and to have a say if not a veto over the posts of war minister or chief of the general staff."

The Archduke took a lively interest in his country's armed forces, but his tendency, in the many international crises that erupted in his lifetime, was to draw back and avoid warfare. In this (though not in much else) he would have been the true political heir of Franz Joseph, who had seen his empire lose crucial wars and whose preference, in the international crises of the early twentieth century, seemed to be for peace.

Franz Joseph, as 1914 began, was eighty-four years old. He had ascended the throne in 1848. Most of his subjects could remember no other ruler. In his old age his image was that of a kindly older gentleman: a grandfather figure. He symbolized continuity with the past and with its values and virtues. While the night still was dark, he arose to perform his duties. He started work each day at 5:00 a.m. and put in twelve or more hours on the job.

With the dutifulness and devotion came a certain stiffness: an unwillingness or inability to give; a lack of flexibility that seemed to characterize the arthritic Hapsburg regime as a whole. Its literature suggests that frustration and repression lay behind the excessive formality of Viennese life; and that the city's most famous psychiatrist, Sigmund Freud, may not have been entirely wrong in suggesting that unacknowledged lusts, illnesses of which people were ashamed, and practices then regarded as perverse were widespread beneath the surface. Franz Joseph, the virtuous emperor, himself infected his beautiful wife with a venereal disease, and spent his life with the actress

Katharina Schratt, a mistress—if that is the accurate word—whom, scrupulously, he never touched except on her shoulder. His only son, his then heir, the Crown Prince Rudolf, died together with a young ballerina of gunshot wounds that it was hard to believe were suffered (as the official version would have it) in a hunting accident. *Mayerling*, a motion picture of the 1930s starring Charles Boyer, told a story that sounded more plausible: a suicide pact between doomed lovers whose society would never permit them to marry one another.

Franz Ferdinand, a cousin who succeeded Rudolf as heir to the throne, was another royal figure who was penalized for marrying the woman he loved.

Tall, dark, poor but proud, Countess Sophie Chotek von Chotkova und Wognin was employed as a lady-in-waiting in an archducal household that Franz Ferdinand visited often. It was assumed that he was courting one of the daughters of the house. Their mother was aghast to discover that this was not so—that it was a mere "blind"— and fired Sophie, the true object of his pursuit. Franz Ferdinand proposed to marry Sophie. The Emperor objected.

Sophie was indeed of the ancient nobility, but her impoverished family had lacked the money to perfect their claim to be included in the list, prepared by the European powers in 1815 (after the Congress of Vienna) of those eligible to marry and transmit royalty. Insisting on marrying Sophie anyway, Franz Ferdinand took her as his spouse in 1900. He was thirty-seven, she thirty-two. Franz Ferdinand was forced to settle for a morganatic marriage, forswearing forever the right of his children to succeed to the throne, and excluding Countess Chotek (later Duchess of Hohenberg) from a position by his side at formal functions (she was banished to a relatively lowly status). Prince Alfred Montenuovo, the Imperial Lord Chamberlain, was the official in charge of court etiquette, and as such seemed to make himself her particular enemy.

Emperor Franz Joseph apparently feared that once Franz Ferdinand became emperor in his turn, he would go back on his word, perhaps obtaining a papal dispensation to do so, and would make Sophie his rightful empress, upgrading the rank of their three children as well as putting them in line of succession to the throne. In the light of that probably justified fear, it seems all the odder that the court officials dared carry on their petty persecutions of Sophie, administering protocol in such a way as to repeatedly humiliate her in public. One day she might well have been able to pay them back; indeed, Franz Ferdinand might have enjoyed doing so himself.

The heir apparent was not likable. Few of his contemporaries had a kind word to say for him. The one thing about him that was (and remains) attractive was his love for his wife and children. When he was asked in 1913 to inspect the armed forces in Bosnia-Herzegovina in maneuvers scheduled for late June 1914—an unappealing request in some respects—one of the reasons he may have accepted was that, because of the special status of Bosnia-Herzegovina—it was in a sort of limbo while Austria and Hungary contested its ownership—Sophie would be allowed to take her place next to him during official proceedings. Ceremonies were planned in the provincial capital of Sarajevo on June 28, their wedding anniversary.

It also should have been not merely noted but underlined by the Hapsburg officials responsible for the planning of events that June 28—at least according to the modern Western calendar—was the anniversary of the First Battle of Kosovo (1389), at which medieval Serbia supposedly lost its independence to the Turks. The Serbs of Bosnia-Herzegovina, restive in any event because of having been annexed by Austria, might well have been expected to take exception to a display of Austrian government on that particular date.

Austrian officialdom had a reputation for efficiency belied by its record in arranging this particular trip. The electricity failed as the Archduke boarded the railroad car. Footmen hastened to light candles. Normally ill-tempered, Franz Ferdinand instead made a joke of it; it looked, he said, as though he were entering "a tomb."

The Archduke and his consort departed in the rain early the morning of Wednesday, June 24. They traveled from Vienna separately, by different routes, and rain followed them. Sophie arrived first at their destination: the spa of Bad Ilidze, outside the Bosnian capital of Sarajevo. Franz Ferdinand came late the afternoon of Thursday, June 25. They stayed at the Hotel Bosna, which had been taken over for the duration of their stay by the authorities. Townspeople had loaned furniture and furnishings to the hotel so that it would look its best for the visitors.

That evening, on the spur of the moment, the visiting couple decided to go into town, shopping. In Sarajevo they browsed along a market street where artisans made and sold their handicrafts and merchants plied their wares. They spent time in a rug shop. The crowds that followed them seemed friendly and welcoming.

The following two days Sophie visited schools, orphanages, and churches, and Franz Ferdinand, as inspector general, supervised war games in which one army simulated fighting another through the unending rain. As the Archduke reported to the Emperor in writing, all performed excellently. Afterwards, Franz Ferdinand invited Hapsburg army and civilian officials and local dignitaries to a formal banquet at his hotel the night of Saturday, June 27: a dinner dance. It was a night to remember.

The hotel served Franz Ferdinand and his guests a cream soup, then soufflés of some sort, and then trout from the local river that had been jellied. Main courses were beef, lamb, and (accounts differ) either chicken or goose, followed by asparagus, salad and sherbet, and then cheeses, desserts, ice creams, and candies. A great range of wines and spirits were served, including champagne, white wines from the Rhine, red wines from Bordeaux, Madeira, Hungarian Tokay, and, penultimately, a *vin du pays:* a full, rich white Zilavka from nearby Mostar, drunk just before the cognac.

It was a summer night, and the windows of the Bosna's dining room were open. On the grass below the Sarajevo garrison band was playing a concert of light music. Through the open windows diners could hear the strains of Strauss's *The Blue Danube*, perhaps the most familiar of Viennese waltzes.

Franz Ferdinand and Sophie had met in Prague, all those years ago, at a dance. Now it was at a dance that they were spending their last night together.

CHAPTER 19: IN THE LAND OF THE ASSASSINS

Franz Ferdinand, as remarked earlier, was a reactionary: he would have liked to turn back the calendar by a century. The Slavs who plotted against him were more reactionary still; they looked back more than five centuries, as remarked earlier, to the First Battle of Kosovo, at which, they believed, the greatness of Serbia had been lost. On June 28, 1914, the conspirators proposed to redeem the defeat of 1389 at the cost of their own lives. Of course it was not really the 1389 battle that had doomed the Christian Balkans; it was the Second Battle of Kosovo—in 1448—that had done so. But the apprentice terrorists who dreamed these terrible dreams may not have known that. There were no scholars among them.

Denizens of the revolutionary underground tend to be thought of as belonging to the political left. But terrorists often occupy a time warp of their own: sometimes they look not forward but backward. They seek to restore kingdoms long since crumbled into dust. They rally to the banners of forgotten causes. They hearken to prophets who preached to the people of a bygone age.

Hence religious fanatics in the caves of Tora Bora in the opening years of the twenty-first century seeking to revive a religion as it was taught in the seventh century. Hence schoolboys in the primitive villages of the Balkans a century ago, hoping to become assassins like the legendary figures of whom they had heard tell in patriotic poetry.

These groups in the terrorist underworld were much the same in format, if not in message. They swore terrible oaths of fidelity, were subject to frightening tests, underwent initiation ceremonies at which blood was drunk from skulls, had a pistol put to their head and obeyed an order to pull the trigger, used code names, and were organized into cells in which only the leader knew members of the other cells. Though their aims differed, they sometimes assisted one another and often borrowed ceremonies, practices, and procedures from one another.

What distinguished terrorists from ordinary assassins was that they did not necessarily desire the immediate consequences of their violence. They killed people that often even they regarded as innocent. Their unique strategy—the strategy of terrorism—was to frighten society into doing something that the terrorists wanted society to do. An ordinary assassin shoots John Doe because he wants John Doe dead. A terrorist assassin shoots John Doe, whose life or death may be a matter of indifference to him, because he wants the authorities to react in a certain way to the killing.

At a time when the rulers of Eurasia repressed free political expression, many young idealists were driven underground. Beneath the empires of old Europe and eating away at their foundations throughout the nineteenth and early twentieth centuries were networks of secret societies. Their members were visionaries, nationalists, army officers, romantics, patriots, idealists, fanatics, or madmen. The societies were illegal and the life they offered was dangerous, but for young people that often was an attraction rather than a drawback: life underground sounded glamorous and looked romantic. Some of the youthful terrorists believed in bombing and assassination, while others believed that individual violence was less effective than mass organization; but a belief they held in common was that society as it existed had to be blown up and blown away before construction of a better world could begin.

Undoing the consequences of the Industrial Revolution was a goal that many of them sought, though they would have put it differently, and to that end they fomented strikes and undertook sabotage. Others were intoxicated by the heady brew of nationalism: overthrowing alien rule. As Z. A. B. Zeman has pointed out, population pressures lent an intensity and an urgency to nationalists' demands. The Hapsburg and other multinational empires were a breeding ground for young political criminals and deranged radicals of right and left.

Kings, presidents, prime ministers, and other leaders of government and society were murdered promiscuously, without exciting as much surprise as such events would cause today. That was particularly true in the backward, semi-tribal southeast of Europe, where peasants lived with their animals, blood feuds were common, and vengeance killings were the norm.

Through the imaginative fiction of a Joseph Conrad or a Dostoevsky, one can try to picture this secret-society world of long ago in the far-distant Balkans. It was the world from which Gavrilo Princip, a Bosnian Serb, emerged: an untalented, but serious-minded teenager whose career choice was to be a martyr. He was an adherent of the Young Bosnia movement, a loose grouping of youthful nationalists. Villagers, products of a feudal society, the Young Bosnians, who belonged to the first literate generation in their province, read and discussed relatively up-to-date and sometimes subversive literature: Walt Whitman, Alexander Herzen, Oscar Wilde, Maxim Gorky, and Henrik Ibsen were among the authors whose works they read. It is difficult to imagine what these schoolchildren, with their emotional roots in Serbian fourteenth-century martyrdom and their economic roots in the Middle Ages, made of Victorian and Edwardian modernism. They were acquainted with the writings, theories, and actions of the Russian revolutionary underground, and of the Nihilists of a half century before, but found it difficult to relate the various socialisms that animated the Russians to the peasant world of the Balkans. However, Princip himself owned a small library of anarchist literature that included the works of Michall Bakunin and Peter Kropotkin. The verses of Nietzsche often were on his lips. A solitary figure, he lived among books rather than people.

Princip was born July 13, 1894, in the hamlet of Gornji Obljaj in the high woodlands of the Grahovo valley. It was in what Zeman has called "the poorest part of a poor province"; it was the Krajina, in western Bosnia, near Dalmatia. The Princip family had lived there for centuries, during which time frontiers and states had come and gone. They were Serbs of Bosnia, closely attached to their land, their church, their communal organizations, and their clan. Gavrilo left the valley when he was thirteen years old to attend school in Sarajevo, the capital of Bosnia.

A slight, dark, curly-haired boy, on the frail side, an ascetic who neither smoked nor drank, he grew a mustache that made him look older but also made him look a bit like an organ grinder. He rejected religion, fought with his teachers, and attended schools only fitfully. He wanted to be a poet, feeling the sorrows of others. It bothered him that he was physically unprepossessing. When he volunteered for Serbian military service in the Balkan wars of 1912–13, he was turned down by a recruiting officer who said, "you are too small and weak." The remark stung him. He never forgave that officer.

During the twenty years of Princip's life, assassination had been a frequent and characteristic manifestation of the split between society and its underworld. Among those killed had been the President of France (1894), the Shah of Persia (1896), the President of Uruguay (1896), the Prime Minister of Spain (1897), the President of Guatemala (1898), the Empress of Austria (1898), the President of the Dominican Republic (1899), the King of Italy (1900), the President of the United States (1901), the King and Queen of Serbia (1903), the Prime Minister of Greece (1905), the Prime Minister of Bulgaria (1907), the Prime Minister of Persia (1907), the King of Portugal (1908), the Prime Minister of Egypt (1910), the Prime Minister of Russia (1911), the Prime Minister of Spain (1912), the President of Mexico (1913), and the King of the Hellenes (1913). On average, one head of state or head of government was murdered every year.

When the nineteen-year-old Princip read or heard in March 1914 or thereabouts that the heir to the Hapsburg Empire was to visit Bosnia in June, he hit upon the project (he claimed) of organizing an assassination. To the end of his life he insisted that it was his own idea. Be that as it may, other restless nationalists had plotted to kill Franz Ferdinand without success on many occasions, most recently in January 1914. There are those who believe that it was not so much that the Archduke was hated by the Young Bosnians—indeed they were badly informed and, in a number of respects, quite mistaken about his views—but that he was an outstanding symbol of the existing order that the students wanted to frighten and to overthrow.

According to another set of informants, it was the belief of the conspirators that Franz Ferdinand advocated "trialism"; he intended to make the Slavs full partners in government along with Austro-Germans and Hungarians. This policy might defuse Serb nationalism and deprive Young Bosnia and the others of their issue.

A contrary theory is that the Serbian nationalists had received false information that Austria-Hungary was on the point of attacking Serbia. The maneuvers in Sarajevo (they told one another) were a mere dress rehearsal. After the Balkan wars, everybody knew that Serbia was exhausted and would require several years to recuperate. Franz Ferdinand (they whispered) planned to take advantage of this helplessness by launching an invasion. They wrongly claimed that in Vienna, in the inner circle of government, the Archduke was the leader of the war party. In fact, he was the leading advocate of peace.

Princip asked friends to join in the plot. The friends agreed. He requested lessons in the use of firearms; again, friends agreed. One friend—a certain Milan Ciganovic—knew "a gentleman"—no name supplied—who could and did supply weaponry: bombs, revolvers, and poison with which to commit suicide after killing their targets. The same "gentleman" ranked high in a secret organization that promised to smuggle them across the frontier from Serbia into Austrian-occupied Bosnia in time for Franz Ferdinand's visit.

The revolvers were four Belgian automatic weapons, the latest issue. The six bombs were of a special Serbian manufacture, tiny, lightweight, and easy both to conceal and to use. The poison was cyanide.

Why did the "gentleman"—Major Voja Tankosic, right-hand man of the head of the Black Hand, a secret society within the Serbian army of which more will be said presently—choose to facilitate the assassination? Is it possible that his organization, through him, recruited Princip and his friends rather than vice versa? Or, if the plot really did originate with Princip, did Tankosic back it because he seriously meant what he said years later: that he did it "to make trouble for Pasic," the Prime Minister of Serbia?

Another of the many versions of the story of the Sarajevo murders supposedly was told by the Black Hand leader Apis to a friend in 1915. The friend published it in 1924. In this account, Tankosic complained to Apis one day: "Dragutin, there are several Bosnian youths who are pestering me. These kids want at any cost to perform some 'great deed.' They have heard that Franz Ferdinand will come to Bosnia for maneuvers and have begged me to let them go there. What do you say? . . . I have told them they cannot go but they give me no peace." To this, Apis responded something like: why not give them a chance? But then, sometime later, reflecting upon it, Apis began to think that it was important to kill Franz Ferdinand, and that the schoolboys lacked the requisite skills. So he sent a message to Princip to abort the mission, intending to send someone more seasoned instead. But Princip insisted on going ahead.

There have been three trials in which magistrates have sat in judgment on the Sarajevo affair: Austrian (1914), Serbian (1917), and Yugoslav (1953). All three were politically motivated, and of their findings, none compels credence. Even the exhaustive research and interviews undertaken by and for the great Italian historian Luigi Albertini in the interwar years resolved nothing. Witnesses saw a chance to settle a score or to advance a cause. Some forgot or confused things. Serbian nationalists have remained proud of the murders; many have wanted to take credit for them, or others perhaps wanted to make themselves seem important by knowing how they really happened. Apis, in asserting that he was personally responsible for the killing, may have believed that he was absolving his country from blame. Or he may have believed that, for one reason or another, he would not be condemned by the Serbian tribunal that tried him in 1917 if the judges realized that he was the patriot who killed Franz Ferdinand. Or the tribunal may have ordered Apis's execution in order to keep him from telling . . . we do not know what.

In the end, all that we know with certainty is that Princip fired the gun.

The sinister group that aided Princip was called *Ujedinjenje ili Smrt* ("Union or Death"). Later it became known as "the Black Hand." It was founded March 3, 1911, by seven nationalists who continued to protest the results of the Bosnian crisis of 1908–09. When the Serbian government accepted, albeit reluctantly, the Austro-Hungarian annexation of Bosnia-Herzegovina, so did the existing government-sponsored nationalist organization, the Narodna Odbrana (National Defense). From being a military-oriented anti-Austrian grouping it converted itself into a largely cultural society.

Dissenters from the decision to accept the annexation later formed the ultra-secret Black Hand in order to carry on the struggle. One of its founding members was a student of the history of European secret societies in France, Italy, Germany, and elsewhere. A self-conscious traditionalism (some might call it imitation) is evident in the constitution (in thirty-seven articles) and bylaws (in twenty-eight articles) of the elite secret society that formally came into existence in May 1911. It modeled itself largely on the Freemason lodges and on Mazzini's Young Italy movement in the nineteenth century.

The Black Hand infiltrated Narodna Odbrana and perhaps other organizations, but it was not widely known itself outside of government circles. Its existence, however, was known to a number of foreign countries. It constituted a leading faction within the military, and was represented within the government. The organization consisted of extremist army officers and extreme nationalist politicians. Its dominating figure (though perhaps never its formal leader) was an army officer, now the powerful chief of military intelligence, named Dragutin Dimitrijevic, a bull-like man code-named "Apis." In 1903, Apis had led a murder party that slaughtered the King and Queen of Serbia in their palace, then threw their mutilated corpses out of the window. During the reign of the murdered king, Serbia had been a satellite of Austria. Under the dynasty that Apis and his colleagues restored to the throne, successive administrations pursued anti-Austrian policies, but not sufficiently so for Apis. Consenting to the Bosnian annexation in 1908–09 was, in his view, "treason."

The Black Hand pursued ultimate goals that were different from Princip's. Apis and his colleagues wanted Serbia to rule all the lands in which Serbs lived. Princip dreamed of creating a federation in which Croatia, Slovenia, and other southern Slavic peoples were united. These differences were not necessarily relevant in the spring of 1914; they were long-range goals.

Whether he knew it or not, however, in the short term, Princip was walking into a political crossfire. The Serbian government and even the Serbian army were split in two. Apis was in the grip of a fierce conflict with the sixty-eight-year-old Prime Minister, Nicola

Pasic, a veteran politician who, like Apis, was a Serb nationalist but, unlike Apis, was cautious. Each led a faction in a fight that was climaxing as Princip initiated his project. In May 1914, Apis persuaded the reigning monarch, King Peter, that Pasic ought to be dismissed. Then Russia intervened. As Serbia's sponsor among the Great Powers, Russia could, to some extent, lay down the law. Nicolai Hartwig, the Russian minister in Belgrade, intervened to retain Pasic as Prime Minister. Hartwig recognized that Serbia needed years of rest in which to recover from the Balkan wars and to consolidate its gains. It was no time for reckless adventurism.

On May 26, Gavrilo Princip set out from Belgrade, and headed toward a prearranged rendezvous with his fellow conspirators in Sarajevo. He traveled for nearly ten days through wild, forbidding country, difficult to traverse. His greatest challenge would be to cross the unfriendly frontier between independent Serbia and Hapsburg-ruled Bosnia. But it all was made easy for him. Agents were waiting to help him at every point along the way. It was a "tunnel" route developed and controlled by Narodna Odbrana and borrowed for the occasion by the Black Hand. On June 4, Princip arrived in Sarajevo to meet fellow conspirators, to prepare, and to rehearse.

The historian Albertini believed that Ciganovic, who had put Princip in touch with Tankosic of the Black Hand, was a police informer. If so, the Prime Minister from afar followed Princip's progress step-by-step. According to one version, the Prime Minister gave orders to border guards to stop Princip at the Serbian frontier— orders that were disobeyed by Serbian officials loyal to Apis. Instead, they let the conspirators pass, and then told Pasic that they had not received his orders until it was too late. In a variation of that version, those same officials then confessed to Pasic what they had done. One way or another, the Prime Minister (it is widely believed) learned that terrorists—Princip and a companion—carrying pistols and bombs had crossed the Drina River into Bosnia, and he either knew or guessed that the Archduke must be the target. But Pasic always denied that he had specific knowledge of what was about to occur.

For Pasic, a wily survivor of some of the world's most treacherous politics, the choices—to the extent that he did know of the plot— were not easy. His country was exhausted after the Balkan wars, and in no position to defy a Great Power. An attack on Franz Ferdinand was bound to trigger some kind of nasty international situation with which Serbia would find it difficult to deal. Of course he could do nothing, in the hope that the inexperienced schoolboys would flunk their test, but whatever they did might at least supply hard-liners in Vienna with a pretext for taking action. If, on the other hand, Pasic warned the Austrians, news of what he had done leaked out, the Black Hand might order him assassinated too, or else might use news of what the Prime Minister had done to label him a traitor. Whatever warning he sent also might be used by Vienna to prove that his government was involved in the plot against the Archduke; was he not admitting it by his very warning that Serbian officials were planning an attack?

In the end, despite his later denials, Pasic may have sent a cable to his legation in Vienna sometime in the first half of June instructing his minister there to inform the Austrian government that "owing to a leakage of information," Serbia "had grounds to suspect that a plot was being hatched against the life of the Archduke on the occasion of his journey to Bosnia. Since this visit might give rise to regrettable incidents on the part of some fanatic, it would be useful to suggest to the Austro-Hungarian government the advisability of postponing the Archduke's visit."

Whether or not Pasic sent such a cable, his envoy did seek such an interview. Minister Ljuba Jovanovic, who may have received the cable, had at least two reasons for not following his Prime Minister's instructions. He was on bad terms with the Hapsburg foreign minister, Count Leopold von Berchtold, the official whom he was supposed to alert, and preferred not to have to meet with him. He chose instead to seek an interview with Finance Minister Leon von Bilinski, under whose administration (at least temporarily) fell the newly annexed provinces of Bosnia and Herzegovina, which the Archduke was scheduled to visit. Security issues, however, were the responsibility of General Oskar Potiorek, governor of the provinces, nominally subordinate to Bilinski but actually feuding with him. Potiorek had deliberately ignored Bilinski in making arrangements for the Archduke's mission to Bosnia.

Jovanovic met with Bilinski on June 21 at noon. He apparently decided to cut out the very heart of the message he supposedly had been told to deliver—that Belgrade had actual information of a plot to kill the Archduke. Instead, he spoke in general terms of the dangers inherent in the visit to Sarajevo and of the possibility that some disaffected Serb might attack Franz Ferdinand. Jovanovic had reason not to tell of the plot to kill Franz Ferdinand; he had been Apis's nominee for foreign minister in the May coup d'état that Hartwig had prevented. Now there were rumors that Apis was scheduling a new coup, perhaps for August, and once again proposed to promote Jovanovic. This was no time for Jovanovic to side with Pasic against Apis.

In turn, Bilinski had reason to dismiss the vague warning he received. He had been ignored in security planning. Responsibility had been assumed by his subordinate, General Potiorek, on the express orders of Franz Ferdinand. If things went wrong on the trip to Bosnia, Potiorek, not Bilinski, would be blamed. Besides, it was difficult to worry much about what might happen to the Archduke: Bilinski had no cause to love him.

In the Serbian capital the Prime Minister tried to find out exactly what was going on, in order to stop it. Apis stonewalled; and Pasic loyalists in the army, the war department, and the interior ministry were unable to shadow Princip's conspirators, who by now were in Bosnia, beyond Serbia's official reach.

Leaders of Narodna Odbrana, the Serb nationalist society, held positions in Pasic's government, and therefore also learned of the assassination plot. They instructed their contact man in Bosnia to stop it from going forward. He failed.

On June 2 the Central Executive Committee of the Black Hand convened. Or maybe it was just an informal meeting of all members who could be brought together on short notice. At the meeting, the members heard of the assistance that Major Tankosic had extended to the Princip group on behalf of their organization. For whatever reasons, they ordered the mission aborted immediately. Apparently the decision was unanimous—except, it seems, for Apis and Tankosic.

Apis dispatched Tankosic's go-between with the Princip group to Bosnia, where he met with Danilo Ilic, who served as technical coordinator for the assassination team. Ilic relayed the order to Princip: call it off! Princip refused.

As of June 20 or 21, Apis may have believed the assassination plan had been cancelled, while Pasic may still have felt otherwise. Ilic repeatedly tried to persuade Princip to obey orders to cancel the attack. But a clash of views in middle June between Apis and Pasic—

whether about the death plot or something else—drove a Black Hand agent to send a new message to Princip revoking Apis's order to cancel and reinstating the operation. The man who brought the message later was accused by Serbia of being an Austrian spy, but the accusation was never proved; in fact, he served as Apis's chief spymaster within Austria-Hungary.

In any event, the conspiracy no longer may have been much of a secret; we are told that the cafés of the Balkans were abuzz with speculations about a plot to kill Franz Ferdinand, and that the cafés were alive with Austrian spies. A century later, we still do not know with certainty who knew what, and when they knew it.

CHAPTER 20: **THE RUSSIAN CONNECTION**

Was Russia somehow involved in the plot against Austria's future leader? In government circles, people asked that question at the time, and in scholarly circles, academics have asked that question ever since.

Russian involvement would have made little sense. Franz Ferdinand was the leading pro-Russian in his government; therefore removing him from the scene would have run counter to Russia's interests. Of course his political views were misunderstood elsewhere, so perhaps they were in St. Petersburg as well. Perhaps the extent of his friendship was not fully understood. But as a champion of monarchism throughout Europe, surely, on fiercely held principle, the Czar would have opposed such a murder.

Russia's Balkan policy, run in the field by Nicolai Hartwig as minister to Serbia (1909–14), was, as noted earlier, susceptible to being viewed as in the nature of a rogue operation. A militant pan-Slav, with long service in and knowledge of the Balkans and the Middle East,

Hartwig "used the Serb cause as a weapon in his struggle against his own government," according to the well-informed French minister in Belgrade. "With the support of conservative and orthodox circles at St. Petersburg" he battled Sazonov, the foreign minister, and "he dragged Russian diplomacy toward the Balkan evolution of the last two years which he had the merit of conceiving and carrying out."

It was Hartwig who had brought the Balkan states together for a time against both Turkey and Austria, and it was generally believed that he dictated policy in Belgrade. But he was unlikely to have approved the Black Hand plot; he had just rescued the Pasic government from Apis, approving the more cautious nonprovocative faction against the hotheads.

It apparently is true that the Russian military attaché in Belgrade, Colonel Viktor Artamanov, worked closely with Apis. The two may have run spy networks together. According to some allegations, at one time Artamanov provided Apis with funds for operations. It is not inconceivable that in some fashion Artamanov became aware that Apis was helping the Bosnian schoolboys. There is a story that Artamanov may also have assured Apis that he had it on good authority that if Austria attacked, Russia would come to Serbia's aid. There is no evidence, however, that anyone in a position to give such a guarantee on behalf of the Czar's government did so.

George Malcolm Thomson, a popular historian, writes in *The Twelve Days* (1964) that Artamanov "was, from an early stage, a party to the Black Hand conspiracy to murder the Archduke." Thomson bases his claim on the research of Albertini, research that does not support such an unqualified allegation. Artamanov denied everything in an interview with Albertini. Albertini did not believe Artamanov's story, but could not disprove it.

A document dated June 12, 1914, found in recently opened Russian Ministry of Defense files, relates that in 1910 Russia extended a subsidy of 4 million francs to the Serbian army's officer corps and that the money had been misused and disappeared long since. The document, which originated from the Russian military agent in Serbia hinted that some of the money might have been improperly siphoned off to the Black Hand; and it appears to confirm that the Russian government, based upon this past experience, would not consider providing any more funds to the Serbian officer corps. The assumption is that Russia would not want to help the Black Hand.

Was there a Russian connection in the Sarajevo affair? If there was, no evidence of it has yet been uncovered.

A few days before the assassination, Prime Minister Pasic received an anonymous letter. Its author speculated that the Austrian government might arrange to have "that foolish Ferdinand" killed during the Bosnian maneuvers, and then blame it on Pasic's government as an excuse to start a war against Serbia. It is not what happened, but it could have been.

CHAPTER 21: **THE TERRORISTS STRIKE**

Sunday, June 28, 1914. Early in the morning, Archduke Franz Ferdinand and his consort, Sophie, prayed at mass in a chapel set up for them at their hotel. Leaving the suburban spa of Ilidze, they then boarded a train to Sarajevo, a trip of less than half an hour. At the railroad terminal on the outskirts of town, they transferred to automobiles, in which they rode the rest of the way. The display of motor vehicles was striking; only recently had the automobile come into common use.

The procession of chauffeur-driven cars entered Sarajevo somewhere between 9:30 and 10:00 a.m., heading for the town hall. The mayor and the chief of police led the way in the first auto. The Archduke and the Duchess followed in the second, a convertible touring car that had been borrowed for their use. With them was the military governor, General Potiorek. The owner of the borrowed car, Count Franz von Harrach, sat in front next to the driver. The rest of the procession—between two and four other vehicles, depending upon whose account one accepts—followed.

The rains had finally stopped. The morning mists disappeared. A dazzling sunshine beamed down upon the anniversary couple: he, brilliantly attired in his many-colored uniform; she, radiant in white. At last side by side at a formal official celebration, they took in the sights and sounds along the route, and the enthusiasm of the cheering crowds and the booming of the twenty-four-cannon salutes.

Later, historians were puzzled by the lack of security precautions. Soldiers ought to have lined the route but did not. Some 22,000 Hapsburg troops were in the vicinity, but General Potiorek detailed only an honor guard of 120 to escort and protect Franz Ferdinand and his party. It was explained later that the general wanted to prove that under his iron-fisted rule, order was so firmly established that policing was unnecessary. If so, what Potiorek proved was the reverse of what he had intended.

Turbulent Bosnia was a borderland. It and its neighbors formed the arena where East met West, where rival clans, nationalities, religions, and empires collided. Bosnia's capital city of Sarajevo, an ancient settlement with roots in the distant past, consisted of a cluster of buildings stretched along both sides of the Miljacka River. It was laced together into a town by bridges. A torrent during the winter, the Miljacka slowed during the summer so that in June the riverbed was beginning to dry up. A British visitor in the late 1930s claimed that the waters of the Miljacka ran red, but that may well have been an optical illusion produced by a reading of history. The road that the motorcade followed into town was the Appel Embankment, which ran parallel to the river. It was bordered on the Miljacka side by a low embankment and on the other side by houses. It was the town's only considerable thoroughfare.

Centuries of rule by the Muslim Ottoman Empire had left their mark on the inhabitants: their dress, habits, and behavior. The appearance of the streets, especially as one turned away from the river into the narrow, winding streets of the interior, was distinctly Oriental.

The skyline of Sarajevo, punctuated by minarets, aglow in the dazzling summer sunshine, served as a reminder that the city often had changed hands. There were a hundred mosques in Sarajevo, and almost as many churches. The synagogues, though less conspicuous, attested to a Jewish presence. A polyglot, multinational, religiously diverse population had learned to live, not only with one another, but

also under whatever flag flew. Dominations and powers were temporary at best, and, as it happened, were about to change once again, as
a result of the events in Sarajevo that June 28.

That morning, Princip had stationed his fellow conspirators along
the Appel Embankment at three places where it was intersected by
bridges. The motorcade driving along the quay therefore would be
running a gauntlet. Princip's older friend Danilo Ilic was to serve as
coordinator with no fixed place of his own, to move his gunmen
when and where needed. Ilic, it will be remembered, had tried with
no success to persuade Princip to follow orders to abort the mission.

At the first of the bridges, the Archduke's procession entered a
danger zone: three conspirators formed a line along the river side of
the quay, and two on the land side. The first attempt on the Archduke's life came from the river side, from Nedeljiko Cabrinovic, who
asked a policeman to point out which was Franz Ferdinand's car.
Then he knocked the cap off his bomb on a lamppost to detonate it.
He threw the bomb wildly at the Archduke's car, hitting the folded-
back hood of the convertible, from which it rolled off to explode
against a wheel of the car following it.

The Countess felt a graze on her neck from the detonator, flying
wide, while an occupant of the car behind, Colonel Erich von Merizzi, an aide to General Potiorek, was wounded on the wrist by flying
shrapnel. The noise of the explosion was alarming, another officer
and a number of bystanders were lightly injured, and the procession
stopped to inquire.

Cabrinovic, the perpetrator, ran from the scene. He jumped from
the embankment and tried to escape in the waters of the shallow
riverbed. Captured by police who pursued him, he swallowed his poison pill, which turned out to be too old to work; its only effect was to
make him throw up.

Princip, who had heard the explosion and shouts from a crowd,
hurried to the spot, where it looked as though all was over. The gen-
darmes had Cabrinovic firmly in custody, and were bustling him off
to the police station. None of the other conspirators was to be found.

What happened to the others is most concisely recounted by A. J. P.
Taylor. "Of the other conspirators, one was so jammed in the crowd
that he could not pull the bomb out of his pocket. A second saw a
policeman standing near him and decided that any movement was too

risky. A third felt sorry for the Archduke's wife and did nothing. A fourth lost his nerve and slipped off home."

Alone, Princip wandered back to what had been his appointed station on the river side of the Appel Embankment at what was called the Latin Bridge. He then crossed the street. Accounts differ as to where he then stood or sat down.

Franz Ferdinand decided to cancel existing plans, which called for his motorcade to maneuver through winding alleys on the way to the museum; but neither did he return the way he had come. After a stop at the town hall for a reception and speeches, he insisted on driving to the hospital to visit Colonel Merizzi, lightly wounded in the Cabrinovic attack. The driver of the lead car either was not told or did not understand this; he followed original plans and turned off the Appel Embankment into a side street to drive toward the museum, and the Archduke's driver simply followed. "Turn back!" General Potiorek shouted. The driver stopped. He considered how best to back out. His car's rear may have been blocked by the rest of the motorcade. He would have had to maneuver slowly in the narrow side street, perhaps putting his vehicle into reverse or trying a U-turn. Meanwhile the vehicle stood motionless. All this happened about five feet from Princip. He was surrounded by onlookers. He must have been astonished, but he thought quickly and seized his chance. He reached for a bomb in his pocket, and became aware that he was too hemmed in by the crowd to swing his arm for a free toss at his target. So he pulled out his pistol and fired two shots at point-blank range, hitting the Archduke's jugular with one and the abdomen of the Duchess with the other. At that distance it was almost impossible to miss.

Princip then turned the revolver on himself, but was prevented from firing it by a bystander who hurled himself on the assassin's arm. It was not clear what had happened. To some the two shots that had rung out unexpectedly sounded like the backfires to which automobiles were prone in those early days. Confusion erupted as the crowd and nearby police battled one another to get at the boyish assassin. Princip swallowed his suicide capsule, then vomited when it did not work. The mob began to beat him and may well have been dragging him off to lynch him. Struggling, Princip used the handle of his weapon to hit back. Eventually the police wrestled him away from the crowd. Thereupon he dropped his bomb. Onlookers shouted out warnings as police reinforcements arrived and cleared the scene.

Meanwhile the limousine with the dying royal couple fled to seek help. "Sophie dear! Sophie dear! Don't die! Stay alive for our children!" Franz Ferdinand called out; and then, more weakly, but repeatedly, "It is nothing," as aides anxiously asked how he felt. The fatally wounded couple were rushed to the governor's residence, only minutes away. They had been shot at about 10:30 a.m.; Sophie died at roughly 10:45 a.m.; Franz Ferdinand, at around 11:00 a.m. It was *not* "nothing."

CHAPTER 22: **EUROPE YAWNS**

Had the crime in Sarajevo been committed even a century earlier, it would have taken weeks or months for word of it to reach faraway places. In the nature of the case, therefore, its consequences might have been far different. But technology had changed things. In the age of the steamship and, above all, the telegraph, news traveled fast. The foreign offices of the world knew of the shootings at once, and within hours condolences began to pour in from places as far away as the White House in Washington, D.C.

While details of the murders remain disputed to this day, some of the main outlines came through accurately at the time. Thus, though the British consul in Sarajevo, muddled by the two assaults, reported that it was the bomb attack that had killed Franz Ferdinand and Sophie, the British ambassador in Vienna had the details right.

In the streets of Vienna, a typewritten account of what had happened was distributed by the Austrian Official Telegraphic Agency almost immediately.

Rumors traveled fast too. A persistent one was that the Freemasons were responsible. A decade later the novelist Thomas Mann continued to attribute the summer of 1914 crisis, at least in part, to them. The "international illuminati," he wrote, "the world lodge of freemasons," played a role in unleashing the war.

German intelligence was suspected; the Hungarian Prime Minister was blamed. Twenty-five years later Rebecca West, the British journalist whose account of Balkan affairs is considered classic, still was echoing the belief that it was someone in the Austro-Hungarian government itself who had arranged it all; how else explain the otherwise puzzling lack of security precautions?

Moreover, the Emperor, though horrified by the crime itself, was not unhappy that Franz Ferdinand was out of the way. He had not wanted to have the Archduke succeed him on the throne. "For me, it is a great worry less," he told his daughter in speaking of the Archduke's death. To a close aide he confided: "God will not be mocked. A higher power had put back the order I couldn't maintain."

Even Berchtold noted in his diary that during the first cabinet meeting after the assassination there was "yes, consternation and indignation, but also a certain easing of mood."

President Poincaré of France was at the Longchamps racetrack when news of the Sarajevo killings was brought to him. He remained to see the end of the races. He then went about his usual routine. Paris was unaffected.

Kiel, Germany.   The Kaiser was racing in a regatta aboard his yacht *Meteor.* On shore the chief of his Naval Cabinet, Admiral von Müller, received a coded cable from the German consul general in Sarajevo relaying the news. Müller immediately set out in the launch *Hulda,* overtook the *Meteor,* and shouted out what had happened.

Deliberations were held aboard. Wilhelm decided to return to Berlin to "take the situation in hand and preserve the peace of Europe."

It must have been a terrible blow to Kaiser Wilhelm. He would have been horrified by the assassination of any royal figure, but in addition he had worked for years to cement his special relationship with Franz Ferdinand. To that end he had been, and showed every sign of continuing to be, a champion of Sophie. Once the elderly Franz Joseph passed away—and that could not be in more than a few years—the two friends and emperors, Wilhelm and Franz Ferdinand, could (in what seemed to be the Kaiser's vision) work together as partners to lead the continent of Europe. Now that dream was smashed. For Germany, it was conjectured, the Hapsburg Empire after Franz Joseph left the scene might be not as close and reliable an ally as it would have been under Franz Ferdinand's leadership.

From Kiel, the London *Times* correspondent cabled to his editor that "German interest in the Austrian problem will be even more intense" than it had been before.

According to a leading contemporary newspaper editor in Vienna, long afterwards, "the death of Archduke Franz Ferdinand . . . came as a relief in wide political circles even to the highest official circles." Bülow, the former German Chancellor, reported that he was told by a Hungarian diplomat that the outrage "was a dispensation of Providence" because the anti-Hungarian Franz Ferdinand might have broken up Austria-Hungary in a civil war.

Monday, June 29. England.   The "Outrage," as the assassinations were called, dominated the foreign reporting published in the morning's London *Times*. According to the newspaper's Sarajevo correspondent, the terrible events in the Bosnian capital were "evidently the fruit of a carefully laid plot."

Franz Ferdinand and Sophie, having "narrowly escaped death" from a bomb thrown at them at 10:15 a.m. by one assailant, were struck down soon afterwards by another, "a high school student" who fired a Browning automatic pistol. The fact that one of the attackers was from Bosnia and the other from Herzegovina pointed to a plot that was widespread. However, no information as to the race or creed of the assassin was available. Both criminals had been "with difficulty saved from being lynched," reported the *Times* correspondent.

The news account was supplemented by background pieces. A sympathetic note about eighty-four-year-old Austrian Emperor Franz Joseph, who had been dealt another blow in the sixty-sixth year of his reign, reminded readers of the violent deaths of his wife, his brother, and his son, concluding, "few can have had to suffer a succession of calamities so grievous as the stricken old man who sits upon the proudest throne on the Continent."

Yet the Emperor showed no sign in public of being stricken. Nor was the Austrian public upset by the news; "there is little trace of public excitement," reported a correspondent in Vienna.

According to the British consul in Sarajevo, "Local paper speaks of Anarchist crime, but act was more likely that of Servian [*sic*] irredentists, preconcerted long ago."

A concise biography of Franz Ferdinand explained that since in his early years he was not expected ever to mount the throne—his cousin Rudolf then was the heir, and presumably would have been succeeded by his future children—there seemed to be no reason to train him in statecraft. His tutors therefore were guided by the principle that his "intellectual faculties . . . should not be overtaxed." By his mid-twenties he was "a good horseman, a crack shot, and a painstaking officer, [but] his knowledge of political and constitutional questions was limited." These latter were matters that he began studying only in 1889 when, on the death of Rudolf, he became heir to the throne. Rudolf had been the Emperor's son; Franz Ferdinand was only a nephew.

In the City of London, securities markets were weak at the opening, but recovered once it became evident that the Vienna exchange and other continental bourses were holding firm.

Sir Mark Sykes, a Tory backbencher who was by no means parochial in outlook—he had traveled widely in the Middle East, an area on which he was one of his party's few experts—spoke for many when he told the House of Commons that it was no time to focus on foreign developments, no matter how gripping; it was "difficult to discuss foreign affairs freely when our home affairs were in such a particularly evil plight."

Tuesday, June 30.   Sykes's sentiments were echoed in a *Times* leader (an editorial) that agreed that what happened in Sarajevo "fills the first place in the public mind" and would "occupy the attention of all students of European politics" but that domestic politics must not be ignored: "our own affairs must be addressed." The *Times* presumably referred to the threat that in a few weeks the United Kingdom might dissolve in a civil war to determine the fate of Ireland—and much else.

The permanent head of the Foreign Office, in a communication to his ambassador in Russia, expressed his wish that the fallout be limited. "The tragedy which has recently occurred at Sarajevo will, I hope, not lead to further complications; though it is already fairly evident that the Austrians are attributing the terrible events to Serbian intrigues and machinations" some good might come of it all: "it is possible that the new heir will be more popular than the late Archduke."

In France, at the first cabinet meeting since the assassinations, the killings (according to President Poincaré's biographer) were "hardly mentioned."

The British ambassador to Italy reported to London: "It has been curious to study here the effect of the abominable assassination at Sarajevo. While ostensibly the authorities and the press have been loud in their denunciations of the crime . . . it is obvious that people have generally regarded the elimination of the late Archduke as almost providential."

Paris could take no notice. It was completely caught up in a scandal, a wonderful scandal. The scandal had everything: sex, violence, international intrigue, love and passion and jealousy and wrongdoing in high places. It was the notorious Caillaux affair.

Joseph Caillaux, who had become Prime Minister of France in 1911, was a left-wing politician who had been forced out of office in 1912 for being, allegedly, too accommodating to Germany. In 1913 he again became a cabinet minister, but was under frequent attack from the right. He was indeed a leading advocate of friendship with Germany—and he was a something of a pacifist.

Caillaux was an old friend of President Poincaré's. In their bachelor days they had been companions in pleasure-seeking. One difference between the two was that Poincaré was discreet while Caillaux was a showoff. When the two men spent a vacation in Italy together, along with their mistresses, the contrast was striking: in the words of Caillaux, "mine I displayed, his he kept hidden."

When, at the age of forty-three Poincaré married, in a civil ceremony, the wedding was so private that few knew of it. Caillaux, however, when he married, proceeded to carry on a clandestine love affair with another mistress, who eventually became his second wife.

Despite the personal friendship between the two men, they had become political adversaries by 1913–14. Having just been elected

President of France, Poincaré, on March 4, 1913, supported proposed legislation to increase the length of military duty in the French army from two to three years. It seemed to be the only way for France to offset Germany's population lead: 70 million to 40 million. Caillaux opposed the measure. The bill was adopted on August 7. Caillaux, who was elected chairman of the Radical party, continued to attack the legislation. So did the somewhat pacifist Jean Jaurès, who had unified the country's Socialists.

The political campaign against Caillaux in 1914 was spearheaded by the most powerful journalist in France, Gaston Calmette, editor of the leading journal of the right, *Le Figaro*. Calmette claimed he would make public certain documents that would show that Caillaux, when he was minister of finance in 1911, had obstructed justice in a financial scandal in which he personally had perhaps been involved. Calmette also threatened to publish the love letters of Caillaux and his second wife, written at a time when Caillaux was still married to his first wife.

More was to come: German cables to Caillaux, dating from the Agadir crisis of 1911, that supposedly showed Caillaux to be sympathetic to Germany had been intercepted by the French foreign office. Calmette supposedly was going to publish these, too, whereupon the German government protested against the interception of its correspondence.

Caillaux now went to his old friend President Poincaré, asking him to prevent Calmette from revealing his dossier, and warned that unless the President did so, he (Caillaux) would disclose what he knew about Poincaré's secret negotiations with the Vatican. These were evidenced by intercepted Italian cables. If known, these would compromise the President with his secularist anticlerical supporters.

Thereupon the French government officially denied the existence of the intercepted German cables, and Caillaux, in return, refrained from revealing the existence of the Italian cables in his possession. All that now threatened Caillaux was Calmette's proposed publication of the love letters.

On March 16, 1914, the second Mme Caillaux went to Calmette's office, asked to see him, waited, and when she saw him, fired six shots from an automatic pistol and killed him.

Her murder trial was scheduled for July 20. In July, therefore, the attention of Paris was riveted on the trial. Leftists and rightists fought in the streets. There was no time and no attention left for the Archduke and his consort.

Poincaré jested that the affair had put new ideas in his head: he might send out his wife to shoot down his own opponents.

If there were any country in Europe in which the killings in Sarajevo should have been felt keenly, it would have been the Archduke's own Austria. People should have been crying in the streets. Yet Z. A. B. Zeman writes that in Vienna "the event almost failed to make any impression whatever. On Sunday and Monday, the crowds in Vienna listened to music and drank wine . . . as if nothing had happened."

The author Stefan Zweig was seated on a park bench in Vienna the afternoon of June 28. He was aroused from the book he was reading by a sudden silence: the distant sound of a band no longer could be heard; the music had stopped. People were gathering around the bandstand, listening to some announcement. Zweig joined them. The crowd was receiving news of the assassinations in Sarajevo. These were Austrians, hearing of the death of their leader-to-be. Yet, Zweig wrote later, "there was no particular shock or dismay to be seen on their faces, for the heir-apparent was not at all well-liked. . . . He was never seen to smile, and no photographs showed him relaxed. He had no sense for music, and no sense of humor, and his wife was equally unfriendly. They both were surrounded by an icy air; one knew that they had no friends. My almost mystic premonition that some misfortune would come from this man with his bulldog neck and his cold, staring eyes, was by no means a personal one but was shared by the entire nation; and so the news of his murder aroused no profound sympathy."

Indeed, in all the capitals of Europe, the reaction to the assassination of the heir to the Hapsburg throne was calm to the point of indifference.

CHAPTER 23: **DISPOSING OF THE BODIES**

Prince Montenuovo, chief controller of the Hapsburg Imperial Household and chief persecutor of Sophie while she was still alive, was in charge of arrangements for the two bodies. He had them shipped to Vienna so as to arrive late at night: 10 p.m. on July 2. Montenuovo expected nobody to meet them so that, unobserved, he could separate the two corpses. The Archduke could be sent to the Hapsburg family Hofburg Chapel, while Sophie could go to Artstetten, a castle where Franz Ferdinand had built a chapel for his wife and himself.

Montenuovo's plan was derailed when the bodies were met at the Vienna train station by the Archduke Charles, Franz Ferdinand's nephew who had succeeded to the position of heir apparent. Charles was accompanied, Albertini tells us, by "the whole officer corps of the Vienna garrison." So both bodies went to Hofburg Chapel for memorial services.

Even so, the Archduke's coffin was higher and larger, and bore "his full insignia" as the second-highest-ranking prince of the empire, while hers bore a pair of white gloves and a black fan—the insignia of her service as a lady-in-waiting.

The children of the couple were forbidden to attend the memorial services for their parents. They did send flowers, one of the only two bouquets allowed.

Foreign royal personages were asked by Vienna not to attend and therefore did not do so. The ceremony occurred on July 3. Afterwards the chapel was closed. In the night the coffins were transferred back to the railroad station but were intercepted; thereafter they were accompanied by a large body of nobles led by Sophie's brother—a group that refused to be excluded.

At Artstetten the bodies of the Archduke and his morganatic wife reached their burial ground, harassed and humiliated in death as they had been in life by the Hapsburg court. It was shabby behavior by the court grandees. It also was shortsighted: it undermined its claim to have been injured by the crime that Gavrilo Princip had perpetrated.

CHAPTER 24: ROUNDING UP THE SUSPECTS

Battered, bleeding, and vomiting, Princip was brought into the police station. Cabrinovic, the bomb thrower, had arrived only a short time before. Following continental legal procedures, an examining magistrate, Leo Pfeffer—a local functionary—had been appointed to investigate Cabrinovic's crime. When the police brought in Princip, the scope of Pfeffer's inquiry was widened. Two such attempts within minutes of one another suggested something larger than a murder; it pointed to a conspiracy.

At first, wrote Judge Pfeffer, Princip, "exhausted by his beating, was unable to utter a word. He was undersized, emaciated, sallow, sharp featured. It was difficult to imagine that so fragile looking an individual could have committed so serious a deed."

Later, under interrogation, Princip regained his voice, and asserted that he had no accomplices and had acted on his own initiative. He denied all knowledge of Cabrinovic. Of himself, he said: "people took me for a weakling. . . . And I pretended that I was a weak person even though I was not."

In turn, Cabrinovic, though he admitted knowing Princip, denied any knowledge of what his friend had done. If Princip, too, had made an attempt on the Archduke's life, it must have been (according to Cabrinovic) because he harbored similar feelings and had arrived at the same conclusions as to what had to be done.

The correspondent of the London *Times* reported on June 29 that Princip and Cabrinovic "are said to have assumed a most cynical attitude during their examination" and to have persisted in claiming that nobody else was involved.

Their story—that two friends by coincidence had tried to assassinate the same public figure, independently of one another, on the same day in the same place, at roughly the same time—was inherently absurd. The reason they had no more plausible account to provide was that they had made no effort to devise one: theirs was a suicide mission; they had swallowed their cyanide; they should have been dead, and therefore in no need of a cover story for the authorities.

As the questionings continued, the police threw out a dragnet. Not merely Cabrinovic's family and the Ilic family with whom Princip lived, but more than two hundred leading Bosnian Serbs were arrested in Sarajevo alone. Princip felt guilty about this; it was wrong, he felt, to stand by and let innocent people be punished for what he had done. In any event (though accounts differ) Cabrinovic had confessed some elements of the conspiracy to Judge Pfeffer. Princip wanted to reveal only the names of fellow conspirators—after all, they had volunteered for a suicide mission.

Ilic, caught up with many others in the police dragnet, volunteered to reveal everything if his life were spared. Unlike Princip, he was over twenty-one and subject to the death penalty. He told the Austrians what he knew.

By July 2, all conspirators had been identified; by July 3, all were in custody, except for a minor figure who escaped to Montenegro and was never apprehended. The prisoners attempted to avoid supplying information that could link them with Serbia. They did not entirely succeed; on July 5, General Potiorek was able to cable his civilian superior, Finance Minister Bilinski, that the conspirators had been supplied with weapons by Serbian Major Tankosic, who also had trained Princip in marksmanship.

Austria's military attaché in Serbia uncovered vital evidence that, if properly followed up, might have tied Princip's conspirators to

Apis—and therefore to the Serbian government. He reported this to his superiors in the war ministry, who failed to forward or communicate it, but merely filed it away.

This evidence of a link to Serbia was suggestive, but by no means conclusive. The Hapsburg government was convinced that Serbia somehow was implicated in the crime, but it had no proof of it. An official from Vienna who traveled to Sarajevo to see for himself cabled home: "There is nothing to indicate that the Serbian Government knew about the plot." Moreover, Vienna was—and remained—mistaken as to the secret society that had backed Princip; it was not the essentially cultural society Narodna Odbrana, but the Black Hand, which Austrians did not mention by name because they did not know of its existence.

The German minister in Belgrade reported to Chancellor Bethmann Hollweg on June 30 that Serbs were worried that they would be held responsible for the murders and that they were "very depressed" but that "Serbia's moral complicity in the crime . . . cannot be denied." He quoted the Russian minister as hoping that whoever did it was not Serbian: "Esperons que ce ne sera pas un Serbe." ("He must have known it!" commented the skeptical Kaiser.)

In his report two days later he told the Chancellor that the Austrian chargé d'affaires in Belgrade, on July 1, on his own initiative, had asked the Serbian foreign office what inquiry was being made into the crime. "Nothing had been done!" was the reply. When he expressed his astonishment, the foreign office contacted the minister of the interior. Searches and arrests then were made in the quarter where some of the conspirators had lived.

That same day Pasic, the Serbian Prime Minister and foreign minister, circularized his ministers abroad to the effect that "Austrian and Hungarian press are blaming Serbia more and more for the Sarajevo outrage." Calling this "absurd" he claimed that in all circles of Serbian society the act "had been most severely condemned." It had not been within Serbia's power to prevent the crime because "both assassins are Austrian subjects." He implored his representatives to use all channels available to them "to put an end as soon as possible to the anti-Serbian campaign in the European press."

Germany's civilian leaders, the Chancellor, the foreign minister, and the ambassador to the Dual Monarchy, instinctively moved to caution Vienna to react with restraint. Not so the Kaiser, who was devastated and enraged. No longer did he, like his friend Franz Ferdinand, minimize the Serbian problem, for he was among those who assumed—without waiting for proof—that the trail of guilt led to Belgrade. "Now or never," he commented. "The Serbs must be disposed of and that right soon!" His words resounded throughout the twentieth century. They have been quoted repeatedly to show that his knee-jerk reaction was what led to the outbreak of world war.

From an agent in the old Serbian fortress town of Nish, the Dual Monarchy Foreign Minister Count von Berchtold heard: "There was practically no sign of consternation or indignation; the predominant mood was one of satisfaction and even joy, and this was often quite open. . . . This is especially the case with the so-called leading circles—the intellectuals, such as professional politicians, those occupied in education, officials, officers, and the students."

As of the first days of July, neither of the quarreling parties seemed to be aware of how matters looked to the outside world. Belgrade, unable to hide the joy of the people of Serbia, did not appear to realize how much more it had to do to persuade others that it was innocent. Vienna did not understand how much more it had to do to persuade others that the Serbian government—not merely rogues in its officialdom—was guilty.

Nikolai Schebeko, Russia's minister in Vienna, initiated an investigation of his own. He dispatched Prince M. A. Gagarin to Sarajevo. Gagarin was struck by the almost total lack of security on the part of local Hapsburg officials. He suspected that they were trying to cover up their own incompetence by accusing the Serbs. The assassins, after all, were not Serbs; they were Hapsburg subjects from Austro-Hungarian Bosnia. It seemed to Gagarin that if Serbs had set out to kill the Archduke, they would have made a much better job of it.

Gagarin's skepticism might have been dispelled had the Austrians been open in revealing the evidence they had uncovered. But the official investigation continued to be conducted in secrecy. Had it been otherwise, had Austria convinced Russia that Serbia was a staging zone for terrorists dedicated to killing royalty, the Czar might have closed ranks with Austria-Hungary and Germany against the regicides. And there would have been no war in 1914, though there may well have been a war in some other year.

PART FIVE

TELLING LIES

CHAPTER 25: **GERMANY SIGNS**
A BLANK CHECK

The truth of the matter was that, with the possible exception of Berchtold, few in Austria-Hungary were sorry that Franz Ferdinand had been removed from the scene. True, the leaders of the Dual Monarchy deplored the killing of royalty, but if someone of the blood had to be sacrificed, the Archduke was everybody's choice to be the one.

Of course the heir apparent was, next only to the Emperor, the most important figure in the Hapsburg Empire. In murdering him, upstart Serbian terrorists threw down a public challenge to the very existence of the empire. If Vienna failed to respond, it would lose by default: such an argument could be and was plausibly made at the time and by many historians since.

It was not, however, the reason that the Dual Monarchy sought to destroy Serbia. It could not have been the reason, for, Franz Ferdinand apart, the Hapsburg leaders wanted to destroy Serbia *before* the assassination. They would have launched their campaign not in 1914, but in 1912 or 1913, had they not been blocked. The opinion of

Europe had stood in their way, as did the fear of Russia and as did the lack of German support.

What the killings gave Vienna was not a reason, but an excuse, for taking action. They provided the Austrians with grounds for destroying Serbia—a pretext that Europe would accept and believe, and with which Europe might well even sympathize. It was a justification that might bring Germany to support them and prevent Russia from opposing them. In the past two men, Franz Ferdinand and Wilhelm II, had stood in the way of mounting a crusade against Serbia, and the assassinations had, though in different ways, removed them both: the Archduke killed, and the Kaiser carried away by a desire for revenge and caught up in unthinking rage.

In the course of the Balkan wars of 1912–13, Austria had developed a fear of Serbia that bordered on the hysterical. The Kaiser had discounted such fears, to Vienna's intense chagrin. Now, at last, the volatile Wilhelm had been turned around by the events in Sarajevo.

In this respect, and from Vienna's point of view, Gavrilo Princip had committed the perfect crime.

Just after the murders, when Germany's ambassador in Vienna ventured to offer advice to his hosts to go slowly and be cautious the Kaiser was enraged: "Who authorized him to act that way? That is very stupid! It is none of his business, as it is solely the affair of Austria what she plans to do in this case." Wilhelm himself now believed that the Balkan situation could be righted only by force.

How would the Hapsburg government respond to events? The official in charge of foreign policy was Leopold von Berchtold. It was to him that the Dual Monarchy—and Europe—looked for the answer.

Aged fifty-one in 1914, the minister was ill-fitted for leadership. Berchtold had accepted office only with the greatest reluctance. Appointed when Aehrenthal died in 1912, he had retained Aehrenthal's fervent young staff members and tended to let them have their way. Indecisive and intellectually shallow, but a person of charm and manners, he was best suited to a playboy life. Born wealthy, he had become one of the richest men in the empire through marriage. He had lands and stables. He was a diplomat by nature but an amateur foreign minister.

In the past Berchtold had equivocated on the Serbia issue. Franz

Ferdinand, after the Konopischt meetings in mid-June, believed that the foreign minister agreed with him that the Dual Monarchy should leave the Serbs alone. But the memorandum that Berchtold had commissioned from his ministry—from Franz von Matscheko in collaboration with Ludwig von Flotow and Johann Forgach, officials in the expansionist tradition of Aehrenthal—advocated a forward policy: a close and active German-Austrian alliance that would take the offensive in Europe against a supposed Russian threat. The memorandum envisaged, among other things, the diplomatic encirclement of Serbia.

Immediately after the assassinations, Berchtold gave orders to revise the memorandum in the light of what had just happened. The new memorandum retained its call for strong measures. Goals stayed the same, but new opportunities might now be available. The word "war" still was not mentioned. But on June 30, Berchtold spoke of the need for a "final and fundamental reckoning" with Serbia.

This was something that had to be discussed with Germany. Austria-Hungary's government was not strong enough to take a stand on its own. In requesting European royalty not to attend the funeral services for Franz Ferdinand, the Vienna authorities made an exception for Wilhelm II; the Kaiser was invited in his capacity as a personal friend of the deceased, yet would be available for policy discussions and decisions. However, German officials feared another attack; out of a concern for the Kaiser's safety, his aides persuaded him to decline the invitation.

How could the Hapsburg government enlist the Kaiser's help in carrying out whichever policy it adopted? The solicitation of German support had to be embodied in a plan and it had to be in writing: such was the advice of Germany's ambassador in Vienna, Count Heinrich von Tschirschky.

Berchtold, as recounted earlier, already had something in writing: his foreign office memorandum, urging that Serbia be encircled, isolated, and crushed, which with some modifications could become the requisite written proposal. The Emperor of Austria, Franz Joseph, agreed to supply a cover letter to Wilhelm. The letter was written, emperor to emperor, man to man. Count Alexander Hoyos, a firebrand in his mid-thirties who served as Berchtold's chief of staff, volunteered to act as courier.

Hoyos had reason to believe that his mission was promising. Only

days before, on July 1, he had conversed at length with Victor Naumann, a German journalist with close ties to Berlin officialdom and
especially to the foreign office. Naumann told him that if ever Vienna
was going to ask Berlin for support, this was the time: the Kaiser was
shocked by the assassinations. Moreover, throughout the government
there was less opposition to initiating a preventive war against Russia
than there had been ever before. (This is interesting because it suggests that on balance Berlin still was opposed to launching such a war.)

This was the time "to annihilate Serbia," Naumann said. In his
view, "if at the present moment, when Kaiser Wilhelm is horrified at
the Sarajevo murder, he is spoken to in the right way, he will give
[Austria] all assurances and this time go to the length of war because
he perceives the dangers for the monarchical principle."

Naumann may have been speaking not just for himself, but for a
group within the German government. Whether he was or not, he
was believed to be both shrewd and well informed. In fact, just before
journeying to Vienna, he had come from a meeting with Wilhelm
von Stumm, a hard-liner in the German foreign office.

In Germany at the time there were those who saw what had happened in Sarajevo as an opportunity for taking action: action by Germany or action by Austria. The Saxon ambassador in Berlin reported
to his home government on July 2 that the German military was
pressing for an immediate war while Russia and France were
unready. These views were widespread, reported Austria's ambassador in Berlin.

Moltke, Germany's chief of staff, vacationing on July 5, saw
another alternative if it were Austria that took the field. "Austria
must beat the Serbs and then make peace quickly, demanding an
Austro-Serbian alliance as the sole condition. Just as Prussia did with
Austria in 1866."

Berchtold cabled the German embassy in Vienna that his envoy
Hoyos, a personal friend of the nephew of Germany's Chancellor,
was en route to Berlin in hopes of seeing the Kaiser and the Chancellor, and would arrive the following morning. It would be a tight
schedule; Wilhelm was to leave on July 6 for his annual North Sea
cruise.

Berlin, July 5. In the morning Hoyos briefed Austria's veteran
ambassador to Germany, Ladislaus Szögyéni-Marich, who then left

for Potsdam and lunched with the Kaiser. Meanwhile Hoyos had lunch with Arthur Zimmermann, under-secretary of the German foreign office. It was at the lower-ranking lunch meeting that the Austrian envoy was most open about his country's real goals. Hoyos spoke openly of war, of wiping Serbia off the map and of partitioning Serbia among neighboring states afterwards. He met with a sympathetic reception.

Meanwhile, at Potsdam, Szögyéni gave Kaiser Wilhelm the two documents that Hoyos had brought with him. The foreign office memorandum concluded by saying that it had been written before the murder of the Archduke and had been confirmed in its analysis by that event. The covering letter was in a more personal and moving vein. Both documents focused largely on Romania, warning of its increasing closeness to Serbia and to Russia. Neither called for specific action, although a stated objective was to be the elimination of Serbia as "a factor of political power in the Balkans."

Wilhelm began the discussion by saying that he would have to consult the Chancellor. After lunch, however, pressed to say more, he did so. He pledged Germany's unconditional support for Austria-Hungary in whatever it chose to do in its conflict with Serbia. He gave what historians have called a "carte blanche," or a "blank check." He said he would back the Dual Monarchy even if Russia intervened. He warned his guest, however, that Austria must strike quickly. He then met with the Chancellor and with such of his military advisers as could be found at short notice in summertime, and did so again the following morning. A consensus emerged in support of Wilhelm's decision. Even the Chancellor was in agreement.

According to the latest scholarship, it was mainly Chancellor Bethmann Hollweg who worked out the terms of the German response. A career civil servant, fifty-seven years old, he had spent a career trying to restrain powerful forces and intemperate personalities.

As Chancellor for five years, he had felt the pressure of army officers who believed war with Russia to be inevitable, and who advocated a preemptive strike before the Russians were ready. He was exposed also to the countervailing pressure from Tirpitz to delay going to war until the distant point when the German fleet could deter Britain. Bethmann was aware that the Kaiser, no matter what he said, in the end usually opted for peace.

Now there was the July 4 written inquiry from Vienna as to whether Germany would protect Austria-Hungary against Russia if Austria-Hungary tried to crush Serbia. What the Austrians wanted to do was not spelled out in writing. It was not clear that they had the nerve to do anything at all. But both sides—Berlin and Vienna—were worried, as it turned out, about what might happen if the requested guarantee were not given.

Each side was conscious of its international isolation. Each was afraid of losing its only real ally. In German government circles one concern was that, after Franz Joseph died, the Hapsburg Empire could disintegrate. Another concern was that, as in the Moroccan crisis of 1911, the Dual Monarchy would not back Germany in its quarrels; it would fight only in its own. In Austria-Hungary, on the other hand, some worried that Germany would walk away from an ally that proved useless because it lacked the courage to fight at all.

The essence of the consensus that developed among the Germans on July 5–6 was that circumstances now were favorable to a bold design: that Austria-Hungary could deal with its Serbian problem without risking a larger war, provided that Vienna struck swiftly. The German response to the Hoyos mission, according to Berghahn's authoritative work, bore the stamp of Bethmann, who apparently devised it. It was Berlin's plan (though the world was to be kept from knowing this) that Vienna undertook to follow. The plan was for Austria to strike rapidly, crush Serbia, and present Europe with a *fait accompli*.

On July 6, Bethmann confirmed to the Austrians the Kaiser's secret commitment to support Austria in case of war.

Most historians have condemned the German pledge as reckless. Samuel Williamson, a leading scholar of Austria-Hungary's role in the origins of World War I, writes: "Germany, by its pledges, had surrendered the direction and the pace of the July crisis" to Austria.

Yet the check may not have been entirely blank. The Germans may have believed that it was their own plan—a quick strike—that Austria would carry into effect, so they were not really turning over decision-making to Vienna. Then, too, there were qualifications to Germany's pledge—or at least Kaiser Wilhelm may have believed that they were implicit. The guarantee was issued in the context of several years of warfare in the Balkans during which Austria already had asked at least three times for the statement of support that Hoyos had received, eliciting one yes and two noes. The Kaiser had certain preconditions in mind for pledging full support to Austria-Hungary in its continuing conflicts with Serbia, preconditions that become clearer if viewed within the context of 1912–14 rather than of 1914 alone.

· Austria-Hungary had to be seen—at least by the German people, and preferably by all of Europe—as the provoked party. That, in Wilhelm's view, had not been the case in the early autumn of 1912 or the late spring of 1914 but had been true in the late autumn of 1912—and now was true again because of the Sarajevo killings.
· Austria-Hungary had to act by itself and with lightning speed.
· The Kaiser clearly believed that Austria intended to punish Serbia for the killings. He either was not told or did not understand that the Dual Monarchy proposed to destroy Serbia—a goal that Wilhelm had blocked in the past when it was openly avowed.
· Circumstances had to be such that Russia, France, and England were unlikely to intervene. That is what the Kaiser and much of his entourage believed to be the case in July 1914. Bethmann, who was designated to watch over the operation against Serbia on behalf of Germany, understood that there was a risk of igniting a conflagration, but believed it to be only a slight risk. Wilhelm believed that for all practical purposes there was no risk at all.
· The Kaiser's conviction was that the crisis would pass quickly: "that the situation would be cleared up within a week, because of Serbia's backing down."
· Alternatively, Wilhelm explained to one of his naval officers, "the Austrian government will demand the most far-reaching satisfaction from Serbia and will, as soon as this is not given, move its troops into Serbia." As he saw it, there would be a quick Hapsburg military occupation of Belgrade, the Serb capital, which was conveniently located on the river that formed the Austro-Hungarian frontier, followed by an imposed peace treaty forcing Serbia to become an Austrian ally.

On July 5–6 neither the Kaiser nor his advisers believed that they were risking much by extending their guarantee. Erich von Falkenhayn, Prussian minister of war, was not convinced that Vienna "was really in earnest" or "had taken any firm resolution." Germany risked nothing because in all likelihood it would never be called upon to make good on its guarantee. The consensus was that "the Russians—though friends of Serbia—will not join in after all." The Kaiser said to Szögyéni that Russia "was not by any means prepared for war," and he told his military advisers that France would "scarcely let it come to a war" because it still lacked heavy artillery. Moreover, he did not believe that the Czar would enter a war on the side of regicides. Falkenhayn asked if additional preparations should be made for a war involving the Great Powers, and Wilhelm said no.

Germany's military leaders had made it clear that, in any case, they were prepared for all eventualities. The Kaiser and his generals may have supported the blank check decision for opposite reasons. He was in favor of it because he believed that war would not result from it, while some of them may have been in favor of it because it raised the possibility that a war *would* result from it.

So it was that, three weeks after refusing to pledge unconditional support to the living Franz Ferdinand, Kaiser Wilhelm avowed such support to the cause of the dead Franz Ferdinand. What had changed was the death of the Archduke. Wilhelm was not alone in this; the leaders of other countries felt the same way. Europe's sympathies now would be against Serbia and with the Austrians—if they struck back immediately, and if they acted alone rather than in collusion with Germany.

But the lies—or at least misleading statements—told by the Austrian and German governments threatened to catch up with them.

Austria-Hungary lied when it claimed to be striking back for the murder of the Archduke. In fact, the killings at Sarajevo had relatively little to do with the Hapsburg desire to crush Serbia. What gave away Austria's lie in the first instance was that it did not attack immediately, which is what one does when one strikes out in anger or in self-defense. Alternatively, one would pursue a full judicial inquiry to its conclusion, and then publish its results to the world, which Vienna lacked the patience to do.

The fact—known now, though not then—that the memo submitted to the Kaiser in support of the plan to go to war was the same memo that had been prepared before the murders in Sarajevo shows that it did not arise from that event.

Austria did not play its part very well. Its behavior in the weeks that followed did nothing to persuade Europe that it was primarily motivated by a desire to avenge the slain Archduke. Disbelief crept over Europe. Vienna's claims appeared less and less credible in the ensuing weeks.

To Germany, the Austrian representatives apparently gave the impression that they would do what the Kaiser insisted upon: act with lightning speed, finishing the matter in a week or two or three.

The Germans counted on it, but the Hapsburg Empire was incapable of fulfilling this expectation. It was another misstatement that was apt to catch up with the Austrians, though perhaps they themselves did not realize they could not perform as promised.

Then there were the Germans, not perhaps lying, but showing a want of candor. The Kaiser and many of his men were certain that none of the other Great Powers of Europe would intervene to halt the expected Austrian strike. They committed to ward off France and Russia in the firm belief that they never would be called upon to do so. They were signing a check that they believed would never be cashed.

CHAPTER 26: **THE GREAT DECEPTION**

In collusion with one another, each of the two parties now played out their assigned roles. Austria decided—apparently acting by itself and spontaneously—to claim to be bringing the murderers and their Serbian sponsors to justice. Striking out in a show of righteous wrath, the Hapsburg armies would be punishing the guilty and also exercising a right of self-defense against further attacks staged from Serbia. Europe, even if it did not applaud, would at least admit that the Austrians had every right to be doing what they were doing.

It was vital that the world should not know of Germany's role or the Kaiser's guarantee. Certainly the two allies acted as though they believed secrecy to be essential. They lied repeatedly in the weeks to come, breaching the trust that was the hallmark of European diplomacy in an earlier age.

Had Germany's participation been discovered in time, Europe would have recognized that Austria was not pursuing the objectives it claimed. It was not avenging a murder victim; it was using the murder as a cloak under which to set back Russia in the Balkans. Europe would have seen what Austria intended was not to punish Serbia but to destroy it; not to defeat Serbia, but to wipe it off the map.

And the world would have realized that Germany was not, like France or Italy, an innocent bystander, but a full participant in Austria's project. The German-speaking combine was not seeking justice for the slain Archduke; instead it was engaging in a power play intended to alter the balance of power in the Balkans in their favor.

So Austria had to attack and subjugate Serbia before anybody fully realized that anything was afoot. Europe had to be lulled into believing that Austria was going to do nothing at all until weeks of judicial inquiry had concluded with the fixing of responsibility on the guilty parties. Unaware of what was planned, Europe would take no precautions. To dupe Europe, the leaders of Germany and Austria would have to become play actors.

It long had been the custom of Europe's leaders to take summer holidays. In early July, Berchtold had the notion (as did Bethmann) of lulling the European world into a sense of illusory security by pretending to follow their normal July schedules. Berchtold told his war minister and his army chief of staff to go away on vacations "to prevent any disquiet." Emperor Franz Joseph resumed his holiday. Chancellor Bethmann attempted the same ruse and made a show of being at his country estate. Tirpitz was vacationing in the Black Forest. Moltke was at the famous spa of Carlsbad, taking the waters. The foreign minister was on his honeymoon. Moltke's and Tirpitz's deputies were on holiday. So was the minister of war.

The Germans, once installed in their vacation retreats, seem to have done their best to remain there and to look innocent. On the advice of the Prime Minister, Kaiser Wilhelm reluctantly went off on his scheduled cruise, though he found the whole exercise in deception "childish!" It seems not to have occurred to him at the time that his Chancellor was dispatching him on his voyage in order to get him out of the way.

The special oddity of July 1914 therefore was that those fateful activities that were going on were not visible. It was like a play in which everything of importance happens offstage.

Early in the morning of Monday, July 6, before embarking, the Kaiser sent for several officers to deliver messages for him. Admiral Eduard von Capelle, Tirpitz's deputy, received a phone call between

7:00 and 8:00 a.m. summoning him. He found Wilhelm in the garden of his palace. Capelle recalled: "The Emperor walked up and down with me for a short while and told me briefly of the occurrences of the day before"—the blank check to Austria, an account of which Capelle apparently was to give to Tirpitz. The Kaiser "did not believe in serious warlike developments. According to his view, the Czar would not in this case place himself on the side of regicides. Besides that, Russia and France were not prepared for war. (The Emperor did not mention England.) On the advice of the Imperial Chancellor, he was going to start on the journey to Northland, in order not to create any uneasiness."

A similar message was sent by the hand of a naval officer, Captain Zenker, to his superiors. "His Majesty had promised" to protect Austria if Russia interfered "but did not believe that Russia would enter the lists for Serbia, which had stained itself by an assassination. France, too, would scarcely let it come to war, as it lacked the heavy artillery for the field armies. Yet though a war against Russia-France was not probable, nevertheless the possibility of such a war must be borne in mind from a military point of view."

Wilhelm was aware that he had a reputation for backing down in a crisis. "This time I shall not give in," he told the armaments manufacturer Krupp.

Aboard ship, the Kaiser did his best to avoid looking like someone awaiting important news. Yet on July 6 he allowed two of his naval officers to understand that in nine days Austria's response to what the Serbs had done would be known. At other times the Kaiser told his officers the situation would be resolved in one week or within three weeks. He told the acting armed forces chiefs: "He did not anticipate major military complications. In his opinion the Tsar in this case would not take the part of the regicides. Moreover, Russia and France were not prepared for war. . . . On the Chancellor's advice he was going on his . . . cruise in order not to give cause for disquietude."

Wilhelm told much the same to the chief of his Military Cabinet and to the Prussian minister of war: "the sooner the Austrians make their move against Serbia, the better, and . . . the Russians—though friends of Serbia—will not join in."

On July 7, the day after Germany signed its blank check, Berchtold convened the cabinet of the Dual Monarchy to seek its authorization to move forward. The cabinet was comprised of the Austrian Premier and his ministers, the Hungarian Premier and his ministers, and the handful, such as Berchtold, who were ministers of the Austro-Hungarian union.

The cabinet deliberated and debated for hours. The Hungarian Prime Minister, Count István Tisza, expressed strong opposition to Berchtold's plans. He was alone in doing so, but he kept the others from taking action. Tisza warned that an invasion of Serbia by the Dual Monarchy "would, as far as can humanly be foreseen, lead to an intervention by Russia and hence to a world war." His alternative plan was for Vienna to draw up a list of demands and "issue an ultimatum only if Serbia did not fulfill them. The demands must be stiff but not impossible to meet." Above all, he argued, the Hapsburg Empire should not allow itself to be drawn into a war.

Instead, the cabinet proposed to present an ultimatum to Serbia—a waste of time, as Berchtold should have realized—that Serbia could not possibly accept, and to follow it up by launching an invasion. Tisza, who was entitled to a veto, held out for making demands that Serbia *could* accept. His preference was for a peaceful solution.

All the ministers were convinced that some Serbian officials were connected in some way with the crime in Sarajevo, though they had no conclusive proof of it, and the Sarajevo trial might not take place for weeks or months. That was too long for Berchtold to wait. He needed to act in a matter of days or perhaps a week or two at most.

For a week, July 7–14, Count Tisza stonewalled. Then his foreign policy adviser persuaded him that Hungary, in its quarrel with Romania, would benefit from the crusade against Serbia. Moreover, Berchtold employed two other powerful arguments. There were those in the German government who would be so disappointed in the Dual Monarchy if it failed to act in a manly fashion that they would see no value in remaining an ally: the German alliance, on which all depended, would be lost. Moreover, Berchtold held out hope to the Hungarian Prime Minister; it was not impossible that Serbia would accept Austrian terms, in which case there would be no war after all. (That was not really true, for Berchtold was determined to force a war on Serbia no matter what Serbia said or did.)

Tisza abandoned his opposition, but it had cost Berchtold a week.

And the Kaiser, it will be remembered, expected matters to be resolved in a week or two, or three at the most.

From London on July 9, the German ambassador reported that he had discussed the Sarajevo aftermath and Austria's possible response with Sir Edward Grey. He stated that Grey "was in a thoroughly confident mood, and declared in cheerful tones that he saw no reason for taking a pessimistic view of the situation."

July 11.   A question for the German foreign office from the Kaiser's yacht: should the customary telegram of congratulations be sent to the King of Serbia on his birthday, July 12? Answer: "As Vienna has so far inaugurated no action of any sort against Belgrade, the omission of the customary telegram would be too noticeable and might be the cause of premature uneasiness. . . . [I]t should be sent."

July 14.   Vienna to Berlin. The ultimatum to be sent to Serbia "is being composed so that the possibility of its acceptance is *practically excluded.*" But it has not yet been put in final form and would not be before July 19. ("Too bad," notes the Kaiser.)

By mid-July, complaints of Austrian indecisiveness seemed to be justified. It was possible to speculate, as Bavarian officials did, that at the conference of July 5–6, Austria-Hungary would have preferred to have the Kaiser *refuse* the blank check—*not* offer full support—so as to have an excuse for doing nothing.

As had so many European diplomats, Baron Giesl von Gieslingen, Austria's minister in Belgrade, had been away on vacation. On July 10 he returned. The Russian representative, Hartwig, promptly called upon him that evening to present formal condolences for the assassinations in Sarajevo. Hartwig denied a rumor that he had failed to mark the occasion by flying the legation flag at half-mast.

Hartwig, who was obese, suffered not only from asthma but also from angina pectoris. It was of the heart pains that he now complained. Official duties would keep him at his post for two days more. Then he could vacation at a spa.

Hartwig inquired what Austria planned to do in response to the events in Sarajevo. Giesl assured him that he need have no fears on Serbia's behalf. Hartwig looked relieved. Then, noiselessly, the Russian diplomat slipped to the floor. A doctor, called immediately, pronounced him dead of a heart attack.

The Giesls sent for Hartwig's daughter Ludmilla. She brushed aside all attempts to comfort her, bitterly calling them "Austrian words." She searched the room; she asked whether her father had been served food or drink (he had not); and she carefully carried away his cigarette butts, presumably to be tested for poison.

The cigarettes had not been tampered with. What had been poisoned in Balkan Europe in July 1914 was the air. It had become a world of lies, plots, and deceit.

CHAPTER 27: **BERCHTOLD RUNS OUT OF TIME**

July 14.   Even though Tisza no longer stood in the way, Berchtold still could not go ahead to attack Serbia. Conrad, the chief of staff, discovered that a leave of absence that had been given to the troops for harvesting of crops would not expire until July 25. An emergency recall would have signaled Vienna's warlike intentions; it could not be done.

To strike before then would be imprudent, the Austrians decided, for another reason. The President and the Prime Minister of France were about to pay a state call on Russia. Therefore the leaders of the two allies would be together, able to concert their response to whatever moves Austria might make. Not wishing to allow this to happen, Berchtold decided to wait until the two Frenchmen had left St. Petersburg and were aboard ship, thus safely out of touch. That meant ascertaining the date that French President Raymond Poincaré and Prime Minister René Viviani planned to leave. He asked his embassy in St. Petersburg to supply him with this information. Having done so, Berchtold planned to present an ultimatum to Serbia on July 23 that would expire July 25.

For use in his proposed note to Serbia, Berchtold wanted information on the latest incriminating evidence uncovered in Sarajevo. One of his officials went to Sarajevo, sifted the evidence, and reported on July 13: It was not what Berchtold would have wished to hear. Much of it was inconclusive. The Austrian investigators had found that "There is nothing to prove or even to suppose that the Serbian government is accessory to the inducement for the crime, its preparation, or the furnishing of weapons. On the contrary, there are reasons to believe that this is altogether out of the question." All that could be found was that the assassins had been aided by persons with ties to government.

To wait for conclusive evidence of Serb guilt to surface was no longer an option. Berchtold would have to go forward with the drafting of his ultimatum without the evidence to back him up.

Yet another delay threatened. Conrad advised that the armed forces would not be ready to invade Serbia until August 12. That would be seven weeks after the assassinations—far too long for launching an attack on Serbia that Europe would excuse as an unthinking reaction.

What was Berchtold to do? What was he to tell Berlin? He had run out of time.

What was happening? Berlin inquired. Vienna did not answer because Berchtold had no reply to give.

CHAPTER 28: **THE SECRET IS KEPT**

Berchtold kept the Germans in the dark, in effect maintaining radio silence. He had a plausible excuse: To achieve surprise in his planned assault on Serbia, he had to keep anyone outside the existing circle from knowing what was going on. As communications could be intercepted and deciphered it was best to communicate as little as possible with anyone.

Keeping the secret proved difficult. The German foreign office passed on to its ambassador in Italy a general sense of Austria's thinking. The ambassador mentioned it casually to Foreign Minister Antonio di San Giuliano. Italians rarely were entrusted with secrets by the Great Powers because of their reputation for indiscretion. Indeed, a historian of the country's foreign policy at the time writes: "Italian diplomats could not even arrange appointments with major European statesmen." Alerted by the German ambassador, San Giuliano passed on whatever he knew to his embassies in Russia, Austria, and Serbia. The Austrians, having broken the Italian code, knew what San Giuliano was telling his diplomats. Historian Samuel

Williamson, who relates this story, conjectures that the Russians, with their sophistication in cryptology, might have broken the Italian code too, and might have alerted Serbia.

The Russians had cracked the Austrian code, had read Berchtold's inquiry as to when the French President and Prime Minister would leave Russia—and could have drawn inferences from this request.

Such leaks were only to be expected as time went on, and as delay led to further delay. A retired Austrian diplomat dropped a hint that was picked up by a British ambassador, who passed on the rumor to a French colleague.

On July 16 the British ambassador to Russia alerted his government to the gathering storm: "Austro-Hungarian government are in no mood to parley with Servia [sic], but will insist on immediate unconditional compliance, failing which force will be used. Germany is said to be in complete agreement with this procedure."

The same day, and in the same city, St. Petersburg, the Italian ambassador told a Russian diplomat "that Austria was capable of taking an irrevocable step with regard to Serbia based on the belief that, although Russia would make a verbal protest, she would not adopt forcible measures for the protection of Serbia against any Austrian attempts."

A number of European diplomats heard disquieting rumors, but only a handful had hard knowledge. Even in Vienna few actually *knew*, and in Berlin even fewer.

In a broader sense, moreover, the secret was kept: the public knew nothing of it. As Volker Berghahn writes of Germany: "only a very small circle of men was involved in the crucial decisions which ended in war," and "when it came to making this decision no more than a dozen people were consulted." The same was true of Austria-Hungary. The plotters went on with their work, silently and hidden from view, while, totally unaware, Europe basked in the sunshine of a lazy summer holiday.

PART SIX

CRISIS!

CHAPTER 29: **THE *FAIT* IS NOT *ACCOMPLI***

On July 16 the Russian ambassador in Vienna cabled his government: "Information reaches me that the Austro-Hungarian Government at the conclusion of the inquiry intends to make certain demands on Belgrade. . . . It would seem to me desirable that at the present moment, before a final decision on the matter, the Vienna Cabinet should be informed how Russia would react to the fact of Austria's presenting demands to Serbia such as would be unacceptable to the dignity of that state."

This, and similar intimations of Austrian designs, disturbed Russia's foreign minister. But Vienna's ambassador hastened to reassure. He told the Russian foreign minister that Austria-Hungary wanted peace. So Russia did nothing.

On July 18, Pasic, the Prime Minister of Serbia, cabled Serbian missions abroad (other than in Vienna) that he was determined not to accept any demands by Austria-Hungary that would infringe on Serbian sovereignty.

The hidden plot that the Austrian and German leaders were in the process of executing was outlined clearly—but in confidence—for the government of Bavaria at the time. The kingdom of Bavaria was the largest and most populous state in the Prussian-led German Empire. In joining Germany, it had "reserved a larger measure of sovereign independence than any of the other constituent states" including a separate diplomatic service, military administration, and postal, telegraph, and railway services.

On July 18, Hans Schoen, a Bavarian diplomat who had been briefed by officials in Berlin, explained at length to his Prime Minister, Count Georg Hertling, the Dual Monarchy's pretense "of being peacefully inclined" and why an Austrian ultimatum could not be delivered to Belgrade until mid-July. Summarizing the demands that would be made in the ultimatum, Schoen observed: "It is perfectly plain that Serbia can not accept any such demands, which are incompatible with her dignity as a sovereign state. Thus the result would be war." That is, there would be war if Vienna actually went through with the plan. Jagow and Zimmermann, respectively number one and two ranking officials at the German foreign office, had their doubts. They "made the statement that Austria-Hungary, thanks to her indecision and her desultoriness, had really become the Sick Man of Europe as Turkey had once been."

"A powerful and successful move against Serbia," Zimmermann had continued, would bring the Dual Monarchy back from the brink. Schoen reported that German leaders "are of the opinion . . . that Austria is face to face with an hour of fate." That, they told Schoen, was why on July 5–6 they had given the Austrians a "blank power of full authority" "even at the risk of war with Russia." In their view the Austrians were surprised by such unconditional support, and might have felt more comfortable if they had been told instead to restrain themselves.

Germany, Schoen made clear, wished that Vienna had not waited so long before doing anything. The Germans were awaiting presentation of the Austrian ultimatum to Serbia. Berlin then would embark upon a diplomatic effort to localize the conflict. All powers should stay out of it, the Germans were going to say, leaving Austria-Hungary and Serbia to work things out for themselves. The Germans were going to claim they knew as little as everyone else of the ultimatum the Austrians would present; they would say it came as a complete surprise—while the Kaiser and others were on vacation.

Archduke Franz Ferdinand and his family

Aerial view of Sarajevo in 1914

The Archduke and Duchess begin their day in Sarajevo, June 28, 1914.

The scene of the first assassination attempt

The royal couple leaves the city hall.

The arrest of
Gavrilo Princip

Emperor Franz Joseph I

ABOVE: U.S. President Woodrow Wilson and
Secretary of State William Jennings Bryan
BELOW: Colonel Edward House,
Wilson's diplomatic envoy

Serbian Prime Minister Nicola Pasic

The leader of the Austro-Hungarian Army, Conrad von Hötzendorf

LEFT: Count von Berch-
told, Austrian minister of
foreign affairs
BELOW: British Prime
Minister Herbert Asquith

LEFT: British Foreign Secretary
Sir Edward Grey
BELOW: David Lloyd George,
Chancellor of the Exchequer

ABOVE: Winston Churchill,
First Lord of the Admiralty
BELOW: Russian Foreign
Minister Serge Sazonov

ABOVE: Czar Nicholas II and French President
Raymond Poincaré
BELOW: In Paris, King George V and President Poincaré

ABOVE: Joseph Caillaux,
Prime Minister of France
BELOW: Mme Caillaux

Kaiser Wilhelm II and General von Moltke viewing maneuvers

LEFT: Chancellor of Germany
(1909–17) Theobald von
Bethmann Hollweg
BELOW: German General
Erich von Falkenhayn

RIGHT: German Admiral Alfred von Tirpitz
BELOW: Prince Karl Lichnowsky, German
Ambassador to Britain, leaving the Foreign
Office as the war begins

Schoen concluded: "The attitude of Russia will, above all else, determine the question whether the attempt to localize the war will succeed." German official opinion, as reported by him, was to the effect that war would not be "acceptable" to either France or England. The Germans, in other words, still believed that Vienna and Berlin could carry through their plot successfully without causing a European war. They thought that they were going to get away with it. This was confirmed by the Berlin representative of Saxony, another of the German states: "one expects a localization of the conflict since England is absolutely peaceable and France as well as Russia likewise do not feel inclined towards war."

As the great web of deception was being woven to its conclusion, in Vienna and Berlin, the Dual Monarchy's ultimatum was being drafted behind closed doors. The Austro-Hungarian foreign ministry began work on the document on July 10. The Germans were kept informed of its progress. The note was ready to be circulated internally on July 19.

Since Tisza's change of heart on July 14, there had been no doubt as to the purpose which the note to Serbia was meant to serve. It was being drafted in such a way as to be rejected. The German ambassador in Vienna reported to his government that "the note is being composed so that the possibility of its being accepted is *practically excluded.*"

Another official of the German embassy followed up with the report of a conversation with the Austro-Hungarian foreign minister: "Count Berchtold appeared to hope that Serbia would not agree to the Austro-Hungarian demands, as a mere diplomatic victory would put the country here again in a stagnant mood." Hoyos at the Dual Monarchy's foreign office told a German colleague "that the demands were really of such a nature that no nation that still possessed self-respect and dignity could possibly accept them."

The ultimatum in its final form was submitted to the Council of Ministers—the cabinet—on Sunday afternoon, July 19. In the words of the historian Frederic Morton, the ministers arrived at Berchtold's palatial private residence for their meeting in "taxis and private automobiles. . . . The cars arrived at intervals, avoiding a dramatic convergence. . . . The scene seemed to point to some weekend social gathering. A passer-by, had he cared to notice, would not have spotted a single official limousine." It was no accident: participants had been ordered to arrive in unmarked cars.

At the meeting, the council ratified the ultimatum to Serbia. The following day a courier brought it to the elderly emperor, Franz Joseph, in his country palace. Franz Joseph read and approved it. At the same time, the text was cabled to the Hapsburg envoy in Belgrade who was scheduled to present it to the Serbian government on the prearranged date.

On a motion from Berchtold, the council had unanimously agreed "that the note should be presented to the Royal Serbian Government on 23 July at five in the afternoon" so that, by its forty-eight-hour terms, the ultimatum would expire July 25 at 5 p.m. In turn, Austro-Hungarian mobilization of the armed forces could be decreed and published overnight Saturday/Sunday, July 25–26.

Berchtold had told his colleagues that he was opposed to any further delays. For one thing, news of Austria's intentions had leaked in Rome, endangering the element of surprise. Moreover, "Berlin was beginning to get nervous."

"Nervousness" perhaps understated the case. For Germany's civilian leaders, Bethmann and Jagow, Austria was proving to be a disappointment and indeed was depriving them of a brilliant victory. The Hapsburg Empire was supposed to have crushed Serbia by now, before the rest of Europe had time to react or respond. The assault was supposed to have taken place. The *fait* was supposed to have been *accompli.*

Yet none of that had been done or even was about to be done. As of July 19, the Austrians were starting—for the first time—to draw up a set of demands to be sent to Serbia. The document then had to be delivered and Serbia's response awaited.

So it was too late now to launch the surprise invasion Bethmann had envisaged. As soon as the countries of Europe saw the sort of ultimatum Berchtold proposed to deliver, they would be alerted. They would know that Serbia was likely to refuse, Austria was likely to go to war, and Germany might well back Austria. The element of surprise would be lost.

One phase in the Austro-German plan to punish Serbia was over: the invasion plan formulated July 6 and never tried. Until July 19 it had meant that Austria would be allowed to crush Serbia with no interference from the European powers because it would have been accomplished before the powers had time to react. Now—after July 19—it had to be changed because it was too late to carry it out as originally planned. In the original scheme, Austria's invasion was to have been completed before the rest of Europe could do anything but send complaining notes after the fact. In the new conception, Europe would have time to react and respond, but would be persuaded to hold off until it was too late. "Localization" was the key word the Germans would continue to use; it meant that the Great Powers, though fully conscious of what was about to transpire, would choose not to intervene on the grounds that it was none of their business. Germany undertook to persuade them that they should let Austria and Serbia resolve their differences by themselves. Clearly speed was required of the Austrians here too, because the longer they took in crushing their smaller neighbor, the more likely it was that one of Serbia's patrons—Russia or France in particular—might begin to think in terms of stopping the unequal conflict.

July 19. The Austrian ultimatum to Serbia was put into its final form. The phase of Austrian and German thinking in which all was going to be decided by a swift attack was over. From July 19 on the German-speaking allies would move forward in full view. Germany shifted into phase two: localization, in its new sense. In this phase Germany would let the other European powers know in advance that there would be a war.

The ultimatum having been formulated, the German government moved immediately to warn the other Great Powers to stay out of the fight that was about to begin while, unconvincingly, disclaiming knowledge of *why* a fight was about to occur or why the Great Powers might be tempted to intervene in it. Jagow placed a note on July 19 in a quasi-official publication, the *North German Gazette*, advising the others "that the settlement of differences which may arise between Austria-Hungary and Serbia should remain localized." This was the start of a diplomatic campaign launched by the German government on behalf of its new tactical goal, conscious localization.

When the French ambassador in Berlin asked Jagow "as to the contents of the Austrian Note," Jagow assured him "that he knew nothing about it." Understandably, the ambassador was "astonished." How could Jagow *not* know? But of course he did.

Fuller statements of the German case for localization were sent on July 21 to Russia, Britain, and France. Vienna, for its part, gave its ambassadors to major countries full statements of the Austro-Hungarian position.

Germany's continued insistence that it knew nothing of what Austria-Hungary planned to do or to demand met with widespread disbelief in Europe's capital cities. Analyzing Jagow's pleas for localization, a British official told Sir Edward Grey: "We do not know the facts. The German government clearly do know. They know what the Austrian government is going to demand . . . and I think we may say with some assurance that they have expressed approval of those demands and promised support should dangerous complications ensue." But the official was confident that "the German government do not believe that there is any real danger of war." According to one source, the official was Sir Horace Rumbold at the Berlin embassy; according to another, Sir Eyre Crowe at the Foreign Office.

The Austrian ambassador in Berlin brought a copy of the ultimatum in final form to Jagow, who later lied and denied having seen it before it went out.* Jagow rechecked calculations and discovered that the Austrians planned to present the ultimatum an hour too soon—while the French leaders were still in Russia. A panicked effort by Hapsburg officialdom, alerted by Jagow, resulted in moving that ultimatum time to an hour later.

Obeying orders, Germany's military leaders remained ostentatiously on vacation, leaving everything to Chancellor Bethmann Hollweg, and to the chief officials of the foreign office, Jagow and Zimmermann, who outwardly affected, as best they could, an air of unconcern.

But they awaited events with different hopes, fears, and expectations. Only a month or so before, Moltke, the gloomy and pessimistic chief of the general staff, had asked Jagow to provoke a world war soon, while Germany still could win it. In two or three years, according to Moltke, it would be too late.

---

*However, in an interview on September 17, 1916, with American journalist William Bullitt, he admitted that he had seen the ultimatum before it was sent. And Zimmermann, Jagow's number two, told a colleague (August 11, 1917) that "it is true that we received the Serbian ultimatum about twelve hours before it was presented." Zimmermann wrote that it was pointless to keep on lying about it, since it "cannot be kept secret forever."

Now Moltke seemingly was prepared to accept the limited but brilliant victory that an Austrian attack would bring—if indeed Vienna would summon up the nerve to proceed with Bethmann's plan and could pull it off. If, however, the German leaders—military and civilian alike—were wrong in their estimate that the war could be localized, and that Russia would stay out, then, unlike the Kaiser and the civilians, Moltke would be happy—maybe even happier—with that result too.

Bethmann, whose role was to preside over affairs while the Austrians carried his strategy into execution, was worried from the start. "An action against Serbia can lead to a world war," he told his confidant Kurt Riezler on July 7. He feared that "whatever the outcome" such a war would turn "everything that exists upside down." The risk of bringing about a global conflict with unforeseeable consequences was "a leap in the dark."

Yet Bethmann felt that Germany had no choice. The portrait that he painted of his country's international position showed a dark and even paranoid vision, with dangers exaggerated. In his own words, it was "a shattering picture." As he saw it, Germany was "completely paralyzed," and its rivals, the allied powers of Russia, France, and Britain, knew it. "The future belongs to Russia which is growing and growing and is becoming an ever-increasing nightmare to us." Even the Dual Monarchy would ally with Russia in order to go with the winner. Germany would be alone and helpless in the world of international politics.

The Chancellor was unnerved by intelligence reports that had reached him about secret naval talks between Britain and Russia. According to German sources, these might have envisaged an amphibious operation in which British forces brought by sea would land in northeastern Germany.

In the memoirs of British Foreign Secretary Sir Edward Grey (by then Viscount Grey of Fallodon), written a bit more than a decade later, the talks were inconsequential. They were undertaken at the request of the French in order to reassure the Russians. So talks were held. No joint operations were planned; no commitments made. What did occur, it would seem, was an exchange of information.

Russia was aware that Britain and France had held naval conversations, in the course of which each had disclosed to the other the dispositions they intended to make of their fleets in the event of war.

Each was free to change those planned dispositions. The Russians now wanted to be treated on a par with the other two countries: to be full allies. When Britain held talks with France, Russia wanted to hold such talks too. The Russians told the French of their desire.

On May 13, Asquith's cabinet had authorized holding such conversations. The ranking serving officer of the British fleet, Admiral Prince Louis of Battenberg, came over to Paris to meet with the Russians some weeks later. Further talks were contemplated, but were obviated by the outbreak of war.

The news leaked out. Questions were asked in Parliament. In reply, Sir Edward Grey reiterated an earlier statement by the Prime Minister that "if war arose between European Powers, there were no unpublished agreements which would restrict or hamper the freedom of the Government, or of Parliament, to decide whether or not Great Britain should participate in a war."

As Grey writes in his memoirs, "The answer given is absolutely true. The criticism to which it is open is, that it did not answer the question put to me. That is undeniable." But, argues Grey, government officials do not habitually make full public disclosure of confidential documents regarding their armed forces.

According to Grey, the Russians overstated the importance of the conversations Britain held with the French. His information was that three secret letters from Russian sources were obtained by the German authorities. These letters suggested that Grey had withheld material information. Given Grey's character and his reputation for truthfulness, if these intercepted letters had been accurate, his lack of candor as seen through skeptical German eyes must have been a source of genuine alarm. For whatever reason, the Germans worried greatly about those talks.

For all of its dangers, the strategy of striking Serbia so quickly as to produce a *fait accompli*, in the view of Bethmann, its author, was the only plausible road out of a situation in which the other Great Powers might turn against Germany and Austria. And this strategy had not been employed. The Austrians had not even tried it.

The Chancellor (according to his confidant) brooded. He reflected on the mistakes Germany had made in foreign policy since the dismissal of Bismarck. Germany had alienated Russia, France, and Britain, making enemies of all of them without *weakening* any of them.

· · ·

In England, the foreign secretary professed optimism about the Austro-Serbian dispute. Sir Edward Grey was perhaps the only member of the cabinet who had reason to realize early on that the Balkan situation was serious. He had been alerted by the strongly pro-British German ambassador in London, Prince Lichnowsky. As early as July 6, Lichnowsky warned Grey that Austria would take a hard line on the Sarajevo matter, and would have Germany's blessing and backing in doing so.

Grey considered working with Germany to restrain Austria. Later, he urged Austria and Russia to hold talks to resolve their differences. Grey did not display any great concern; the Foreign Office showed less. As reported by the German ambassador in London, Grey "believed that a peaceful solution would be reached." He urged moderation, and stressed the importance of Austria proving that the accusations made against Serbia were true.

Britain, too, was in the grip of passions at home, occasioned by the question of what to do with Ireland. The British remained oblivious to danger from abroad. External threats seemed to be evaporating. "The spring and summer of 1914 were marked in Europe by an exceptional tranquility," Winston Churchill, England's civilian chief of the navy department, later remembered. The thirty-nine-year-old boy wonder of English politics was an activist—even an adventurous—First Lord of the Admiralty, yet he looked ahead to calm waters.

Churchill was not then the imposing figure whom the later twentieth century revered. He had risen far and fast in politics, but was regarded as something of an upstart by his cabinet colleagues, almost all of whom were a decade or more older. He seemed always to be in the headlines and in the limelight. His energy was boundless— enough to exhaust those around him, and even in the cabinet he would never stop talking. He was enthusiastic to the point of childishness. Yet his gifts were undeniable. Even then, it could be seen that he had talent; only decades later would it be seen that he also had genius.

In 1914 he was applying his abilities to the seemingly hopeless question of Ireland. As he later wrote: "The strange calm of the European situation contrasted with the rising fury of party conflict at home." As it became clear that Home Rule for Ireland would finally be enacted, Liberals and Conservatives became caught up in the blood feud of their respective clients, the Catholics of the south of

Ireland and the Protestants of the north: the Ulstermen. Both sides recruited and trained paramilitary formations. Ulster purchased arms in quantity from Germany, and war equipment for rival militias was reported to be illegally imported from abroad.

Overwhelmed by events, London ordered troop reinforcements and naval support. Understandably, "the military commanders, seeing themselves confronted with what might be the opening movements in a civil war, began to study plans of a much more serious character." The complication was that the officer corps in the British army was disproportionately drawn from Protestant Ulster, and it could be speculated that the army, at least in part, might back Northern Ireland and the Unionist party against Asquith's Liberal government. "These shocking events caused an explosion of unparalleled fury in Parliament and shook the State to its foundations," writes Churchill. "We cannot read the debates that continued at intervals through April, May, and June, without wondering that our Parliamentary institutions were strong enough to survive the passions by which they were convulsed. Was it astonishing that German agents reported and German statesmen believed, that England was paralysed by faction and drifting into civil war, and need not be taken into account as a factor in the European situation?"

On July 20, King George V convened an all-party conference to assemble at Buckingham Palace the following day. On the twenty-first he opened the meeting with a brief statement. He pointed to the dangers that had led him to convene the conference. "The trend," King George said, "has been surely and steadily toward an appeal to force, and today the cry of Civil War is on the lips of the most responsible and sober-minded of my people." He appealed to the party leaders to arrive at some peaceful compromise.

The conference did indeed show the differences to be narrow, but they remained intractable nonetheless. The conference broke down, and the conferees disbanded Friday morning, July 24. According to the Prime Minister, King George "came in, rather *émotionné*, and said in two sentences . . . farewell, I am sorry, and I thank you."

That afternoon, cabinet members assembled and went back to work on a proposed definition of the border between Home Rule Ireland and British Northern Ireland. When they had finished their deliberations, Sir Edward Grey turned their attention to the Serbian crisis.

CHAPTER 30: PRESENTING
AN ULTIMATUM

There had been an ominous semi-break in communication between Austria and Serbia since the Outrage; for all practical purposes they were not talking to one another, or at least not very much. The Austrian investigation of the murders was being conducted in secret, and while all but one of Princip's band were swiftly taken into custody, the proceedings against them moved forward in weeks, or indeed months, rather than days.

Meanwhile (since the common assumption was that Serbia was in some part to blame) Serbia awaited with dread whatever punishment was being prepared or proposed. From sources in London the Serbian government heard on July 17 that "a kind of indictment is being prepared" for "alleged complicity in the conspiracy which led to the assassination of the Archduke." From Vienna came the rumor on July 20 that Austria was preparing to go to war.

The Serbian population was the reverse of helpful to its government in this respect. They showed no remorse, while the opposition press gave every sign of being pleased by the killings.

To outsiders, the Serbian government seemed unwise in not making at least a show of energetically pursuing those who had aided the killers. True, the two main criminals were Austrian subjects; true, they were being tried in an Austrian judicial proceeding which had not yet concluded. However, the real reason for Serbian inaction may have been that the government had much to conceal. If it became known, for example, that Pasic had learned of the death plot in time to have averted it—if indeed that was the case—the Prime Minister would have been condemned by the Black Hand for warning Vienna, however feebly, and by Austria for not having warned effectively enough. Indeed, if Pasic had let the truth come out in any investigation commissioned or sanctioned by him, the Black Hand might well have killed him.

Moreover, Serbian elections were scheduled for August 14. Pasic had to campaign as a fiery nationalist. The country was in no position to stand up to the Hapsburg Empire, but if Pasic let the electorate know that he was willing to make concessions or compromises in order to avert a conflict, he was likely to lose votes. He somehow had to perform the impossible feat of moving in two opposite directions at once.

Baron Giesl von Gieslingen, Austro-Hungarian minister to Serbia, telephoned the Serbian foreign ministry on Thursday morning, July 23, out of courtesy. He wished to alert the Serbian government that between four and five he would be delivering an important message to the Prime Minister.

Giesl then received a cable from his own government concerning the mistake that Jagow had caught: the French leaders would not yet have left St. Petersburg. He was ordered to postpone his delivery time to 6:00 p.m.

When Giesl finally arrived, it was to find that the Serbian Prime Minister was not in Belgrade; he was out of town, campaigning for votes in the election—or at least so he said. Pacu, Serbian minister of finance, was delegated to act in the Prime Minister's absence. But Pacu did not speak French, the language of diplomacy. It therefore would not be possible for Giesl to communicate with him.

The secretary general of the foreign office, Slavko Grvic, stepped in to translate. But Pacu, faced with the document being served upon him, refused to accept it. Giesl placed it on the table and told Pacu to do what he wanted with it, and then left.

When Giesl departed, Pacu and his colleagues tried to get in touch with Pasic. It took about two hours. Over the telephone his associates then summarized for the Prime Minister the harsh terms of the document that Giesl had served upon them. (See Appendix 1, pp. 307–12, for the Austrian note in full.) Pasic decided to return by train promptly, and called a meeting of the cabinet in Belgrade the next morning at 5:00 a.m. Nicolai Hartwig, the Russian envoy upon whose advice the Serbians generally relied, had died two weeks before and had not yet been replaced; the Serbs were on their own.

The cabinet ministers met all day, through the night, and then all through the following day. Urgency was imposed upon them, for the Dual Monarchy's note demanded a reply within forty-eight hours. Pasic turned to other governments for counsel and help, but there the time was even shorter: Hapsburg couriers had delivered copies of the note to the powers only the morning of July 24.

And without even waiting for a reply, on July 23 the Hapsburg army had opened its war book: its outline of administrative measures and its designation of responsibilities that would come into effect on commencement of hostilities.

The news arrived in London in time for the cabinet meeting that had been devoted to trying to pick up the pieces of the failed Buckingham Palace conference on Ireland. The differences between the two sides, according to Winston Churchill, had been reduced to a question of the boundaries of two Irish counties, Fermanagh and Tyrone. But on this question there was a hopeless deadlock, and a civil war threatened.

In the oft-quoted lines of Churchill:

> The discussion had reached its inconclusive end, and the Cabinet was about to separate, when the quiet grave tones of Sir Edward Grey's voice were heard reading a document which had just been brought to him from the Foreign Office. It was the Austrian note to Serbia. He had been reading or speaking for several minutes before I could disengage my mind from the tedious and bewildering debate which had just closed. . . . This note was clearly an ultimatum; but it was an ultimatum

such as had never been penned in modern times. As the reading proceeded it seemed absolutely impossible that any State in the world could accept it, or that any acceptance, however abject, would satisfy the aggressor. The parishes of Fermanagh and Tyrone faded back into the mists and squalls of Ireland, and a strange light began . . . to fall upon the map of Europe.

It was the first time that month that the cabinet had heard mention of foreign policy. Churchill was one of only two in the cabinet other than the Prime Minister alerted by Grey in advance of the meeting.

During the meeting, as was his custom, Prime Minister Asquith wrote a letter to his confidante, Venetia Stanley. He told her that the European situation "is just about as bad as it can possibly be. Austria has sent a bullying and humiliating ultimatum to Serbia, who cannot possibly comply with it, and demanded an answer within forty-eight hours—failing which she will march. This means, almost inevitably, that Russia will come on the scene in defence of Serbia and in defiance of Austria; and if so, it is difficult both for Germany and France to refrain from lending a hand to one side or the other. So that we are in measurable, or imaginable, distance of a real Armageddon."

But he closed on a reassuring note: "Happily, there seems to be no reason why we should be anything more than spectators."

At the conclusion of the meeting, Churchill, in turn, wrote to his wife that "Europe is trembling on the verge of a general war. The Austrian ultimatum to Serbia being the most insolent document of its kind ever devised." But he too foresaw no role for Britain to play in the coming conflict, and wrote mainly to say that he would join his family at the beach over the weekend.

Meanwhile Grey focused first on the forty-eight-hour deadline. "I had never before seen one State address to another independent State a document of so formidable a character," he told the Austrian government; and whatever the merits of the dispute, the first thing to be done was to postpone or eliminate the deadline.

At Grey's request, the German ambassador, Lichnowsky, came by to see him. Lichnowsky reported that Grey was "greatly affected by the Austrian note, which, according to his view, exceeded anything he had ever seen of this sort before." He believed that "Any nation that accepted conditions like that would really cease to count as an independent nation." ("That would be very desirable. It is not a nation in the European sense, but a band of robbers!" commented Kaiser Wilhelm, reading Lichnowsky's report.)

The private comments of the three statesmen, if read as though they were a conversation, reveal the widening gap in their opinions:

LICHNOWSKY: "One could not measure the Balkan peoples by the same standard as the civilized nations of Europe. . . ."

KAISER: "Right, for they aren't!"

LICHNOWSKY: "Therefore one had to use another kind of language with them."

GREY: "Even if able to share this opinion [it would not] be accepted in Russia."

KAISER: "Then the Russians are not any better themselves."

Grey asked German support for a prolongation of the deadline, and suggested that England, France, Germany, and Italy should mediate the conflict. "Superfluous," commented the Kaiser. "Grey has nothing else to propose." But, the German ruler noted in the margin of Lichnowsky's report, he himself would mediate the conflict if, but only if, Austria asked him to do so.

From St. Petersburg, Foreign Minister Sazonov sent a circular cable to the concerned countries asking them to act together in obtaining a postponement of the deadline. Sazonov also asked Austria for the results of the official inquiry into the Sarajevo murders, in line with Vienna's early promise to make the report available to the other powers.

In Vienna, on July 24, Berchtold met with the Russian chargé d'affaires, Count Kudashev, and delivered a soothing message: "nothing was further from our thoughts than the wish to humiliate Serbia"; and the Dual Monarchy "did not aim at a territorial gain but merely at the preservation of the status quo."

Literally, Berchtold was telling the truth: Vienna did not intend to annex Serbia; it ruled too many Slavs already. But he was deliberately misleading: Austria-Hungary, according to Berchtold's chief aide at the foreign office, intended to partition Serbia but to take no part of Serbia for itself.

Kudashev asked what would happen if Serbia's reply was not acceptable to Berchtold's government. Berchtold's answer: Austria's minister in Belgrade would close his legation and depart with staff. "Then it is war," exclaimed Kudashev.

The following morning Kudashev returned to ask for an extension of the deadline Austria had set. The Austrian government refused. Kudashev then cabled Berchtold, who was en route to a meeting with his emperor, repeating his request for an extension. Berchtold refused.

As Vienna and Berlin had calculated, Paris was unable to react meaningfully to the Austrian note. President Poincaré, Prime Minister and Foreign Minister René Viviani, and Bruno Jacquin de Margerie, senior official at the foreign office, were still at sea. Jean-Baptiste Bienvenue-Martin, minister of justice, and caretaker head of government, seemed unable, or unwilling, to take a strong line, or indeed any line at all, despite the assistance of Philippe Berthelot, number two official at the foreign office.

Because the French voice was not heard, German and Austrian envoys apparently felt encouraged to believe that France might stand aside in the days to follow. Instead, what was happening was that Bienvenue-Martin was forwarding at least some dispatches to the traveling President to deal with, and Poincaré decided upon an immediate return to Paris.

When news of the Austrian ultimatum reached him in St. Petersburg, Sazonov burst out: "C'est la guerre européenne" (It's the European war). Meeting with the Austrian ambassador, he put it in blunt terms. "I know what it is. You mean to make war on Serbia. . . . You are setting fire to Europe. . . . Why was Serbia given no chance to speak and why the form of an ultimatum? . . . The fact is you mean war and you have burnt your bridges. . . . One sees how peace-loving you are."

The Russian Council of Ministers met and decided to try to persuade Austria to extend the July 25 deadline. It decided also to advise Serbia to offer the least possible resistance to any Austrian agreement. Finally, it decided to ask the Czar to agree, at least in principle, to partial mobilization of the armed forces. Without going into details (although historians have been doing so ever since), "partial mobilization" consisted of a number of measures, some feasible and others not, none of which would have significantly helped to defend

Russia and most of which put Russia in a less advantageous position than before. It was an essentially political concept, muddled and unclear, intended to convey the message that Russia was resolved to act if necessary, but did not wish to alarm or provoke Germany or Austria as a full mobilization—a real mobilization—would have done.

Russia, as so often had been the case, was a mystery to the European world in 1914. Its immense size and seemingly Oriental foreignness were frightening. It was the largest of countries, and the size of its population—170 million—was intimidating. Yet its ministers saw Russia in July 1914 as vulnerable.

The pace of its industrialization and its growing railroad network and its modern rearmament program, in large part financed by France, started with Russia so far behind as to make progress seem far greater than it was. In Western Europe, and in Germany in particular, the future Russian threat loomed large. In the spring of 1914, the British ambassador to Russia advised London that "Russia is rapidly becoming so powerful that we must retain her friendship at almost any cost."

But as the historian D. W. Spring reminds us, "this was not how the Russian government and public saw their position in the world in 1913–14." They saw their country as surrounded by "ten states with half the world's population," of which "three or four were directly hostile." Its government was largely ineffective. For the most part, the country remained backward: a peasant economy a century or so behind the times. Such industrialization as had taken place did so to the accompaniment of social strife; in St. Petersburg in July 1914, "180,000 industrial workers out of a total of 242,000 were on strike."

Although the masses played no role in foreign policy decision-making, there was a sort of public opinion, however weak, that found expression in the Council of Ministers meeting of July 24.

It was one of those rare moments of concord. The press, government ministers, and the public all seemed to be of one mind. Russia wanted Serbia to make whatever concessions were necessary. Russians wanted peace and knew that they were not prepared for war. On the other hand, there was a consensus that in the past Russia had made concessions to the German-speaking powers in the interests of peace, but had found that such concessions only encouraged Berlin and Vienna to ask for more. The summer of 1914 seemed to Russia to be a good time to experiment with the opposite approach. This time, in a nonprovocative way, the Russian ministers intended to stand firm.

One unstable element, however, was introduced into decision-making by the indecisiveness of Czar Nicholas II. The Russian monarch was a weak character inadequately prepared to assume the crown, of whose costly errors—notably the disastrous war against Japan—he was all too well aware. He had inherited autocratic powers but had been compelled to proclaim his position to be that of a semi-constitutional emperor.

The emotional focus of Nicholas's life was his home: the wife and daughters he adored, and the son Alexei, not quite ten years old in July 1914, whose hemophilia hung like a sword over the monarchy.

Nicholas, whatever his feelings for Serbs as fellow Slavs, was bound to feel strongly about regicides. His grandfather Alexander II, who had freed the serfs, was subject to more than a half dozen assassination attempts before the fatal one.

Moreover, Nicholas had begun his reign somewhat under the sway of Kaiser Wilhelm. Nicholas was crowned in 1895 at the age of twenty-six. Wilhelm, nine years older, had occupied the German throne six years longer. "Willy" influenced "Nicky" for a decade, giving him dangerously bad advice, turning his mind to conquests in the Far East that led to the disastrous war with Japan (1904–05) that brought about Russia's near-collapse as a Great Power. It culminated in the revolution of 1905.

At the end of 1905 and of Wilhelm's influence, the Czar fell under the spell of another dangerous figure, the peasant religious healer Gregory Rasputin, who offered hope of curing the hemophiliac heir apparent. The trusting and vulnerable imperial couple, Nicholas and his wife, Alexandra, who cared more for the life of their son than for anything else, seemed to be placing the Czarevich's fate in the hands of Rasputin, he of the deep voice, hypnotic eyes, and soothing touch. Physically powerful, Rasputin was driven by almost insatiable lusts; scandalmongers were kept busy adding women's names to the list of his conquests, which was said to include the Empress Alexandra and one of her daughters, which the monk's wife, left at home in Siberia with their four children, took pride in: "He has enough for all," she boasted.

The hold exercised by this fraudulent and wicked magician over the royal family brought the monarchy itself into disrepute as the July crisis of 1914 approached. It was predictable that at least some section of the public would blame Rasputin's influence for the tragic turn in Russia's destiny in and after 1914.

In fact, Rasputin consistently advocated peace. In the Balkan war crisis of 1908 he had said: "The Balkans are not worth fighting for." In 1914, recovering in his peasant village from an assassination attempt, he angered the Czar by cabling him, after hostilities already had begun: "Let Papa not plan war, for with the war will come the end of Russia and yourselves and you will lose to the last man."

In London on July 24 the Russian ambassador told the German ambassador "in strict confidence" that it was "scarcely possible" for Russia "to advise the Serbian Government to accept" the ultimatum "unless she was to sink to the level of a vassal of Austria." He said: "Public opinion in Russia would not tolerate that." Vienna's intentions now were clear. "Only a government that wanted war could possibly write such a note."

Rumors reached Berlin that the ultimatum was being attributed to Germany. From its foreign office streamed denials. To German envoys in Paris, London, and St. Petersburg it cabled instructions to deny the charge. "We exercised no influence of any kind with regard to the contents of the note." Nonetheless Berlin was "unable to counsel Vienna to retract" because retraction would cause Austria-Hungary to lose prestige.

From its ambassador in Vienna, Germany learned that Berchtold had called in a Russian envoy for a soothing talk, at which the Austrian foreign minister had denied having any desire to upset the balance of power or to disturb Russia. He appealed for a united front of Europe's monarchs against the common danger arising from a "Serbian policy conducted with revolver and with bomb."

Reading an account of this conversation, Kaiser Wilhelm noted his disapproval. Of Berchtold's profession of good intentions toward Russia, he commented "absolutely superfluous! Will give the impression of weakness and the impression of an apology." Calling Berchtold an "Ass!" the Kaiser noted: "Austria must become preponderant in the Balkans as compared with the little ones, and at Russia's expense; otherwise there will be no peace."

. . .

France's foreign policy leaders knew little of what was happening. By Austria's design, they were aboard ship when the crisis erupted. The President, the Prime Minister who also served as foreign minister, and their chief foreign policy aide were aware that the messages were not getting through. They were not aware that they were being jammed by the Germans.

The French leaders had come from conversations with the Czar and the Russian government. Little is known of what was said. But Poincaré's policy from the outset had been to restrain Russia from doing anything that could provoke Germany. The President was keenly aware that France was in no military position to fight a war. There is no reason to believe that he said anything different during his stay in Russia.

However, once the French leaders departed, their country's remaining spokesman in St. Petersburg played the part of a sort of rogue ambassador. Maurice Paléologue, who had presented his credentials only five months earlier, was a personality in his own right, whose tendency was to pursue his own foreign policy. He left Russia's government with the impression that France would back it unconditionally. A recent study of French prewar diplomacy by M. B. Hayne tells us that, unlike others, Paléologue believed that the French and Russian armies were at their peak. Assuming that Germany intended to force a European war, he advocated fighting it as soon as possible. In that respect, he was a sort of Moltke. It is not evident how much he influenced the decisions the Russian leaders made, for they distrusted him.

An inquiry from Vienna to Berlin dated July 22 did not arrive until the twenty-fourth. The Hapsburg Empire was about to break all relations with Serbia. No Austrian officials would be left behind. How, then, would the Dual Monarchy declare war on Serbia? Who would actually deliver the declaration? Would Germany do it on Austria's behalf?

From the foreign office, Jagow replied that it would not be a good idea: "Our standpoint has to be that the quarrel with Serbia is an Austro-Hungarian internal affair." Yet Berlin and Vienna were discussing modalities of declaring war even before the Austrian ultimatum was delivered, let alone answered, let alone answered unsatisfactorily.

CHAPTER 31: SERBIA MORE OR LESS ACCEPTS

A "pretty strong note," the Kaiser, aboard ship, remarked to the chief of his Naval Cabinet, Admiral von Müller. The emperor had learned about the Austrian ultimatum. But "it means war," responded the admiral. No, said Wilhelm, Serbia would never risk it.

The Regent of Serbia, Prince Alexander, visited the Russian legation in Belgrade the night of July 23–24 "to express his despair over the Austrian ultimatum, compliance with which he regards as an absolute impossibility for a state which had the slightest regard for its dignity." His hopes lay with the Czar, he said, "whose powerful word could alone save Serbia." Pasic, the Prime Minister, also stopped in at the Russian legation, later, en route to the 5 a.m. meeting of available cabinet ministers.

But Russia offered nothing more than moral support. From St. Petersburg, Sazonov, speaking only for himself, said that his country would offer help, but did not specify what form that help would take. In the end the Czar's government suggested that Serbia—if resistance were hopeless—should retreat rather than resist, and rely on the sense of justice of Europe to rectify matters. Neither Russia nor its ally France was ready to fight, especially for Serbia.

At first the Serbian government was inclined to be defiant. As the ministers thrashed things out they fell into a more realistic mood.

It was common ground among the Serbian leaders that their country would be crushed in a war against the Dual Monarchy. Only Russia, or a combination of the neutral powers, could save them. Such support would be difficult to obtain in any event, and all the more so because there was so little time: the Serbian response was due at 6 p.m., July 25. Pasic and his colleagues were at work continuously, veering between total acceptance of the ultimatum and the temptation to add conditions or qualifications that would allow them later to slip out from under Vienna's rigid requirements.

As language was added, changed, and crossed out, the text became less and less legible. Yet it had to be readable enough so that the translator could do his job. Revised and retyped many times, it still remained messy as the deadline approached. The typist was inexperienced; the typewriter broke down. With less than two hours to go, an attempt was made to start again in longhand.

The final document looked more like a first draft, with words crossed out, inkblots, and the like. As nobody else volunteered to carry it, Pasic did so himself, hurrying to the Austrian legation to hand Serbia's reply to Giesl before the 6 p.m. deadline. He may have been slightly late. Giesl read it quickly, standing up. He already had destroyed his papers and packed his bags. An automobile was poised to drive him to the railroad station. He went through the brief forms of breaking off diplomatic relations, and then left to catch his train.

The response to the ultimatum, it was believed outside of Austria-Hungary, accepted all conditions but one. In fact, it contained a number of reservations. (See Appendix 2, pp. 313–16.) It hardly mattered, for the Dual Monarchy was just going through the formalities.

The shipowner Albert Ballin later remembered the "disappointment" in the German foreign office when the news arrived that Serbia had accepted—followed by "tremendous joy" when a correction was received: Serbia had *not* fully accepted. Should the Kaiser be recalled? No, said Ballin's foreign office source: "on the contrary everything must be done to ensure that he does not interfere in things with his pacifist ideas."

Berchtold took the position that his note to Serbia was not an ultimatum because a declaration of war did not automatically follow when the time limit expired. As late as July 25, Berchtold was telling the Russians that the Austrian break in relations with Serbia would not necessarily lead to a war: "our demands could bring about a peaceful solution."

But then a cable arrived from his ambassador in Berlin, reminding him that Germany expected Austria to commence hostilities. "Here every delay in the beginning of war operations is regarded as signifying the danger that the foreign powers might interfere. We are urgently advised to proceed without delay."

Might convening a conference of the neutral powers prevent the outbreak of war? Sir Edward Grey sounded out opinion on the question. The conference that Grey had convoked in London in 1913 had brought peace, however temporarily, to the Balkans; perhaps it might do so again. But was it the right time to put forward such a proposal? For the moment, the quarrel concerned only Austria and Serbia; it was not yet between Austria and Russia.

To Grey's surprise, the Russian ambassador guessed that his government would not agree to a conference. If Germany, Italy, France, and Britain were to mediate between Austria and Russia, it would look, he said, as though France and Britain had split from their Russian ally. When the question was put to St. Petersburg, however, Sazonov made no such difficulty.

Grey sent notes to his ambassador in St. Petersburg on July 25 outlining his position. He wrote: "I do not consider that public opinion here would or ought to sanction our going to a war over a Serbian quarrel. If, however, war does take place, the development of other issues may draw us into it, and I am therefore anxious to prevent it." In view of Austria's actions, he wrote, Austria and Russia almost inevitably would mobilize against one another; and that is when a four-power mediation might be opportune.

It was a Saturday. Grey felt the threat of war was not immediate enough to keep him from the countryside. He placed matters in the hands of his assistant and left town.

. . .

A cable from Germany's envoy in Belgrade described the confusion and dismay of the Serbian government in dealing with the Austrian ultimatum. Kaiser Wilhelm was delighted. "Bravo! One would not have believed it of the Viennese! . . . How hollow the whole Serbian power is proving itself to be; thus it is seen to be with all the Slav nations! Just tread hard in the heels of that rabble!"

July 25. St. Petersburg.   Evening. The Russian General Staff inaugurated the "Period Preparatory to War," the first step on the road that, if further steps were taken, could lead to mobilization.

Paris.   The acting government of France took its first military preparedness steps. Secretly, it recalled its generals to duty on July 25; it canceled leaves of officers and troops July 26; and it ordered the bulk of its army of occupation in Morocco to return to France on July 27.

Berlin.   The foreign minister, Jagow, told German journalist Theodor Wolff that "neither London, nor Paris nor St. Petersburg wants war."

PART SEVEN

COUNTDOWN

CHAPTER 32: **SHOWDOWN IN BERLIN**

Germany's leading military figures had been ostentatiously on leave in July. So had the Kaiser, the Chancellor, and the foreign secretary. In fact, they returned to Berlin from time to time, often secretly. And their aides kept the military officers well informed.

After the Austrians had set a fixed date for their ultimatum, Berlin quietly signaled its leaders to return. They did so from July 23 onward, returning singly but then seeking each other out.

In a sort of movable secret conference, about which we know from the reports of the Saxon and Bavarian military attachés, Germany's military leaders on the one hand, and the civilian leaders, the Chancellor and his foreign office officials on the other, debated what to do next. Their best information was that Austria now claimed it would be at least two more weeks—perhaps August 12—before it could attack Serbia. The Germans, military and civilian alike, were disgusted by Austria's indolence.

The Chancellor and his civilian colleagues conducted a holding

operation. They asked for more time for their plans—and Vienna's—
to work. They held out for a reprieve of at least a few days before
changing plans.

The generals in large part were led by Moltke and by Erich von
Falkenhayn, the war minister, who played a main role in arguing that
Germany take military action against Russia and its allies.

Moltke played a curious role, often changing his mind, at times
holding back, yet arguing forcefully that this was the time to go to
war because circumstances were more favorable than they ever would
be again. In Berlin, the structure of the eventful and decisive week, in
broad terms, seems to have been that the country's leaders, returning
from weeks in the countryside, spent from Sunday afternoon to
Monday night (July 26–27) bringing themselves up to date and
exchanging views, from Tuesday through Thursday (July 28–30)
thrashing matters out among themselves, and from Friday through
Monday (July 31–August 3) swinging into action. These were showdown days in which Germany's leaders fought among themselves,
changed their minds, and risked strokes or heart attacks in the violence of their fears and rages.

Germany's overlapping army leaders—Chief of Staff von Moltke,
War Minister von Falkenhayn, and Military Cabinet Chief von
Lyncker—were among the several key officials debating the issues of
war and peace after the return from vacation. For Moltke the arguments were particularly frustrating, in part because the civilian leaders shared neither his point of view nor his objectives, and in part
because he knew things they did not—things he could not tell them.
In 1997, Holger Herwig wrote that "the almost complete destruction
of Moltke's papers 'precludes formal connection between Moltke's
mind-set and the push for war in 1914.' " That would seem to be no
longer true. The recent publication of Annika Mombauer's biography, based, as noted earlier, in part on previously unused documents,
makes it possible to interpret Moltke's thoughts, words, and actions.

A Saxon officer who spoke with Moltke's deputy on July 3 reported
that he received the impression that the Great General Staff "would
be pleased if war were to come about now." In Mombauer's words,
the July crisis "seemed to present an opportunity rather than a
threat." That might explain why for a time in late July, Moltke held
back, to the surprise of belligerent colleagues. He did not fear Rus-

sian mobilization; he devoutly desired it. If it meant delaying his own plans for a few days, it would be well worth it; it could mean the difference between winning and losing. Moreover, Moltke received information that Russia's mobilization preparations were on a smaller scale than had been thought.

Yet Moltke was almost uniquely aware that time was running out for his country. Germany was committed to follow Moltke's own grand strategy, of which few people were aware. The Kaiser and (until July 31) the Chancellor, Bethmann, were among those in the dark, as was Falkenhayn. None of them knew what Moltke really had planned for his opening moves in the war.

With remarkable consistency, and for a long time, Moltke had believed that Germany ought to launch a preventive war against Russia and its ally France immediately. But he had also continued to think that such a preventive war could be waged successfully only if the German people could be persuaded that Russia had started it: that Russia was attacking Germany.

So at times he argued that Germany should hold back and wait for Russia to make the first move—which is to say, to mobilize. But as the week went on, he swung around to the opposite view: strike immediately.

Moltke was a pessimist. He feared that Germans, especially Prussian Germans, would eventually be overwhelmed by the sheer number of Slavs unless action was taken promptly. He often had urged starting a war against Russia, before the Czar modernized and rearmed his empire. Yet Moltke also foresaw that in the modern age a war among Great Powers would destroy Europe.

Until April 1913, Germany had an alternative war plan to wage war against Russia only. No longer was that true. Moltke had his general staff prepare a current war plan in 1913–14 to deal with one eventuality only: a two-front war against France and Russia. He had good reason to keep details of the plan a closely held secret.

It will be remembered that in the first phase of the Moltke plan, which followed some (but not all) of the main lines of Schlieffen's 1906 memorandum, Germany was to employ a large force in invading France through Belgium while a smaller but still significant force blocked the path along which the Russians could be expected to attack. Now, in 1914, Russians were able to move much more quickly and in greater force than had been the case when Schlieffen had composed his memorandum and when Moltke had taken office. That made it all the more imperative that the entire Austrian army should be deployed along the Russian front to help shield Germany when war began.

Clearly that was a reason Moltke always had been a leading advocate of the Austrian alliance, and why he developed a warm personal relationship with his opposite number in Austria-Hungary, Conrad. It was also why he assured the Austrians of Germany's support if Russia attacked. But he did not reveal what would be required of Austria-Hungary.

Moltke kept his secrets, and Conrad kept his. As Conrad saw it—or at least so he claimed later—Austria would crush Serbia while Germany deterred Russia from interfering. His enemy—Austria's enemy—was Serbia; he had no desire to fight Russia. What Moltke did not tell Conrad was that if war came, Austria would have to subordinate its conflict with Serbia in order to devote itself entirely to the combat on the Russian front.

Moltke had another secret. It was one he could not share even with the Kaiser, the war minister, or the chief of the Kaiser's Army Cabinet. It had been devised for him, in large part, by his former assistant, Erich Ludendorff. It was the plan to seize the fortress of Liège (in Belgium) by surprise the moment that war was declared. Unless that were done, the invasion of France and Belgium probably would fail—and with it, the war. Had France or Belgium somehow forestalled Germany's move, it therefore would have been a catastrophe.

As the military historian John Keegan tells us, the fortresses of Liège and Namur, interdicting passage of the Meuse River, were "the most modern in Europe." They were "constructed to resist attack by the heaviest gun then existing. . . . Each consisted of a circle, twenty-five miles in circumference, of independent forts, arranged . . . to lend each other the protection of their own guns." He tells us that at Liège there were four hundred guns, arrayed in twelve forts, "all protected by reinforced concrete and armour plate" and garrisoned by forty thousand troops.

The sooner Germany started the war, the better for the Liège operation. Every day it was postponed was a day in which France or Belgium might divine or anticipate Germany's move. On the other hand, Moltke had always argued that Germany had to postpone declaring war against Russia until Russia could be made to appear the aggressor.

Which was it to be: sooner or later? In the last week of July 1914 Moltke changed his mind from hour to hour and day to day, visibly agonizing.

CHAPTER 33: JULY 26

The Foreign Office building, situated at the corner of Downing Street and rebuilt in the 1860s as an Italianate palace to suit the Regency tastes of Lord Palmerston, did not house the sort of demanding institution that required long hours of its employees. They could sleep late; we are told by Zara Steiner, a historian of the Foreign Office, that on weekdays "official hours were from twelve to six."

On weekends one left for the country. On the weekend in question the Prime Minister and the foreign secretary—and practically everybody they knew—were in the countryside as usual. Asquith was playing golf, and Grey was fishing for trout. Winston Churchill was with his wife and children on the beach, building sand castles. So it was remarkable that the head of the Foreign Office, Sir Arthur Nicolson, in London, should have gone to his office to work on July 26, a Sunday.

The telegraphed dispatches that awaited him contained grim news. Serbia had ordered mobilization the day before, even before replying to the Austrian ultimatum; and from Vienna came reports that Austria had broken relations with Serbia. "War is thought imminent. Wildest enthusiasm prevails in Vienna," cabled the British ambassador from the Hapsburg capital.

From St. Petersburg: "Russia cannot allow Austria to crush Serbia and become predominant Power in the Balkans." According to the cable, Serbia had ordered mobilization and Russia had ordered preliminary preparations for mobilization. Historians in the years to come were going to become experts on mobilizations, endlessly disputing the nuances of difference among various forms of readiness for war: of preparatory stages, of mobilizations less than full, and of other postures short of marching on or firing upon a neighboring country.

Nicolson swung into action. He had two expedients in mind, but they were mutually exclusive: if he pushed one, he blocked the other. So he had to choose. The one he did not adopt was to campaign for direct talks between Austria and Russia, the two Great Powers that were directly concerned. Instead, he proposed convening a conference in London of the ambassadors of the uninvolved Great Powers—Germany, Italy, and France, meeting with Britain—at which the quarrel between Austria-Hungary and Serbia could be resolved peacefully. This was the process that had brought a halt to the Balkan wars of the year before. From his country house, Grey sent his go-ahead to Nicolson, who cabled the suggestion to the relevant foreign capitals.

Asquith told Venetia Stanley that he was concerned that "Russia is trying to drag us in." He wrote to her: "The news this morning is that Serbia had capitulated on the main points, but it is very doubtful if any reservations will be accepted by Austria, who is resolved upon a complete and final humiliation. The curious thing is that on many, if not most of the points, Austria has a good and Serbia a very bad case. But the Austrians are quite the stupidest people in Europe (as the Italians are the most perfidious) and there is a brutality about their mode of procedure which will make most people think that it is a case of a big Power wantonly bullying a little one. Anyhow, it is the most dangerous situation of the last 40 years."

That was not necessarily the view of Asquith's cabinet. That night, Chancellor of the Exchequer David Lloyd George was reported to have told a friend otherwise: "He said that Austria had made demands which no self-respecting nation could comply with . . . he said the situation was serious, but that he thought there would be peace—in fact, he thought so very strongly."

In *Britain and the Origins of the First World War* (1977), Zara Steiner, looking at the weeks following the assassinations of June 28, 1914, suggests: "Only a calendar of events would catch the sense of rising tension and illustrate the interaction between all the capitals which ended in the breakdown of the European state system."

There is a strong element of truth in that insofar as Berlin and Vienna were concerned. But there was no rising of tension day by day in, for example, Paris or Rome or London. Austria and Germany successfully kept the secret of their plot from the other Great Powers for almost four weeks. From the killings the morning of June 28 until the morning of July 24, there was no significant rise in the level of tension.

Then, suddenly, on the midsummer weekend of July 24, a full-blown war crisis was sprung on Europe's leaders. It caught them unawares. Until July 23, the British cabinet had spent no time at all on foreign affairs; on July 26 the Chancellor of the Exchequer still believed that peace would be preserved.

In Russia, two weekending statesmen ran into each other that Sunday: the German ambassador found himself about to board the same train as Sazonov, the Russian foreign minister. It happened because their summer houses were near to one another. The ambassador took advantage of the situation to persuade Sazonov to reject Britain's proposals to convene a conference of the powers: "a European forum." It would be "unwieldy," argued the ambassador; the machinery would work too slowly. Instead, Russia should negotiate directly with Austria. (London, it will be remembered, had decided not to launch a campaign for direct negotiations because it would block the more promising proposal for a conference.) According to Germany's ambassador, Austria "does not think of swallowing Serbia, but only wants to give her a well-merited lesson." Sazonov, reported the ambassador, promised to follow the advice: no conference; direct negotiations.

Sazonov took a conciliatory line. He expressed willingness to see almost all of Austria's demands granted. In fact, he proceeded to postpone acting on the British conference proposal while he explored the possibility of direct negotiations with the Dual Monarchy. But Austria refused to make any concessions. Sazonov had been persuaded to waste a vital couple of days.

Britain.   Members of the naval reserve left for home immediately after their exercises. The fleets themselves were scheduled to disperse Monday morning. Sunday, First Sea Lord Prince Louis of Battenberg spoke twice by telephone with First Lord of the Admiralty Winston Churchill, who was at the seashore. Prince Louis gave him news of Austria's rejection of the Serbian reply.

Either Churchill or Prince Louis then ordered the fleets not to disperse but to remain as they were. Churchill came to London, arriving at 10 p.m. He went to see Foreign Secretary Grey to ask whether it would be helpful if he made a public announcement of the order that had been given. Grey said yes. Churchill did so. It was a shot across the bow, aimed at attracting Germany's attention.

Contrary to the views of his closest associates at the Foreign Office, who were skeptical of German intentions, Grey tended to give Berlin the benefit of the doubt. His strategy in 1914, as in 1913, was to move toward a joint Anglo-German approach on the theory that otherwise the Germans would see Britain as forming a bloc with France and Russia. In other words, precisely because of the informal alliance among Britain, France, and Russia, Britain had to move in the first instance toward Germany so as not to appear to be taking sides.

Nonetheless, Berlin rebuffed Grey's conference proposal, claiming that it would be an arbitration, a laying down of the law to Austria. Grey denied it, but Jagow refused to accept the denial. Meanwhile a statement was published in Germany's quasi-official publication, the *North German Gazette*, backing Austria fully.

Nicolson, the British foreign office head, told Grey that "Berlin is playing with us." Though Nicolson did not say so, Grey's strategy would prove futile if Germany, instead of being a neutral like England, was a hidden belligerent—in fact, Austria's secret backer. And that, indeed, was the case.

Paris.   The political director of the French foreign ministry told the German ambassador that "to any simple mind Germany's attitude was inexplicable if it did not aim at war." The ambassador denied it, but he knew nothing; Berlin had left him in the dark.

Vienna. Berchtold was urged by Jagow in Berlin to declare war immediately, before the other powers stepped in to impose a peace settlement. In turn, the Austro-Hungarian foreign minister attempted to put pressure on his army chief, Conrad, who had been a persistent advocate of going to war in the past. Conrad claimed not to be ready. In Conrad's account:

> BERCHTOLD: We should like to deliver the declaration of war on Serbia as soon as possible so as to put an end to diverse influences. When do you want the declaration of war?
> I: Only when we have progressed far enough for operations to begin immediately—on approximately August 12.
> BERCHTOLD: The diplomatic situation will not hold as long as that.

Conrad replied that Austria had to hold back. Looking just at the Russian situation—what did Russia intend?—it was necessary to wait until at least August 4 or 5. "That will not do!" Berchtold exclaimed.

Germany's ambassador to Russia reported that he had held a long conference with Sazonov. The Russian foreign minister had been "conciliatory." He had stressed that he was ready to exhaust every means necessary to prevent a war. He "urgently entreated" Germany, too, to do whatever was needed to accomplish that goal. Though the Serbs were fellow Slavs, Russian policy was not guided solely by its "sympathies." It was guided by the need to uphold the balance of power and to protect those interests that were vital.

The German ambassador reported: "I particularly pointed out . . . that if Austria was really seeking a pretext for falling on Serbia . . . we should already have heard of the commencement of some action on the part of Austria."

It was an ingenious way of taking advantage of Austria's maddening slowness to move. Vienna's civilian government *was* trying to get its army to act, and Germany, too, was pushing the Austrians to take up arms.

Berlin. Moltke, the chief of staff, was back at work with his chief deputy from the morning of July 26. Moltke then went to the Auswärtiges Amt, the German foreign office, to review matters with Jagow. During the course of the meeting, Moltke supplied Jagow with a draft ultimatum to Belgium to be used if and when war began. This envisaged a conflict with France, not with Serbia: a major war rather than a local one.

Finally, Moltke met with the Chancellor, who had been on the telephone almost continuously ever since returning the day before.

According to his wife, Moltke was "very dissatisfied" with the situation he found on his return. So were the other officers who returned that weekend and who had been holding meetings and exchanging views. In the three weeks that they deliberately had stayed away, Austria was supposed to have crushed Serbia, but instead had not even made the first move. Russia, which was to have been kept out of things, was taking preliminary military measures. Bethmann's plans were falling apart. The presentation of a *fait accompli*—his original plan—had not occurred. Localization of the conflict—his improvised second plan—was not occurring either: Britain was considering diplomatic initiatives, and Russia was thinking of taking action.

CHAPTER 34: JULY 27

Kaiser Wilhelm II insisted on returning from his cruise in northern waters. He cut short his voyage when it became evident that his government was not keeping him fully informed. Bethmann, trembling figuratively if not literally, met him on his arrival to proffer his resignation. Wilhelm would not let him off so easily. According to Bülow, Bethmann's predecessor, the Kaiser said something like: "You have cooked the broth and now you will eat it." Later, settled in his palace at Potsdam, Wilhelm brought himself up to date on the diplomatic cables, and met with the leaders of his government and of his armed forces.

According to the plan formulated largely by Bethmann on July 5–6, Wilhelm should have returned to find the Hapsburg army in occupation of Belgrade, supervising the carrying out of terms of surrender that had been agreed to by a crushed Serbia. It all would have happened too quickly for outside powers to prevent it. It would have been too late for them to do anything about it. Russia and its allies would have bowed before the inevitable.

But that was not what had happened. What Wilhelm found was that Austria-Hungary had passed up a chance to humble Serbia peacefully. Now Serbia was readying to take a stand, the British fleet was mobilized, and Russia had taken the first step toward preparation for war. Britain was pushing for a diplomatic conference that might settle the dispute on a basis less favorable than the terms Austria already had rejected on July 25.

As they returned from their staged holidays, the leaders of the German-speaking powers had to decide upon their next move. This was to prove a decisive week. What key members of the German and Austrian governments identified as their immediate danger was that Grey might succeed in his four-power mediation proposal, thus preventing the outbreak of war. In the foreign offices of Vienna and Berlin, July 27 saw the beginning of a peace scare.

For itself, Germany had rejected Grey's conference notion. The German government agreed to forward the proposal to Austria-Hungary, however, while it secretly sabotaged Grey's efforts to get Vienna to agree.

Bethmann explained to one of his officials why he felt obliged even to forward the proposal. "As we have already rejected one British proposal for a conference, it is not possible for us to refuse" to pass on the latest idea. "If we rejected every attempt at mediation the whole world would hold us responsible for the conflagration and represent us as the real warmongers. That would also make our position impossible here in Germany, where we have got to appear as though the war had been forced upon us." Bethmann, who heretofore had been speaking of Austria going to war, suddenly was speaking of *Germany* going to war.

The German government forwarded Britain's peace plans while privately advising the Austrians to pay no attention to them. The Austrian ambassador in Berlin cabled Berchtold in Vienna with a message "in strictest privacy" from Jagow, who said that Germany would soon forward to Vienna mediation proposals from Grey. "The German government assures in the most decided way that it does not identify itself with the propositions, that on the contrary it advises to disregard them, but that it must pass them on, to satisfy the English government." Berlin hoped to keep Britain from siding with France and Russia: "If Germany candidly told Sir E. Grey that it refused to communicate England's peace plan, that objective might not be achieved."

Jagow reported that Grey had asked him to forward a plea for modification of Austria's ultimatum. He explained to his colleagues that he had sent the message to his ambassador in Vienna without instructing him *to deliver it* to the Austrians. Thus, Jagow concluded, he could truthfully tell Grey that he had forwarded the British note "to Vienna."

Bethmann continued to take the line he had the week before: the other powers should stay out of the conflict between Austria and Serbia. Britain should use its influence, therefore, to persuade Russia to accept "localization." Grey pointed out that Serbia, in its reply to Austria's demands, had conceded practically everything; and Grey ascribed this to the pressure Russia had brought to bear upon Serbia. At Britain's request, Russia had restrained Serbia; now Britain was asking Germany to use its influence to restrain Austria.

But Germany rejected Grey's proposal. Jagow claimed that Russia and Austria were about to enter into negotiations, and that their outcome should be awaited before any other move was taken. As before, he was using a negotiations proposal to block the conference proposal.

London.   At a cabinet meeting that morning Grey told his colleagues that the moment had come to make up their minds whether they were prepared to stand by France and Russia if it came to a war. This was the first cabinet conclave devoted entirely to the war crisis in Europe. The governing Liberal party tended to be pacifist in outlook. No treaty bound Britain to come to France's aid, and the cabinet overwhelmingly was opposed to intervening in a European war.

Grey was still focused on preventing the outbreak of war, but believed that if he could not prevent it, Britain would have to participate in it. Prime Minister Asquith was strongly disposed to support his foreign secretary, but his chief concern was to keep his Liberal party united behind whatever policy was adopted.

After the cabinet meeting, Winston Churchill set about formulating plans for ensuring the readiness of the naval service. He was in his element. He had battlefield experience in India and the Sudan, and as a civilian his remarkable deeds in the Boer War had helped launch his political career. Though not a warmonger, he gloried in the clash of arms.

That afternoon he set about placing guards at vulnerable points, and taking precautions against surprise attacks. His Admiralty joined with the War Office in convening a small group to consider how best to ask the press for self-censorship; there was to be no disclosure of information useful to an enemy.

The press lord George Riddell, who was among those present, later recorded in his diary that a government spokesman "apprised us that the continental situation was becoming very serious. He said that it might be necessary to move troops and ships . . . secretly" and asked how to keep the news from becoming public. Riddell drafted a letter to the newspapers which was promulgated "and was the first official intimation to the Press of the impending war. The result was remarkable. No information was divulged, and the Germans were unacquainted with what was being done."

That night Churchill put his forces on informal alert. To the far-flung fleets of the Royal Navy around the world he cabled: "Secret. European political situation makes war between Triple Alliance and Triple Entente Powers by no means impossible. This is *not* the Warning Telegram, but be prepared to shadow possible hostile men-of-war. . . . Measure is purely precautionary."

Paris. The German and Austrian ambassadors in Paris were kept in the dark about their own government's plans and thinking. This added an extra measure of confusion to events as seen in that effectively leaderless capital, whose heads of government still were at sea.

Apparently, the Austrian ambassador was amazed that his own government had rejected Serbia's note of near-surrender. He told his superiors in Vienna: "The far-reaching compliance of Serbia, which was not regarded as possible here, has made a strong impression. Our attitude gives rise to the opinion that we want war at any price."

London. Lichnowsky, Germany's ambassador in London, as an Anglophile, was not always taken into Berlin's confidence. By July 27 he was strongly questioning the judgment of his superiors. How could he advocate localization of the conflict, as the foreign office told him to do, when the feud between Serbia and Austria could *not* be localized—and when Britain knew that? Austria-Hungary had picked its quarrel in such a way as to force Russia to intervene. The small war might be leading to a big one. "Our entire future relations with England depend on the success" of Grey's move for a conference. If Berlin were to sacrifice everything else to its Austrian alliance, then "it would never again be possible to restore those ties which have of late bound [Britain and Germany] . . . together."

Grey's tendency in a crisis had been to reach out for a partnership with Germany in dealing with it. Lichnowsky's point to his home government was that, if Berlin kept on course, in the future Grey would no longer do so. Senior officials at the British Foreign Office already were critical of Grey in this regard. So were some foreign leaders.

At dinner that evening, a Russian diplomat told a British statesman that "war is inevitable and by the fault of England; that if England had at once declared her solidarity with Russia and France and her intention to fight if necessary, Germany and Austria would have hesitated."

Berlin. At least since the war council of December 1912, Germany's military leaders had focused on blaming Russia for the European conflict they foresaw and regarded as inevitable. This had been, and remained, Moltke's line. It was echoed on July 27 by Admiral von Müller: Germany should, he told his diary, "remain calm to allow Russia to put herself in the wrong, but then not to shrink from war if it were inevitable." Bethmann agreed with the military on this: "In all events Russia must ruthlessly be put in the wrong," he told Wilhelm.

Vienna. The British ambassador, after conversations with other ambassadors, cabled Grey that "the Austro-Hungarian note was so drawn up as to make war inevitable; that the Austro-Hungarian government are fully resolved to have war with Serbia; that they consider their position as a Great Power to be at stake" and that "this country has gone wild with joy at the prospect of war with Serbia."

CHAPTER 35: JULY 28

Vienna. Pursuant to a decision reached July 25, Austria-Hungary ordered partial mobilization on July 28. Half of the Hapsburg armies eventually were ordered to take up positions along the Serbian frontier. This was done in conformity with the Austrian General Staff's plan for war against Serbia only. It was a gamble on localization. Conrad requested Berchtold to ask Germany to prevent Russia from intervening.

Germany's leaders continued the discussions that had begun over the weekend. By July 28, it was clear that despite differences among them, they were in the mood to take action. They were disposed to give up on waiting for Austria to do something. For themselves, they were resolved to move. According to the war minister, "It has now been decided to fight the matter through, regardless of the cost." They were not talking about fighting Serbia. They were talking about fighting Russia and France.

The most extreme position was taken at times by Moltke. As he had in the past, he argued for a preventive war. His position was that war was inevitable, that time was running against Germany, and that within two years or so the odds would shift: in 1914, Russia and France could be beaten, but in 1916 or 1917, Germany might lose. Germany, therefore, should strike now.

The July crisis, as Moltke saw it, had evolved, happily for Germany, in such a way as to place it in a "singularly favorable situation." Harvests were in, the annual training of recruits had finished, and Russia and France would not be really ready for two years. Austria had put itself in a position such that it could not help fighting at Germany's side, and that was absolutely vital. As Moltke summed it up: "we shall never hit it again so well as we do now."

On the morning of July 28, Kaiser Wilhelm, who had returned from his cruise the day before, read—for the first time—the Serbian reply to Austria's note. It persuaded him, he wrote in longhand to Jagow at the foreign office, that Austria had gotten almost everything it wanted. In his view it was "a capitulation of the most humiliating kind," and as a result, *every cause for war* falls to the ground." A few sentences later he repeated himself: "every cause for war has vanished."

There no longer was any need to start a war. In fact, according to Wilhelm, unlike Berchtold "*I* would never have ordered a mobilization on that basis.

"Nevertheless, the piece of paper, like its contents, can be considered as of little value so long as it is not translated into *deeds*. The Serbs are Orientals, therefore liars, tricksters, and masters of evasion." So it should be agreed that the Austrian army would temporarily occupy a part of Serbia including Belgrade, as a hostage, until Serbia kept its word. On that basis, wrote the Kaiser, "I am ready to mediate for peace." This resolution of matters would give the Hapsburg armies, once in possession of Belgrade, the satisfaction of appearing to have scored a success. In mediating for peace, wrote Wilhelm, he would be careful to safeguard Austria-Hungary's honor and self-esteem.

The Kaiser ordered Jagow to inform Vienna that he was prepared to mediate the Austria-Serbia conflict on the basis he described. The Austrians were to be told that there no longer was any reason to go to war. The Kaiser also notified Moltke, in writing, of the same conclusion.

As Christopher Clark, one of the Kaiser's recent biographers, writes: "Perhaps the most striking thing about this letter to Jagow of 28 July is that it was not acted upon. . . . His instructions to Jagow had no influence on Berlin's representations to Vienna. Bethmann did cable Vienna, repeating some of Wilhelm's views, but omitting the most important one: that Austria should stop, not go to war, and let the Kaiser mediate the quarrel with Serbia instead."

A Bavarian general noted in his diary that there was "unfortunately . . . peaceful news. The Kaiser absolutely wants peace. . . . He even wants to influence Austria and to stop her continuing further."

According to War Minister von Falkenhayn, the Kaiser "made confused speeches which give the clear impression that he no longer wants war and is determined to [avoid it], even if it means leaving Austria-Hungary in the lurch." But Falkenhayn reminded the Kaiser that he "no longer had control of the affair in his own hands." In other circumstances this would have seemed shockingly insubordinate. But ever since the *Daily Telegraph* affair of 1908,* the emperor's position had been precarious. In May 1914, only two months before Falkenhayn's reminder, Edward House, President Wilson's envoy, had reported from Berlin that the "military oligarchy" were supreme, were "determined on war," and were prepared to "dethrone the Kaiser the moment he showed indications of taking a course that would lead to peace." Of course Wilhelm, whose grip on reality was fragile at best, may not have been fully alive to the perils of his position. Alternatively, House may have exaggerated.

But there can be little doubt that much was going on of which the emperor was unaware. Indeed, among the things that Wilhelm did not know was that, the day before, Jagow had cabled Vienna urging—indeed, practically ordering—the Austrian government to declare war on Serbia immediately. Jagow warned that the English proposal for a conference to keep the peace could not be resisted much longer. The German foreign minister neither consulted the Kaiser before sending this warning nor informed him afterwards that it had been sent.

In Austria, too, a reluctant monarch was gotten around. Emperor Franz Joseph was hesitant about declaring war, and his ministers were obliged to obtain his assent in order to do so. Berchtold

*See p. 73.

obtained that assent by reporting—falsely—that Serbian troops had opened fire on Austrian forces. Actually—and it was only one isolated incident—it was Austrian troops who fired on Serbs.

Vienna. It was WAR. The decision had been reached the day before. Responding to the pressure from the German foreign office, Austria at long last declared war on Serbia. According to the German ambassador, it was done "chiefly to frustrate any attempt at intervention."

As with so many things, the Austrians did it awkwardly. Sending the declaration of war by an envoy under a flag of truce was not feasible because, until the declaration was received, the countries were not yet at war, so a white flag was inappropriate. Having no representative in Belgrade anymore, the Hapsburg government sent its declaration to the Serbian government by cable. There was no assurance that it would be received—or would be received by the right party. In the event, the Serbian government, once it received the curious telegram, cabled to the major European capitals to inquire whether it was a hoax. The declaration of war made reference to the alleged attack by Serbian troops on Austrian forces.

Conrad, Austria's chief of staff, had opposed issuing the declaration. He wanted to wait two weeks or so until his armies were ready to march. But, overtaken by international diplomacy, Austria-Hungary had run out of time.

That night the Austrian artillery, briefly and ineffectively, bombarded Belgrade across the narrow Danube River frontier.

Paris. France knew nothing of the war crisis; the news of which everyone spoke was that Mme Caillaux had been acquitted!

St. Petersburg. Russia initiated mobilization in four military districts that previously had been alerted in "preparation for war steps."

Unaware that it was his own foreign office that was undoing his efforts to restrain the Austrians, Wilhelm sent a message to the Czar. In it he reminded his cousin that "we both, you and I, have a common interest, as well as all Sovereigns" in punishing the Serbs for killing members of a ruling family. "In this, politics play no part at all." But, the Kaiser continued, "On the other hand, I fully understand how difficult it is for you and your government to face the drift of public opinion." Russian nationalism, incalculable, but a force nonetheless, was a fact of political life for Nicholas. (Whether or not Wilhelm knew it, pressure to mobilize also was being exerted by Russia's General Staff.) The Kaiser told the Czar of his "hearty and tender friendship" and assured him, "I am exerting my utmost influence to induce the Austrians to deal straightly."

This message—the first in the Willy/Nicky correspondence that took place after Austria declared war on Serbia—crossed with one from the Czar: "Am glad you are back . . . I appeal to you to help me. An ignoble war has been declared on a weak country. . . . [S]oon I shall be overwhelmed by pressure brought upon me . . . to take extreme measures which will lead to war. To try and avoid such a calamity as a European war, I beg you in the name of our old friendship to do what you can to stop your allies from going too far."

London. Grey swung back to the view that direct negotiations between Russia and Austria afforded the best possibility of keeping the peace.

Berlin. Bethmann turned his attention to putting Germany in a position to fight a major war. Domestic discord was the chief obstacle, so now the government entered into talks with the Socialist Democratic party (S.P.D.) aimed at securing agreement from working-class representatives to remain loyal in the event of war. This was a genuine concern. The Executive Committee of the S.P.D., denouncing "the frivolous provocation of the Austro-Hungarian government," had called out its supporters into the streets. Its newspaper predicted that war would bring revolution in its wake. Demonstrations in Berlin on July 28, which the police attempted to break up, brought violence to the capital itself and looked to be merely a foretaste of more disturbances to come.

However, Bethmann scored a success in negotiating an agreement with the S.P.D. leadership to fall in line behind the government in this moment of national danger.

Meanwhile, the Kaiser, still unaware that his decision for peace had been sabotaged by his subordinates, confusedly wondered whether he had acted too late. He remarked that "the ball is rolling" and "can no longer be stopped."

London. Churchill reported to King George V the various measures taken by the Admiralty to place the navy "upon a preparatory precautionary basis." After detailing many of the steps taken, he assured his monarch: "It is needless to emphasize that these measures in no way prejudice an intervention or take for granted that the peace of the great powers will not be preserved."

At midnight Churchill wrote to his wife: "My darling one and beautiful, everything tends towards catastrophe and collapse." Britain was not, he continued, "in any serious degree responsible for the wave of madness which has swept the mind of Christendom."

Prime Minister Asquith wrote to his confidante, Venetia Stanley, that he had just been told that the French government was ordering heavy sales of securities on the London Exchange in order to raise cash: "It looks ominous." The English house of Rothschild, with whom the order was placed, refused to execute it. Then Asquith received a cable reporting "that Austria had ordered war!" Venetia Stanley sometimes told the Prime Minister that there were days when she would like to trade places with him; this, he suggested, probably would not be such a day.

CHAPTER 36: JULY 29

Potsdam. Willy cabled Nicky that Russia really could stay out of the conflict. "I think a direct understanding between your government and Vienna possible and desirable" and—the Kaiser did not know that this was untrue—"my government is continuing its exertions to promote it." Wilhelm cautioned, however, that if Russia were to take military measures that threatened Austria, such measures would bring war rather than peace.

Nicky replied, indicating what puzzled him was that what he was hearing from the Kaiser was not what he was hearing from the Kaiser's ambassador. "Please clear up this difference," he wrote. Nicholas urged that the Austro-Serbian conflict be referred to The Hague* for adjudication. "I trust to your wisdom and friendship."

Questions arose in the minds of Austrian generals now that it was recognized in Vienna that Russia really might intervene if Serbia

*His reference would have been to the Permanent Court of Arbitration, established at The Hague by the Convention for the Pacific Settlement of International Disputes (1899).

were threatened with destruction. These questions were directed to German Foreign Minister Jagow. A couple of days before, he had given official assurances to the Russian government that Berlin had no objection to a Russian partial mobilization so long as it was not directed against Germany.

The Austrians now pointed out to their German colleagues that a partial Russian mobilization had been ordered that was directed against Austria. Were it to remain in effect would that not mean that when Austria sent its armies against Serbia, the Dual Monarchy would be left defenseless against a Russian attack from behind? Conrad still hoped that Germany would deter Russia, and rashly made his dispositions on the assumption that Germany would succeed in doing so.

In conversation with a Russian envoy, Jagow therefore reversed his position. In view of Russia's partial mobilization, "Germany was likewise obliged to mobilize; there was therefore nothing left to be done and the diplomatists must now leave the talking to the cannon." If this was intended to persuade the Russians to roll back their partial mobilization, it failed of its purpose.

Moltke delivered to his government a memo he had written on the current situation. He had expected, as had his military colleagues, that Austria would not commence hostilities for another couple of weeks. Like the Kaiser, he had not known that Jagow had been pressuring Vienna to act at once. Therefore Moltke had been taken by surprise by the Austrian declaration of war. In his memo, he analyzed the consequences of Austria's move. When Austria moved, it was bound to initiate a series of events that would bring Germany into a war against Russia. According to Moltke, "the civilized states of Europe will begin to tear one another to pieces." It now would take a miracle to prevent the outbreak of a "war which will annihilate the civilization of almost the whole of Europe for decades to come."

Yet it was a price he was prepared to pay. His question to his government essentially was, did it still believe that it could localize the conflict and thus avert the dire consequences he foresaw?

The Kaiser summoned Germany's military leaders to Potsdam to discuss his conversations with Bethmann. The Kaiser said that his Chancellor, in the words of Tirpitz, who was there, "had collapsed completely" and Wilhelm had "expressed himself without reserve regarding Bethmann's incompetence."

Bethmann, in fact, had set two chief goals for himself. One of them had been to secure acceptance of the war policy by labor and the Left—which he had done. The other was to get Britain's pledge of neutrality—which he had not done. Keeping Britain out of the war was important to Bethmann though not at all important to Germany's military leaders.

According to Tirpitz, at the Potsdam conference, "The Kaiser informed the company that the Chancellor had proposed that, in order to keep England neutral, we should sacrifice the German fleet for an agreement with England, which he, the Kaiser, had refused."

It was decided at the conference to do nothing until Vienna responded to the Kaiser's proposal to halt in Belgrade and then stop the war. Bethmann had finally sent the proposal, while sabotaging it. He had forwarded it with instructions to his ambassador to make sure the Austrians understood that Germany did not wish to "restrain" them; he wanted to underline for Vienna that the proposal was only for propaganda purposes.

But after the Kaiser had upbraided Bethmann at Potsdam and the Chancellor had collapsed emotionally, Bethmann tried desperately to reverse himself. He threw himself into an effort to get Vienna to do precisely what he had let Vienna understand only the day before that it should not do. At 10:18 p.m. he sent an open cable to Austria-Hungary asking if his halt-in-Belgrade message of the day before had been received. Twelve minutes later he impatiently cabled again.

By now the Chancellor was aware that, independently of one another, both Britain and Italy had proposed plans to keep the peace that were quite similar to the Kaiser's halt-in-Belgrade plan. It now looked as though, if only Bethmann and Jagow had loyally carried out Wilhelm's instructions the day before and brought Germany's full weight to bear upon its ally, the war crisis would have been resolved.

Instead, on the evening of the twenty-ninth, Bethmann, if he were to escape the Kaiser's wrath, had to hope that Austria-Hungary, too, would be willing to change course.

To his ambassador in Austria, Bethmann now cabled: "We are, of course, prepared to do our duty as allies, but must decline to let ourselves be dragged by Vienna, irresponsibly and without regard to our advice, into a world conflagration." He told his ambassador to persuade Berchtold that Austria should at least make a show: "In order to prevent general catastrophe, or at any rate put Russia in the wrong, we must urgently advise that Vienna should initiate and pursue conversations."

But at the same time Moltke was cabling Conrad to urge a full Austrian mobilization. Perhaps this showed Moltke's justified concern that Austria might mobilize against Serbia rather than Russia.

Yet Berchtold was right to ask, as he did when he saw the Chancellor's message: "Who rules in Berlin—Moltke or Bethmann?" One cabled war while the other cabled peace. In any event, Bethmann was too late. His cable arrived hours *after* Vienna, responding to Moltke, ordered full mobilization.

Earlier that day, in London, Grey had asked the German ambassador to come by to see him. The foreign secretary and Lichnowsky conversed as old friends, but in contemplating the outbreak of a European war, Grey "did not wish him to be misled by the friendly tone of our conversation—which I hoped would continue—into thinking that we should stand aside" and that "I did not wish to be open to any reproach from him that the friendly tone of all our conversations had misled him or his Government into supposing that we should not take action."

In diplomatic language, this threatened war. But Grey knew that, at least for the moment, his government was not behind him on this.

It was in the course of this conversation with Lichnowsky that Grey made his own halt-in-Belgrade proposal, which was so similar to Kaiser Wilhelm's. When Lichnowsky reported this to him, the Kaiser commented: "We have been trying to accomplish this for days, in vain." He did not know that Bethmann and Jagow had undercut him in Vienna on July 27 and 28, and that the proposal had been urged seriously only for hours, not days.

Lichnowsky reported that London was firmly convinced that "unless Austria is willing to enter upon a discussion of the Serbian question a world war is inevitable." In Grey's view, "If war breaks out it will be the greatest catastrophe that the world has ever seen." The Kaiser's comment on this was that it would be England's fault; all Britain had to do was give the word, he said, and France and Russia would quiet down and there would be no war." "England *alone*," he wrote, "bears the responsibility for peace and war."

"It is one of the ironies of the case," wrote Asquith to his friend Venetia Stanley, "that we being the only Power who has made so much as a constructive suggestion on the direction of peace, are blamed by both Germany and Russia for causing the outbreak of war. Germany says: 'if you say you will be neutral, France and Russia wouldn't dare to fight,' and Russia says: 'if you boldly declare that you will side with us, Germany and Austria will at once draw in their horns.' Neither of course is true."

That day the cabinet approved issuing a general alert, which was sent to British bases around the world. Various and extensive precautions were taken. In technical terms, the "War Book" was opened by the secretary to the Committee of Imperial Defence. Yet most cabinet members intended to keep Britain out of the conflict.

Winston Churchill feared that opinion in the cabinet and in the governing Liberal party was still inclined to neutrality. Secretly he sent word to his closest Conservative friend, F. E. Smith, asking him to sound out his party's leadership on the possibility of forming a coalition government supported by pro-intervention Liberals—in all likelihood a minority within their own party—and all Conservatives. Smith undertook to speak to the other party leaders when he was scheduled to see them two days later for a country weekend.

Churchill had more pressing concerns. As First Lord of the Admiralty, he worried that the navy was vulnerable to surprise attack. He wanted to move the fleets to their wartime stations in the well-protected north. But, he later recalled, he did not want to ask cabinet approval for such a move, which might be construed as provocative. Instead, he went to see the Prime Minister with his proposal, and decided to construe a sort of grunt from Asquith as approval.

The move was made in secrecy, and the crucial part of the journey to safety took place at night—in Churchill's account, "as darkness fell, eighteen miles of warships running at high speed and in absolute blackness through the narrow straits, bearing with them into the broad waters of the North the safeguard" of Britain's forces.

Paris. Jean Jaurès, pacifist idol of the French Left, was assassinated by a nationalist fanatic. For more than a week, Jaurès had been praising the efforts of the Poincaré-Viviani government to keep the peace. Unexpectedly his death unified the country behind its government.

Berlin. At a late hour—indeed, close to midnight—Bethmann summoned the British ambassador, Sir Edward Goschen, to his residence. The Chancellor asked Goschen to transmit an offer to London: if Britain agreed to remain neutral in the war that might soon commence, Germany would respect the independence and integrity of Holland, and would not seek to acquire French territories—a pledge from which the French colonies were excluded. Goschen did convey the message to the Foreign Office, where it was received the following morning and angered Grey when he read it.

CHAPTER 37: JULY 30

France's Ambassador Paléologue in St. Petersburg has been blamed for years by historians—wrongly, we now believe—for having failed during the night of July 29–30 to notify his government that Russia was mobilizing. Research by Jean Stengers has shown that the Russians—distrusting Paléologue—did not tell him. When France *did* learn of the impending move, it was too late to stop the Russians.

Thursday, July 30, was a day that many historians later were to regard as fateful, and it began badly. The night before, the German government, belatedly falling in with the Kaiser, had sent a message to Vienna telling Austria-Hungary to accept the halt-in-Belgrade formula for pulling back from war—either that or lose Germany's support. But Berchtold claimed to be unable to give a reply for the time being. It was especially frustrating because, as Wilhelm noted, Germany, Britain, and Russia all seemed to agree on the halt-in-Belgrade proposal.

Wilhelm felt discouraged. News reached him that Austria-Hungary was willing to hold talks with Russia; "all too late, I fear" was his comment. "Begin! Now!" he exclaimed. Interpreting such remarks, in his own fashion, Bethmann urged Berchtold to at least go through the motions of seeking a peaceful settlement, for otherwise—if Vienna said no—Bethmann argued, "It will hardly be possible any longer to place the guilt of the outbreak of a European war on Russia's shoulders." The Kaiser was attempting to mediate an end to the crisis only because "he could not refuse to do so without creating the incontrovertible suspicion that we wanted war." He added that if "Vienna declines everything, Vienna will be giving documentary evidence that it absolutely wants a war . . . while Russia remains free of responsibility. That would place us, in the eyes of our own people, in an untenable position."

Meanwhile the Kaiser was enraged by the response his mediation efforts were receiving in St. Petersburg because he misunderstood what was happening. At dawn he awakened to find a message from Nicholas informing him that Russia had ordered the partial mobilization decided upon on July 25: the mobilization in four districts facing Austria-Hungary. According to the Czar, "the military measures which have now come into force were decided five days ago." They were, in other words, the measures Russia's Council of Ministers had envisaged but not immediately adopted when informed that Vienna had rejected Serbia's partial acceptance of the Austrian ultimatum. Russia had stood still ever since, giving negotiations a chance. These were not *new* measures or additional measures; they were the only measures Russia had taken—and they had *just* been taken. Mobilization was only about to begin.

Wilhelm misunderstood. He believed the Czar was informing him that Russia had been mobilizing for five days, and therefore was ahead of Germany, which was still hanging back. "So that is almost a week ahead of us," protested the Kaiser. "And these are supposed to be of defense against Austria, who is not attacking him!!! I cannot commit myself to mediation any more, since the Czar, who appealed for it, has at the same time been secretly mobilizing behind my back." To Nicholas's plea, "We need your strong pressure on Austria," Wilhelm scribbled, "No, there is no thought of anything of that sort!!!"

The Czar, according to Wilhelm, "has simply been acting a part and leading us up the garden path!"—leading the Kaiser to conclude: "That means I have got to mobilize as well!"

But the Kaiser later replied in a civil tone to the Czar. Wilhelm said: "I have gone to the utmost limits of the possible in my efforts to save peace. . . . Even now, you can still save the peace of Europe by stopping your military measures."

The German ambassador in St. Petersburg warned the Czar that mobilization by Russia would bring about German mobilization. In this, the German government was overreacting. Russian mobilization did not pose the deadly danger that German mobilization would. For Germany, mobilization meant war; for Russia, as its government explained to the Germans, it did not. "Russia's armies," as an academic authority recently has pointed out, could "remain mobile behind their frontier almost indefinitely." And the German government really knew that.

St. Petersburg.   Sazonov telephoned the Czar to ask for an immediate appointment. He then traveled to Tsarskoe Selo, the Czar's palace, where he solemnly advised his monarch that war had become unavoidable and that general mobilization was required. Reluctantly, the Czar agreed and Sazonov gave the necessary orders.

The German military plenipotentiary at the St. Petersburg embassy reported: "I have the impression that they [the Russians] have mobilized here from a dread of coming events without any aggressive intentions and are now frightened at what they have brought about." To Kaiser Wilhelm, that apparently had the ring of truth. "Right, that is it" was his comment.

The Czar, reacting to the Kaiser's messages, rescinded full mobilization. He ordered his generals to swing back to partial mobilization. What next? The Russian Council of Ministers did not meet, but individual leaders offered their views to their sovereign. There were persuasive voices on all sides. Sazonov joined with the generals to urge a general mobilization, which the indecisive and unhappy Czar, changing his mind again, finally ordered. The Russian army's chief of staff famously said, "I will . . . smash my telephone" so that he could not "be found to give any contrary orders for a new postponement of general mobilization."

Bethmann understood that Russia's move was no cause for alarm. He told the Prussian State Ministers that "although the Russian mobilization had been declared, her mobilization measures cannot be compared with those of the West European states . . . Moreover Russia does not intend to wage war, but has only been forced to take these measures because of Austria."

The German and Austrian chiefs of staff were in touch with one another, and Moltke cautioned the impatient Conrad: "War must not be declared on Russia." Instead the two German-speaking empires should "wait for Russia to attack."

Meanwhile Bethmann was arguing for postponement while Moltke, who had tended toward postponement half of the time that week, reversed himself. Now Moltke suddenly was in favor of going ahead. "His changes of mood are hardly explicable or not at all," noted a disgusted Falkenhayn.

By the evening, the Kaiser had learned of Grey's warning to the German ambassador in London the evening before. Grey, speaking only for himself, gave his opinion that if France were endangered, Britain would intervene. Since it was widely known in government circles that Germany, in the event of war against Russia, planned to attack and crush France first before turning around and invading Russia, Grey was saying that England would support its fellow Entente powers, Russia and France, against the Triple Alliance powers, Germany and Austria. Once again the Kaiser exploded in rage. "Irresponsibility and weakness are to plunge the world into the most terrible war, aimed in the last resort at ruining Germany," he claimed. "For no doubt remains in my mind: England, Russia and France . . . are in league to wage a war of annihilation against us, taking the Austro-Serbian conflict as a pretext . . . the stupidity and clumsiness of our ally has been turned into a noose for our necks. . . . And we have fallen into the snare."

London. The keenly awaited debate on Ireland, scheduled to be held in the House of Commons in the afternoon, was expected to lead to a civil war in Britain. But earlier in the day the Opposition's leaders met with Asquith and reached agreement to show a united front in view of European dangers. This was a turnabout too fast for the rank and file to grasp. Violet Asquith, the Prime Minister's daughter, along with her stepmother, Margot, attended the Ladies'

Gallery of the House, and found it "packed with expectant and excited women" who gave "a gasp of astonishment" when the Prime Minister rose to speak of postponing the Irish debate. "These words produced bewilderment in the Ladies' Gallery," noted Violet. "Many of its occupants had been busily engaged in preparations for the impending civil war—attending Red Cross classes, rolling bandages and making splints and slings, etc. One Ulster matron Lady M. (whose figure was particularly well adapted for the purpose) was reputed to have smuggled rifles galore into Belfast under her petticoats." They were aghast at the news of postponement and uncomprehending.

Paris.   Back from their long voyage, and not yet caught up on all the news of what had happened during their absence, France's leaders attempted to apply the brakes to fast-moving events. With President Poincaré's approval, Prime Minister Viviani cabled to the Russian government cautionary advice: "in the precautionary measures and defensive measures to which Russia believes herself obliged to resort, she should not immediately proceed to any measure which might offer Germany a pretext for a total or partial mobilization of her forces." France itself pulled back its armed forces six miles from the Franco-German frontier.

London.   "The European situation is at least one degree worse than it was yesterday," noted the Prime Minister, "and has not been improved by a rather shameless attempt on the part of Germany to buy our neutrality during the war by promises that she will not annex French territory (except colonies) or Holland & Belgium. There is something very crude & almost childlike about German diplomacy. Meanwhile the French are beginning to press in the opposite sense, as the Russians have been doing for some time. The City, wh. is in a terrible state of depression and paralysis, is for the time being all against English intervention. I think the prospect very black today."

CHAPTER 38: JULY 31

Jules Cambon, France's veteran ambassador in Berlin, cabled his government that Germany was about to start a war without waiting for Russia to mobilize first.

News of the Russian general mobilization reached Vienna but failed of its effect; it did not deter the Hapsburg Empire from proceeding, however slowly, with its intended invasion of Serbia. The combined cabinets of the Dual Monarchy—its Common Ministerial Council—met, considered the news, and determined to go ahead as planned despite the likelihood that in doing so it would provoke Russia to intervene.

In apparent disregard of the Russian threat, Hapsburg armies continued to march south toward Serbia. Conrad had planned, if the Czar ordered mobilization, to shift troops to the Russian front; unaccountably, he did not do so. This placed the whole burden of defending Austria against Russia on Germany's shoulders, which may have been the point. Samuel Williamson suggests Conrad aimed at attacking Serbia as soon as possible to make sure that fighting started before diplomats could intervene.

At noon the news reached Berlin that Russia was mobilizing against Germany as well as against Austria. The Kaiser had just finished cabling the Czar that "the peace of Europe may still be maintained by you, if Russia will agree to stop the military measures which must threaten Germany and Austro-Hungary." He offered to continue his mediation efforts.

The Czar replied: "I thank you heartily for your mediation which begins to give one hope that all may yet end peacefully. It is technically impossible to stop our military preparations which were obligatory owing to Austria's mobilization. We are far from wishing for war. As long as the negotiations with Austria on Serbia's account are taking place my troops shall not make any *provocative* action. I give you my solemn word for this."

Meanwhile, Franz Joseph cabled the Kaiser his thanks for his mediation offer but said it came too late: Russia had already mobilized and Austrian troops already were marching on Serbia.

Paris.   That evening the German ambassador to France presented an ultimatum to René Viviani in his capacity as foreign minister. France's ally Russia must rescind its proclaimed mobilization, warned the German, or accept the responsibility of bringing on a conflict. Viviani, along with President Poincaré, had been at sea, and knew nothing of the Russian mobilizations. He called St. Petersburg for information.

St. Petersburg.   Near midnight, the German ambassador to Russia delivered an ultimatum: stop the mobilization within twelve hours, or Germany would mobilize too—and, unlike Russia's, Germany's mobilization would bring the countries "extraordinarily near to war."

London.   "There is still hope," Winston Churchill wrote to his wife, "although the clouds are blacker and blacker. Germany is realizing I think how great are the forces against her and is trying tardily to restrain her idiot ally. We are working to soothe Russia."

Asquith had lunch at Churchill's, along with Lord Kitchener, Britain's most famous general, who was spending a few weeks in England before returning to Egypt, where he served as proconsul. Kitchener told the civilians that Britain had to back up France. But that was not the general view. Asquith confided that "general opinion at present—particularly strong in the City—is to keep out at almost all costs."

Lloyd George, leader of the radical wing of the governing party, was perhaps the only member of the cabinet with a following strong enough to challenge the Prime Minister, and he told a political intimate that "I am fighting hard for peace. All the bankers and commercial people are begging us not to intervene. The governor of the Bank of England said to me with tears in his eyes 'Keep us out of it. We shall all be ruined if we are dragged in.' "

Winston Churchill was made aware by at least one well-placed Liberal member of Parliament, Arthur Ponsonby, that there was "very strong" and "very widespread" sentiment within the party against intervention. At the same time, however, he received from F. E. Smith of the Conservatives, an indication that the Opposition party would support the government if it took up arms against a German invasion of France through Belgium. In his reply, Churchill told Smith: "I cannot think war will be averted now. Germany *must* march through Belgium, and I believe that the bulk of both parties will stand firm against that."

Paris.   France's army commander, General Joseph Joffre, asked permission from the government to order general mobilization. The cabinet refused its permission.

CHAPTER 39: AUGUST 1

Paris. Joffre once again asked his government for permission to order an immediate general mobilization. Instead, the cabinet authorized him to do so the following day.

London. At the morning cabinet meeting, Winston Churchill asked if he could order full mobilization of the fleet. But the cabinet, deeply divided, refused its permission. Of those whose instincts were against war, Lloyd George was the key figure; if he were won over, he could bring others with him.

According to the Prime Minister, "the bulk of the party" were opposed to intervening militarily in any circumstances, but that "Ll. George—all for peace—is more sensible & statesmanlike for keeping the position still open." Churchill had been a follower of Lloyd George for years, and during the meeting they passed notes to one another. In one of them, the radical leader held out hope: "If patience prevails & you do not press us too hard . . . we might come together." "Please

God," replied Churchill. "It is our whole future—comrades—or opponents."

"I am most profoundly anxious that our long cooperation may not be severed," Churchill wrote at another point. ". . . I implore you to come and bring your mighty aid to the discharge of our duty." And again: "All the rest of our lives we shall be opposed. I am deeply attached to you & have followed your instinct and guidance for nearly 10 years."

Meanwhile Churchill directed a torrent of rhetoric at the rest of the cabinet. He was notorious for not letting anyone else get a word in edgewise. "It is no exaggeration to say," Asquith told a confidante, "that Winston occupied at least half of the time" of the meeting.

Berlin. The Chancellor addressed the Bundesrat, the assembly of the German states, and presented his government's case. He explained that Russia, rather than continue negotiations with Austria, had mobilized its military forces. In reply, Germany had delivered an ultimatum to the Russian government: either agree by noon to demobilize or else Germany would mobilize. Germany also had sent an ultimatum to France to remain neutral—and to give adequate assurances of remaining so—or else Germany would declare war on it, too. This ultimatum to France was scheduled to expire at 1 p.m. The Bundesrat gave Bethmann its unanimous support.

Noon came and went, and there was no Russian reply. Nearly an hour later Germany cabled its declaration of war to its ambassador to Russia, for delivery in St. Petersburg, worded in the alternative, so that he could claim either that the Czar's government had rejected the ultimatum or had failed to reply to it.

Tsarskoe Selo. It was midday in Russia, and Czar Nicholas received news of Germany's mobilization. Quickly he cabled his cousin Wilhelm: "I understand that you are compelled to mobilize but I should like to have the same guarantee from you that I gave you myself—that these measures do not mean war."

But, of course, the Czar was wrong. In the world of 1914, not even generals and cabinet ministers understood the difference between the various types of military precautionary messages that had been adopted by the various countries. One, however, in its unmistakable clarity stood out from the others: for Germany, mobilization meant war—within twenty-four hours if not before.

Berlin. By four in the afternoon there still was no reply from Russia. Falkenhayn and Bethmann drove to see the Kaiser. They had decided the night before that war had to be declared even if Russia proposed to negotiate. But they found the Kaiser reluctant to do so. There was a time when that would have proved a fatal obstacle to their plans, but no longer was that true. During the last week in July, Wilhelm's instructions had been disregarded by his own Chancellor and foreign minister, his military leaders, and the Austrian Emperor and his government. Wilhelm's orders still counted for something, but not for everything.

The Kaiser agreed to sign the mobilization orders, which took effect the following day. Moltke had drafted for Wilhelm a speech to the German people. Bethmann, who arrived late, was angry at Moltke for having usurped the prerogative of the civilian authorities. Moltke, visibly nervous, told an aide: "This war will turn into a world war in which England will also intervene. Few can have any idea of the extent, the duration, and the end of this war. Nobody today can have a notion of how it will end."

As the Kaiser and his military chiefs finished their discussions and prepared to disband, word arrived from the foreign office that an important message from Great Britain was in the process of being decoded. Admiral Tirpitz suggested to the two army chiefs that they wait to read it. Instead, they hurried off with their signed mobilization order. They might as well have stayed, for they were soon ordered to return.

The message from London disrupted the German government's plans. The cable came from Berlin's ambassador there, Prince Lichnowsky, who repeated assurances which he mistakenly believed that Sir Edward Grey had given to him. England seemed to be saying that if Germany left France alone, England and France would remain neutral in Germany's war against Russia.

The Kaiser and his aides were jubilant. This practically ensured victory, as they saw it. Moltke, as chief of staff the officer in charge of operations, found himself in a minority of one. As he recalled it soon afterwards, "The Kaiser said to me: 'Then we simply deploy in the east with the whole army.' "

It drove Moltke to despair. The Kaiser seemed incapable of understanding the current war plan, which was to hurl the bulk of Germany's forces, via Luxemburg and Belgium, against France, while holding off Russia with a smaller force in the east. A quick victory over France would be followed by a rapid transfer of Germany's armies from the French front to the Russian one. Not since April 1913 had the general staff maintained a current plan of deployment for a war solely against Russia.

The army was already in the process of moving to attack France. Rescinding the orders, Moltke argued, would create chaos. After a violent argument between the Kaiser and the chief of staff, a compromise was reached: mobilization would proceed, and the troops would move in France's direction, but then be available to be redeployed en masse to the east if an agreement were made for Britain and France to remain neutral.

That left a major problem unresolved. In the German war plan, the initial move by the Kaiser's armies would be to seize the railroads of neutral Luxemburg before France could do so, and then deliver an ultimatum to neutral Belgium to stand aside and let the German armies pass through in order to invade France. Germany was a guarantor of Belgium's neutrality and of Luxemburg's.

Now that France was going to stay out of the war, this had to be changed. According to Moltke, "the Kaiser, without asking me, turned to the aide-de-camp on duty and commanded him to telegraph immediate instructions . . . not to march into Luxemburg. I thought my heart would break." With England and France refusing to be drawn into war, "The final straw," Moltke exploded, "would be if Russia now also fell away." Germany would be deprived of enemies!

Meanwhile, the Kaiser and his Chancellor sent messages to London to seal the bargain: Wilhelm to King George V, and Bethmann to the British government. But, as King George wrote in his cabled reply, "I think there must be some misunderstanding." No such offer of British and French neutrality had ever been made.

After reading King George's telegram, the Kaiser told Moltke: "Now you can do as you will." Moltke promptly cabled to his forces to proceed with the invasion of Luxemburg.

At 7:00 p.m., German troops seized their first objective: a railroad station and telegraph office inside Luxemburg. At 7:30 p.m. other

German troops came to recall them, telling the first contingent that they had been dispatched in error; the cable from King George was awaited. Then, in response to the later telegram from Moltke, orders again were countermanded and once again the German invasion of Luxemburg went forward.

London. Authorized to do so by the cabinet, Grey, albeit in diplomatic language, warned the German ambassador that a violation of Belgian neutrality might very well bring Britain to intervene.

St. Petersburg. The German ambassador delivered his country's declaration of war to the Russian foreign minister. In his confusion he served a document that incorporated both versions with which Berlin had supplied him: the claim that Russia had not replied, and the claim that the Russian reply was unsatisfactory.

London. Churchill, through his Tory friend F. E. Smith, had invited Bonar Law, the Tory leader, to dine with him and with Sir Edward Grey at the Admiralty. Smith had asked Sir Max Aitken, Law's closest friend, to join the party. But Law declined, and Grey at some point instead went off to join the Prime Minister. In the event, Churchill dined at the Admiralty alone.

After dinner, at about nine-thirty, Smith and Aitken came by, and found Churchill with two friends. They fell into a discussion of the crisis. News arrived that the Germans were postponing their ultimatum to Russia and opinions differed as to the significance of the news. Three of the men played a rubber of bridge with Churchill. Aitken sat out.

The cards had just been dealt and play begun when a red official dispatch box was brought in to Churchill. He took out a key and unlocked it. In it was a single sheet of paper "singularly disproportionate to the size of the box," as Aitken was later to write, on which was written: "War declared by Germany on Russia."

Churchill turned over his bridge hand to Aitken and walked over to 10 Downing Street. He found the Prime Minister closeted with Grey and other advisers.

Churchill told Asquith that he was going to order full general mobilization of the fleet. He knew, of course, that the cabinet had refused him permission to do so that morning. He personally would answer to the cabinet the following morning for what he was about to do.

The Prime Minister said nothing. Churchill returned to his offices, and spent the rest of the night making sure that, whatever might happen, the Royal Navy would be ready.

Later that night London received word from its embassy in Berlin that the Kaiser claimed his efforts to keep the peace were being undermined by Russia's full mobilization. Was there anything George V could do to help?

Asquith quickly drafted a note to the Czar in King George's name, called a taxi, and raced to Buckingham Palace at one-thirty in the morning to obtain his monarch's signature. "The king was hauled out of his bed," the Prime Minister noted in his diary, "and one of my strangest experiences was sitting with him clad in a dressing-gown while I read the message and the proposed answer."

Berlin.   Newspapers in Berlin and in Hamburg carried the story of the "naval alliance" between Britain and Russia. Allegedly the Russians hoped to win Royal Navy agreement to dispatch transport ships to Baltic ports before the outbreak of war. They were to carry Russian troops who would invade northeastern Germany.

But as the talks between Admiral Prince Louis of Battenberg and the Russian admiralty had been scheduled for August, they had not yet started to take place. According to the German press, Prince Louis did not manage to come to St. Petersburg: "the war that Russia thrust on us prevented" the British-Russian naval alliance from being concluded.

"The war that Russia thrust on us": That embodied what Germans came to believe. When news of Russia's mobilization first was known, the Bavarian military attaché confided to his diary: "I run to the War Ministry. Beaming faces everywhere. Everyone is shaking hands in the corridors: people congratulate one another for being over the hurdle." The German people, the political parties, the labor unions, the press, all had been fooled into believing that Russia had started the war. Another diarist, chief of the Kaiser's naval staff, made everything more clear: "The mood is brilliant. The government has managed brilliantly to make us appear as the attacked."

The German government announced that Russian invaders had crossed into German territory. The German people believed it.

CHAPTER 40: AUGUST 2

London. The British cabinet, which met exceptionally on a Sunday, began by moving somewhat in the direction of involvement in the developing crisis. It was in session from 11:00 a.m. to 2:00 p.m., but then convened again at 6:30 p.m.

In the morning session the ministers ratified Churchill's order mobilizing the fleet. It considered, but rejected for the time being, dispatching an expeditionary force to the Continent, as had been envisaged in secret Anglo-French army staff talks a few years earlier of which most members of the cabinet had been ignorant.

In between the morning and evening sessions, Grey advised the French ambassador that should the German navy attack the undefended French Atlantic coast, the British navy would offer France protection.

In the evening session, the cabinet learned of Germany's violation of the neutrality of Luxemburg. The British government took the view that its responsibility to Luxemburg was collective—that is, it was obliged to act only if the other guarantors did so as well. Belgium was a different matter; the guarantee of neutrality arguably was individual, and Grey had already alerted the German ambassador to Britain's position on the matter. Yet Germany's invasion of Luxemburg presaged an invasion and occupation of Belgium too. Indeed, as the cabinet reconvened at six-thirty, a German ultimatum was being received in Brussels. Asquith ordered mobilization of the army.

The shift in political sentiment over the course of the day was remarkable. That morning Asquith had set down in writing, in a personal letter, his own view of the European situation.

(1) We have no obligation of any kind either to France or Russia to give them military or naval help.

(2) The despatch of the Expeditionary force to help France at this moment is out of the question & wd serve no object.

(3) We mustn't forget the ties created by our long-standing & intimate friendship with France.

(4) It is against British interests that France shd. be wiped out as a Great Power.

(5) We cannot allow Germany to use the Channel as a hostile base.

(6) We have obligations to Belgium to prevent her being utilised & absorbed by Germany.

This formulation of the Prime Minister's public policy objectives in the gathering European storm may be taken as almost comprehensive. But it represented only his personal views, which were not shared by his Liberal party. He reckoned that "a good ¼ of our own party" in the House of Commons "are for absolute non-interference at any price."

Before the morning cabinet meeting he had received an assurance of firm support from the Conservative leadership for his policy of backing up France. This placed Asquith in the peculiar position of being supported in his foreign policy largely by his political opponents. His overriding political object was to keep his Liberal party united behind whatever decisions the cabinet eventually made, while trying to bring the cabinet around to his own and Grey's point of view.

Berlin. Moltke sent to the foreign office some suggestions "of a military-political nature" to which he attributed "some value from a military point of view." If England entered the war, Moltke suggested, Germany should incite uprisings against Britain in South Africa, Egypt, and India, thereby converting a European war into a world war. Germany's secret alliance with Turkey, just being concluded, should be made public; and Italy should state whether or not it would stand by its allies Germany and Austria. Sweden and Norway should be urged to mobilize against Russia, bringing pressure to bear. Japan should be urged to move against Russia in Asia. Switzerland already had mobilized; and, Moltke confided, the Swiss chief of staff had secretly drafted documents that would, if ratified, place the Swiss army under Germany's command.

The foreign office announced that France and Russia already had commenced hostilities. It transpired that this was not true.

Rome.   The German ambassador learned from the Italian foreign minister, the Marchese di San Giuliano, that Rome had decided to remain neutral. San Giuliano explained that the treaty of alliance with Germany and Austria obliged Italy to come to their aid only if Germany or Austria were attacked. But the conflict in which they were engaged in the summer of 1914 was "a war of aggression" on their part. Italy, therefore, would stand aside. In a later account of this interview, San Giuliano stated that "the war undertaken by Austria . . . had, in the words of the German ambassador himself, an aggressive object."

Italy's military chief said that his country could not go to war in any event because its armed forces did not have enough uniforms.

Basel.   German sources reported to Berlin that Swiss authorities had arrested French agents who were sending carrier pigeons to France with reports of German troop movements.

Luxemburg City.   The Grand Duchess of Luxemburg, Marie Adélaïde, cabled the Kaiser: "At this moment the Grand Duchy is being occupied by German troops." She protested and asked Wilhelm to respect the country's rights. In reply, Germany's Chancellor claimed: "Our military measures in Luxemburg indicate no hostile action against Luxemburg, but are solely measures for the protection of the railroads under our management there, against an attack by the French." He promised full compensation.

London. The German ambassador advised his government: "The question as to whether we are going to violate Belgian territory in our war with France may be of decisive importance in determining that of England's neutrality."

In fact, by the time of the British cabinet meeting that evening there was broad agreement that the issue was Belgium. The legal situation was not entirely clear: did one guarantor of Belgium's neutrality have to act even if none of the other guarantors did so? The cabinet felt that if the violation of Belgian neutrality were substantial and if Belgium itself fought back against the invaders, Britain was bound to come to its aid.

Brussels. Alarmed by Germany's incursion into Luxemburg, Belgium's foreign minister called upon Germany's resident minister to ask reassurance. Grey already had asked both France and Germany to pledge their continuing support of their treaty obligations to protect Belgian neutrality. France had given the pledge; Germany had not. Now the German minister was evasive.

He had to be. He did not yet know what was contained in his sealed instructions that a messenger had delivered to him on July 29 with orders not to open them until told to do so. He was told to do so on August 2. The German minister retrieved his instructions from his safe and unsealed them. Inside was an ultimatum that he was ordered to serve upon the Belgian government, which he duly delivered that evening. It gave Belgium twelve hours in which to reply. Drafted July 26 but purporting to have just been written, the German note complained of entirely imaginary French troop movements and demanded that Belgium allow German forces to pass through its territory in order to engage the French.

London. Meeting that evening, the British cabinet learned that Germany had invaded Luxemburg and seemed poised to invade Belgium. The Prime Minister ordered the army to mobilize.

CHAPTER 41: AUGUST 3

Brussels. Early Monday morning King Albert of the Belgians rejected Germany's ultimatum. Assuming command of his country's relatively modest armed forces, he ordered the destruction of the bridges and tunnels the German troops would expect to use in their invasion.

Luxemburg City. Proclamations circulated throughout the city by German invasion forces announced: "Since France, without regard to the neutrality of Luxemburg, has opened hostilities against Germany from Luxemburg territory," German forces had done so too. The head of the Luxemburg government called the German government in protest that "this statement is founded on error. There is absolutely not a single French soldier in Luxemburg territory."

London. The cabinet, in its morning session, was told of the German ultimatum to Belgium. "The Germans, with almost Austrian crassness" had moved against Belgium, Asquith noted privately. The swing in ministerial opinion was dramatic. Belgium had become the issue. The week before, the cabinet had been overwhelmingly opposed to intervention. At the time they had wanted to stay out; now they felt compelled to go in. Lloyd George, formerly for peace, took the lead in arguing for war. Opinion in the cabinet was almost unanimous. Nonetheless, Asquith and Grey continued to make decisions without asking for or receiving a vote.

That afternoon Grey addressed the House of Commons. London was packed with vacationers; it was a Monday day off, known to the British as a bank holiday. Parliament itself was packed with members and visitors; the House of Commons, according to Barbara Tuchman, "had gathered in total attendance for the first time since Gladstone brought in the Home Rule Bill in 1893." "Grey made a most remarkable speech—about an hour long—for the most part almost conversational in tone," wrote Asquith. Grey had not had time to write it out in advance. He narrated the history of the crisis, but when he came to the issue of Belgium it was clear that he had the House of Commons overwhelmingly behind him in favor of intervention.

Only a week before, Britain had been on the verge of civil war on the issue of Ireland. Now, after Grey had finished speaking, John Redmond, the principal leader of the Irish nationalists, rose to assure the government that it "might tomorrow withdraw every one of their troops from Ireland" because "the armed Nationalist Catholics in the South would be only too glad to join arms with the armed Protestant Ulsterman in the North" to defend the shores of the United Kingdom.

What happens next? Violet Asquith asked her father, while independently, Winston Churchill asked Grey the same question. The Prime Minister and the foreign secretary both gave the same answer: deliver an ultimatum. Indeed, at a cabinet meeting convened after the House of Commons session, that is what was decided.

CHAPTER 42: AUGUST 4

London. At 9:30 a.m. Grey sent a telegram to Germany protesting Germany's ultimatum to Belgium and demanding that it be withdrawn.

As news arrived confirming Germany's intention of invading Belgium, Grey, at 2 p.m., sent Berlin an ultimatum demanding German compliance with Belgium's neutrality to be confirmed by midnight. The cable was sent to the British ambassador, who was able to deliver it only at 7 p.m. At some point Grey realized that the ultimatum did not specify whether it was to expire at midnight British time or continental time, and it was decided that it should be continental time, giving Germany five hours in which to reply.

Germany never replied.

Germany's invasion of Belgium, bringing Great Britain into the war, converted what had been a continental war into a world war. The British Empire extended all the way around the earth and so, now, would the warfare. Moltke's memo on August 2 to the German foreign office made it clear that the German government understood that.

In view of the paramount importance of the British decision, it is all the more remarkable how, in that pre-democratic age, the decision was reached. Parliament did not vote. The cabinet played little role. As A. J. P. Taylor tells us, King George V "held a privy council at Buckingham Palace" the night of August 4 "which was attended only by one minister and two court officials" and which "sanctioned the proclamation of a state of war." More astonishing, when viewed through modern eyes, "The governments and parliaments of the Dominions were not consulted." Instead each "governor general issued the royal proclamation on his own authority, as did the viceroy of India." Canada, Australia, New Zealand, South Africa, India (which then included Pakistan and Bangladesh), and much of Africa were swept up in a war without first being asked.

Peculiar in a different way was the situation of Germany, which was fighting Russia, France, Britain, Luxemburg, and Belgium—all supposedly to prop up Austria, which, as of August 4, was still at peace with all of them. Yet Germany was *not* at war with, or fighting against, Serbia, the only country with which Austria *was* at war and which, according to Vienna, was the country that posed the threat to Austria's existence.

The following day, we are told by the historian Hartmut Pogge von Strandmann, there was "a panic in Berlin" as German troops continued to advance alone and without allies. Moltke told Tirpitz on August 5 that if Austria continued to shy away, Germany—only days after declaring war—would have to sue for peace on the best terms it could get.

On August 6, Vienna overcame its reluctance and declared war against Russia.

No wonder that, from the very outset, the belligerents felt obliged to explain to their own peoples, and to the peoples of other countries, the seemingly muddled logic that had brought them to the battlefield and, in Austria's eyes, to the wrong battlefield.

CHAPTER 43: **SHREDDING THE EVIDENCE**

Michael Howard, the military historian, writes of 1914: "Probably no few days in the history of the world have been subjected to such scrutiny as those between June 28, when the Archduke was assassinated, and August 4, when Britain declared war." Yet gaps remain in the record. Suspicious historians are bound to turn detective and to ask what the gaps mean. For the suppression or destruction of evidence in itself is evidence, and the challenge is to discover: evidence of *what*?

A case in point is the week that began the morning of June 28. Austria-Hungary was deciding how to react to the assassination of its heir apparent. Its foreign minister, Count von Berchtold, the prime decision-maker in what ensued, is the first person whose private papers we would want to consult. It may tell us something that we learn from Holger Herwig, author of a magisterial work on Austria and Germany in the First World War: "It is interesting to note that Berchtold's official diary at the Foreign Office is conspicuously devoid of entries for the period between 27 June and 5 July 1914."

There is a one-week gap. It suggests that in the week after June 27, Berchtold was doing something that he knew he might someday want to disavow. Interesting, too, is that Austrian intelligence, in Vienna's war archives, contains records that stop June 28, and do not resume for a whole year. When Germany justified itself on August 3, two days after declaring war, by publishing documents, "half of the thirty documents were blatant forgeries."

During the First World War all sides wanted to prove that they had not started it; afterwards, everyone wanted to avoid "war guilt," especially the Germans, on whom it was officially fixed in the Treaty of Versailles of 1919, after the Armistice. The German authorities instigated the suppression of relevant portions of Moltke's papers.

The result was that even in the decades after the war, evidence tended to be destroyed rather than recovered, and even if recovered, rewritten or restructured. Moreover, the authorities under successive German regimes up to and including the Nazi government carried on a massive disinformation campaign which has been described by Herwig in detail in his essay "Clio Deceived."

The diaries of Kurt Riezler, private secretary to the German Chancellor, illustrate the difficulties that research scholars face. Riezler died after leaving instructions that his diaries should be destroyed. The personal papers of Bethmann had been removed or destroyed a decade or two earlier. After many maneuvers and arguments, the Riezler papers were rescued. But examination showed that while the diaries before and after the summer of 1914 were in small exercise books, the key months of July and August were recorded, instead, on loose paper and in another manner, strongly suggesting that these centrally relevant sections had been rewritten—and had been substituted for the original. The papers of Müller, head of the Kaiser's Naval Cabinet, though they survived, were expurgated.

Germans were not alone in destroying or falsifying their records. In the first weeks of the 1914 war the French foreign office issued a *Yellow Book* justifying all that it had done—a work of which Albertini in the 1940s was to write: "it musters 159 documents, many of them altered, mutilated, or falsified." Of a similar effort by St. Petersburg, Albertini writes that the Russian *Orange Book* "gives 79 documents, some considerably faked." And Serbia's archives were closed for half a century. No minutes were kept of Serbian cabinet meetings for 1914.

But nowhere was suppression or destruction of records, diaries, and the like carried out so widely throughout the following decades as in Germany. Thus all records of telephone conversations and notes of other verbal communications are missing for the period in question from the German foreign office. On the German side the two key turning points were the July 5 conversations with the Austrians, resulting in the "blank check," and the discussions among German leaders the week of July 27 that led to the decision to go to war. All records of both are missing from the foreign office. Missing, too, we are told by a leading researcher in this field, Imanuel Geiss, are all records of the Kaiser's conversations with military and political leaders during July. For that matter, there are no records of Germany's conversations in Berlin with foreign powers.

Appropriately it is German scholars, beginning with the courageous Fritz Fischer in the 1960s, who have taken the lead in discovering or restoring bits and pieces of the record, and who often have done so through enterprising and imaginative fieldwork. Thus in the early 1970s, John Röhl, a leading authority on Wilhelmine Germany, published two documents of considerable importance "discovered in a chest in the cellar of Hemmingen Castle in Württemberg, and in a washing-basket in the attic of Hertefeld manor-house, in western Germany close to the Dutch border," he writes, "while I was searching for letters." The two documents had been hidden away for half a century.

On the whole, we have to draw the obvious and commonsense conclusion that documents destroyed or hidden probably were embarrassing or incriminating, and that the effort to blot out or falsify the record was undertaken in order to deny responsibility for the war.

As will be seen, however, modern scholarship has made it possible, despite the massive destruction and falsification of evidence, to uncover much of the truth about what really happened.

PART EIGHT

THE MYSTERY SOLVED

CHAPTER 44: ASSEMBLING IN THE LIBRARY

An inquest into the circumstances surrounding the outbreak of hostilities in 1914 results in findings that read, in some respects, like a murder mystery. There is the *simple* question of who did it: who, if anyone, was behind the boy who pulled the trigger. There also is the *complex* question of who did it: who, if anyone, deliberately manipulated the resulting situation in such a way as to destroy the existing European order.

The old-fashioned detective story that became so popular with the generation that emerged from the Great War, in Britain in particular, often ended with all the surviving characters assembling in one room. There, in the ship's lounge or in the ballroom of the hotel or in the library of a country house, Agatha Christie's Hercule Poirot or some similar private detective would explain what really had happened and would answer the ultimate question: who did it?

For us, in our own inquiry, the room in which we gather to sum up must of necessity be a library. Those who played a role in the July crisis are no longer alive. They can no longer answer our questions in person. Luigi Albertini, the Italian historian who died in the opening years of the Second World War, was perhaps the last researcher of the events of 1914 who could conduct his inquiries by sleuthing in the way that detectives do: by taking statements from the witnesses and suspects, questioning them, comparing their accounts, and pursuing contradictions and discrepancies. His volumes are the last of the police procedurals.

A new era opened, beginning in the 1960s, with the publication of the pioneering research of Fritz Fischer, who dug in the archives as archaeologists dig in the field. His example was followed and led to discoveries. Memories had been lost but files were found. Now, year after year, decade after decade, disclosures are made, fresh insights are afforded, hidden documents are recovered and displayed in the light of day. No longer, it is true, do participants speak to us, but a literature does.

Thousands of volumes have been written about the origins of the First World War, but of these, perhaps fifty or a hundred from the post-Fischer era, taken together, give at least in its main details a truthful account of what happened in that seminal summer of 1914, with the consequences of which we still live.

CHAPTER 45: **WHAT DID NOT HAPPEN**

In the post-Fischer era, scholars have revised many of the opinions that used to be held about the origins of the Great War. But scholarship has not percolated effectively into the consciousness of the wider public. Much of what people continue to say and think about the events of July 1914 is now questioned or disputed by scholars.

According to the most recent and convincing scholarship, it was not the case, as the man in the street seems to have believed at the time, and as Englishmen and others were to write later, that the European world of June 1914 was a sort of Eden in which the outbreak of hostilities among major powers came as a surprise. On the contrary, as its political and military elites recognized, Europe was in the grip of an unprecedented arms race; internally the powers were victims of violent social, industrial, and political strife; and general staffs chattered constantly, not about whether there would be war, but where and when.

Even the emerging trouble spots, far from coming as a surprise, could be discerned in advance. The chancelleries of Europe expected that the unsettled Balkans soon would be ready for another round of warfare in which the Ottoman Empire might disappear from Europe altogether. German leaders worried (and some of Russia's leaders hoped) that the Hapsburg Empire might collapse as well. Austria-Hungary worried that it might not be able to contain a Slavic tide. Germany was levying taxes to accelerate its military programs at rates that were unsustainable; it looked very much as though it had either to launch a war soon or stand down. What nobody knew was *when* there would be war: in which year or, for that matter, which decade.

The Europe that took up arms in the summer of 1914 had not been a calm and peaceful place. It was riven by a thousand enmities, and was conspicuously bellicose.

Nor was it the case, at least in my view, that the march toward war began on June 28, 1914, and at Sarajevo. It was the Second Balkan War (1913) and its aftermath that persuaded Berchtold and his foreign office that Austria-Hungary had to destroy Serbia. It will be remembered that Vienna started drafting the memorandum-plan to crush Serbia two weeks *before* Sarajevo.

As for Germany, it was Russia's military, railroad, and industrial buildup after 1905 that awakened in its generals an urgent desire to launch a preventive war against Russia and its ally France. That was why they looked back on 1905 with regret: both Russia and France had been temporarily powerless in that year, and could have been defeated easily. The roots of Germany's move can be dated, therefore, to sometime in the decade 1904–1914, when its military leaders first began to advocate preventive war. The move itself took place suddenly in the last week of July 1914, when they seized their chance and opted for provoking the preventive war of which they had long dreamed.

In the aftermath of the June 28 killings, Vienna believed them to be the product of a plot conceived in, and organized by, Serbia. That turns out not to have been entirely true. Serbia bore some responsibility, but not all.

The murder, as we have seen, was committed by one person, a Bosnian, and therefore an Austrian, not a Serbian subject. He acted probably (but not certainly) on his own initiative, though he was assisted by others. His act—we now can confirm—was made possible by support from dissident officers in the Serbian army.

There is no question that the bullet that killed Austrian Archduke Franz Ferdinand in Sarajevo the late morning of Sunday, June 28, 1914, came from the weapon wielded by the schoolboy terrorist Gavrilo Princip.

Princip, though he claimed otherwise for a few days after his capture, did not act entirely alone. He may well have originated the idea of murdering Franz Ferdinand, as he maintained to the end, but he headed a team. The others were, like himself, young amateurs motivated by nationalist or fringe ideologies. Another member of his band attempted the assassination but failed. In the end Princip acted alone. There was no third bullet. There was no grassy knoll.

The assassination plot could not have succeeded without the essential support provided by the Serbian secret society, the Black Hand, which supplied weapons, marksmanship training, and the use of an "underground railroad" to smuggle Princip and a colleague past frontier and customs posts, from Serbia into Bosnia. The Black Hand, in turn, called on the support of low-level Serbian government officials and on the resources of the Serbian nationalist cultural organization Narodna Odbrana.

Apis and his chief lieutenants, the active heads of the Black Hand, were high-ranking army officers who had infiltrated the Serbian government. It was a military-political faction conspiring against the Prime Minister; so he was not responsible for what they did.

Rumors circulated at the time and for decades afterwards that Russia provided financial support to the Black Hand and to the Sarajevo plotters. These appear to be baseless. Junior attachés of the pan-Slav faith may have known of Apis's aid to Princip and may have expressed sympathy, but they were individuals who did not represent their government in the matter. Russia's pan-Slav man in the Balkans, Hartwig, minister to Serbia, supported Prime Minister Pasic against the Black Hand, and surely that would have foreclosed the possibility of any aid by the Russians to the terrorist team.

Princip, who killed Franz Ferdinand, did so for a muddle of misinformed reasons. Although the Archduke was the most pro-Slav member of the Hapsburg hierarchy, the youth believed that he was anti-Slav. Princip feared that the annual military maneuvers Franz Ferdinand was inspecting masked an invasion force that would launch a surprise attack on Serbia (untrue). Princip had heard that the heir was a moderate whose attractive policies might bring all the Slavs of the Balkans under Austrian control.

Like other terrorists, Princip must have believed that killing government leaders would demoralize the ruling classes. He had hoped to assassinate another Hapsburg official before he heard about the Archduke's planned arrival.

Apis, who facilitated Princip's deed, seems to have had not much more information about the policies for which Franz Ferdinand stood than did Princip. But the question of Apis's motivation is more complex. As A. J. P. Taylor has pointed out, Princip and his schoolboy friends, at the time they made themselves known to agents of the Black Hand, could hardly have inspired much confidence as a band of killers. They were adolescents and amateurs with no military training or experience, and with no knowledge of weaponry. How were they going to break through the bodyguard of what should have been one of the most heavily guarded political figures in Europe? Indeed, only a series of blunders and coincidences that could not possibly have been expected led to the success of Princip's plot.

Might it not have been more probable that, as Taylor suggested, Apis decided to facilitate the plans of the little band of teenage incompetents *because* he assumed they would bungle it? If so, without providing Austria with a pretext for taking action, the attempted assassination might have seriously embarrassed the Serbian Prime Minister—Apis's enemy—especially in the upcoming August 14 elections. So while the world always has thought of the murders in Sarajevo as an episode in international affairs, they may have been intended at the time more as a maneuver in Serbian domestic politics.

Austria-Hungary's actions, from the Outrage of June 28 until its declaration of war against Serbia on July 28, were widely believed to have been inspired by a desire to punish the guilty. Critics argued that Vienna was rushing to judgment too soon—that it was condemning Serbia on the basis of insufficient evidence.

In fact, as we know now, Austria-Hungary did not care whether Serbia was guilty of the murders or not. If anything, members of the imperial court came close to welcoming the assassinations. The government of Austria-Hungary, neither angered nor saddened by the death of the Archduke and his consort—in fact, relieved that the unloved couple had been removed from the scene so conveniently—used the events of June 28 as an excuse for doing what it planned to do anyway. Better yet, the assassinations provided an opportunity to secure the support of Germany, which was vital to the success of Austria's plan to attack Serbia. As of June 28, German approval was all that was missing.

Kaiser Wilhelm ordinarily would have refused to support Austrian aggression. He had refused such support before. But he—practically alone—genuinely *was* outraged by the killing of his friend, or at least he seemed to be. Evidently he was carried away. Like his Homeric idol Achilles, he changed his mind and opted for a war to avenge his best friend.

Later, it became a commonplace among historians that the assassinations in Sarajevo served as a mere pretext for making war against Serbia. They were a pretext, but not a *mere* pretext. The murders were important in themselves, for by eliminating the Archduke, and by changing the mind of the Kaiser, they neutralized the opposition of the two people who probably would have continued to stop the Hapsburg government from moving to crush Serbia.

The next key events in the run-up toward war with Serbia occurred July 5–6, when Kaiser Wilhelm and his government extended a blank check to Austria-Hungary. Rightly, historians have condemned this: a government is responsible for its decisions, so a blank check gives one set of decision-makers power without responsibility, and the other, responsibility without power.

But Germany was given no cause to regret its folly in issuing a blank check; in practice the check never was used. Crudely put, Austria, instead of recklessly making decisions for the ally, went on taking orders from Germany. Chancellor Bethmann devised the invasion strategy that Berchtold and his government undertook to follow; and it was Berlin, not Vienna, that mounted the "localization" diplomatic campaign that followed it.

It is true that the Austrians did not call off the war when the Kaiser ordered them to do so in late July, but when the Austrians *did* declare war on Serbia on July 28, it was because the German foreign minister told them to do it.

· · ·

The blank check was never presented for payment, but it would be wrong to say that its issuance proved irrelevant. It was only because of the security it provided that Franz Joseph, Berchtold, and Conrad set out on the path that led to war against Serbia.

It was the Kaiser who decided to give the blank check. His military and civilian leaders approved the decision, and shared in his responsibility for it. For all the hatred directed his way by the Allies in the 1914–18 war—"Hang the Kaiser!" was a popular chant in Britain—it was the only respect in which he was among those principally responsible for the outbreak of war.

The Kaiser, blustering, threatening, and unbalanced monarch though he was, did not want to lead his country and Europe into war. On the contrary, his was the major force for peace within his country's government. Wilhelm and Franz Ferdinand were the two most obnoxious public figures in Europe, but they were the ones who kept hotheads in check and, in the end, always opted for peace. Only when they were removed from the decision-making process, Franz Ferdinand permanently and Wilhelm temporarily, did the pro-war faction find its window of opportunity open. Even in the blank check matter, the Kaiser did not believe that he was initiating a war among the Great Powers. He believed he was encouraging Austria to make war on Serbia, but that none of the other powers would go to war. He appeared to be certain of that.

The very name historians have attached to the thirty-seven days from the Sarajevo events to world war—the "July crisis"—tends to mislead. It suggests mounting tension, day by day, but, as remarked earlier, that is not how events played out.

The July 5–6 blank check conference and its decisions were secret, and the German and Austrian governments were successful thereafter in pretending that no preparations for Serbia's downfall were under way. So Europe, unaware, was not alarmed, either mountingly or otherwise.

A copy of the Austrian ultimatum to Serbia was delivered to European foreign offices on July 23 or 24, and it was only then that the crisis began to detonate. For Russia and Britain it was July 24; for France it was nearly a week later, when Poincaré and Viviani returned from Russia.

· · ·

The ultimatum that Austria-Hungary served on Serbia on July 23 shocked Europe. The opinion was widespread at the time that no country that accepted it could thereafter remain independent.

But after the experiences of the brutal twentieth century, historians have grown callous; they no longer find the Austrian demands outrageous. We still object to the time period; the Serbs should not have been given an ultimatum. But we find Serbia in large part culpable.

Serbia harbored, and perhaps even nourished, terrorist groups. It had been the staging and training ground for the death squad that had killed the Hapsburg heir apparent. Moreover, the Serbian people clearly had rejoiced in the assassination.

Austria's decision to deal with this by invading Serbia, dismantling terrorist logistical supports, disbanding organizations that had supported attacks on Austria, and seeking to bring the guilty to justice, has a twenty-first-century ring to it. In 2001 the United States government, with the aid of its NATO allies, acted similarly in Afghanistan at the outset of our new millennium.

It is basic to international law that each government must keep armed forces from using its territory as a base to attack other countries. But if a government is powerless to enforce the law within its own domains—if it cannot keep its territory from being used to harm other countries—then it forfeits its right to sovereignty in this respect, and the injured foreign country can send in its own troops to punish the guilty and to prevent further attacks. It was in exercise of that right that General John Pershing's American forces were ordered to pursue Pancho Villa's band into Mexico after Villa's 1916 raid on U.S. territory.

At the time it was believed that in its reply, Serbia had agreed to almost all of Austria's terms. Historians no longer believe that. Readers can judge for themselves by reading the notes (Appendixes 1 and 2).

Facing the voters of his turbulent nationalist country on August 14, Prime Minister Pasic needed to convince them that he was making few concessions while, in replying to Vienna, he had to appear to agree to practically all the concessions demanded. The document therefore was drafted to be ambiguous.

Russia has been blamed by some historians for encouraging Pasic to avoid a full surrender. The current view among historians is that

Russia gave no such counsel, and, if anything, encouraged Serbia to make its peace with Austria.

The point to grasp is that it did not matter what Pasic wrote in reply to the ultimatum: Austria had decided in advance not to accept the Serbian reply, no matter what it was. The ultimatum, in fact, had been drafted with the aim of making it practically impossible for Serbia to accept.

Austria continued to move slowly but straight ahead, as it had since July 5–6. It served its ultimatum on Serbia July 23, rejected Serbia's reply July 25, and declared war on Serbia July 28. Thereafter it took steps to prepare to engage the enemy.

It has been widely believed for a long time that the political structure of the European world in 1914—in particular an allegedly overly rigid alliance system—caused the conflict to enlarge and bring in the Great Powers. In retrospect, that seems not to have been true. Italy was bound to Germany and Austria in the Triple Alliance, but nonetheless remained neutral in 1914 and thereafter joined the Allies. Great Britain, on the other hand, had no treaty of alliance with France and Russia but united with them nonetheless. Treaties, therefore, did not determine which countries decided to fight on which side.

The pacts of alliance did not bring countries into the war. If anything, the alliance system (as Kurt Riezler, Bethmann's secretary, observed) was a restraint on adventurism and conduced to peace, for each country tended to discourage its allies from running risks on issues in which only one of them had serious interests. France usually discouraged Russia in the Balkans, while Russia cautioned France in Morocco. Partners held one another back because neither wanted to fight the quarrels of the other.

Treaties normally were defensive, the one country promising aid only if the other were attacked. That changed crucially in 1909. Ignoring the language of the 1879 treaty of alliance, Moltke, backed by his government, asserted that Germany was *bound* to stand with Austria even if it had started the war.

Was it this German disposition to support an ally, right or wrong, that brought about the overthrow of the European order in 1914? It might have, but it did not: Germany did not blindly back up Austria in its aggressiveness; on the contrary, it *led* Austria into aggressiveness and ordered it to go further and faster. The Austrian alliance did not pull Germany into war; it was the German alliance that pushed Austria into the war: the war against Russia and its worldwide allies.

What, then, caused the war? Or who?

On the afternoon of July 31, as Germany prepared to commence hostilities, Chancellor Bethmann, in an address to his cabinet, concluded by saying that "all the Governments—including that of Russia—and the great majority of the nations are in themselves pacific, but the situation had got out of hand."

The situation had got out of hand! There was the most persuasive of explanations. It sounded fair and impartial. It absolved from blame statesmen, many of whom indeed were not to blame. And, best of all, it provided a plausible answer to the otherwise baffling question of what had caused the war—and what "cause" means in that context. But, as historian Marc Trachtenberg and others have argued powerfully, it will not do, for the decision-makers *did* understand the consequences of their actions.

It is true to say that France, Russia, and Serbia were not fully in control of their situation. All of them wanted to remain at peace, which, however, was not an option available to them. But it was not because of the unintended consequences of mobilization or the exigencies of railroad timetables or the requirements of alliance systems that a war was forced upon them in the summer of 1914. It was because they were attacked. They were attacked by Germany and Austria.

It often is said that what led to war was Russia's decision to mobilize. That could have been true in other circumstances. It was not true in the circumstances of the summer of 1914. The German government had determined to go to war *before* Russia mobilized; therefore the German decision could not have been caused by the Russian decision. And, far from fearing Russian mobilization, the German leaders hoped for and waited for it: it was their excuse and enabled them to obtain the essential support of their own people.

Sazonov, the Russian foreign minister, knew that if Russia mobilized, Germany, blaming Russia, would declare war; and he did not opt for mobilization until he was convinced that if Russia did not mobilize, Germany would do exactly the same thing: blame Russia and declare war. So the mobilization question had to be considered in St. Petersburg solely on the merits as a military measure.

If, as the evidence now shows, the Austro-Hungarian government deliberately forced a war on Serbia, and began it by launching an unprovoked attack, and if, as the evidence now shows, the German government deliberately forced a war on Russia, France, and Belgium, and began it by launching an unprovoked attack, does it mean that Austria and Germany should have been convicted of war guilt? No—not in the world of 1914.

Guilt, in this context, was a postwar concept but not a prewar one. War, until the Great War of 1914, was a normal and usual international activity. It was considered, for example by Theodore Roosevelt in passages quoted earlier, as healthy and desirable. We no longer feel that way, but it would be unfair to judge the men of 1914 by our standards rather than by their own.

Moreover, Moltke and his colleagues, and Berchtold and his, did not think of themselves as starting wars that could be avoided—wars that, but for them, would not have occurred. As they saw it, they were merely precipitating in 1914 wars that in any event would have erupted later. It was only the *timing* of the conflicts for which they were responsible, not for the conflicts themselves.

Finally, only the small governing cliques of Germany and Austria-Hungary were responsible for bringing about their respective wars. The people they led had nothing to do with it.

It used to be said that the rigid requirements of Germany's Schlieffen plan, inexorable as a ticking clock, forced Germany and therefore Europe into a war. That was the theme of much literature on the subject. We now know that, in the relevant sense of the word "plan," there was no Schlieffen plan. What Schlieffen imagined in his memo was a mere scenario. Germany initiated the war pursuant not to Schlieffen's memo, but to Moltke's operational plan of deployment.

CHAPTER 46: THE KEY TO
WHAT HAPPENED

Much happened in that long-ago summer of 1914, a summer which in many ways is still with us. The question is, what happened to bring about a world war?

There are aspects of the story that always have been puzzling. In a sense this was only to be expected: enormous quantities of vital evidence have been destroyed precisely because they would supply the answers to our questions. But so much of the past has been recovered by the great scholars of the post-Fischer era that we may be able, now, to fill in the blanks in the reasonable certainty that we have got it right.

We know how the conflict between Austria and Serbia burst out into the open. Austria had resented Serbia ever since 1903, when a coup d'état in Belgrade caused a change of orientation in that Balkan kingdom, transforming it from Austrian satellite to Russian ally. We know that in the Balkan wars that ended in 1913, Austria developed a mortal fear of Serbia. The record is clear that in the middle of June 1914 the Hapsburg foreign ministry, on orders from its chief, was at work on a memorandum that called for the elimination of the Serb threat; a plan that would require German support. Therein lay the problem. For when Germany's emperor was asked to give his full support of Austria in the middle of June 1914, he declined to do so.

The entirely fortuitous assassination of Franz Ferdinand and Sophie, just as the memorandum was drafted, supplied an emotionally powerful argument that led the Kaiser to change his mind. It was pure accident, but as a result of it Wilhelm and his officials extended to Vienna on July 5–6 a carte blanche that the Kaiser had refused to grant only weeks before.

At the time, the blank check did not appear to be as fateful a commitment as it does in retrospect. All that Germany had undertaken was to keep the other European powers from interfering while Austria-Hungary took action against Serbia. The Kaiser and many of his officials saw no risk in making their pledge; they were absolutely certain—and with good reason—that the other countries would do nothing if Austria-Hungary acted quickly. Other German officials—notably Falkenhayn, the war minister—believed that Germany would not be called upon to do anything because Austria-Hungary would not act.

Coming out of the July 5–6 meetings and embarking, as were other key figures on a stage-managed vacation, Kaiser Wilhelm had estimated that it would take between one and three weeks for Austria-Hungary to dispose of Serbia. Returning from their vacations three weeks later, Germany's military leaders found their worst suspicions confirmed: Austria had not finished off Serbia while they were gone. Postponing once again, Conrad, leader of the Hapsburg armies, now estimated that his forces would not be ready to march for weeks; he now set the date at August 12.

That was the situation to which Germany's generals returned to begin their informal consultations with one another the last week in July.

That is the story of Austria's mortal duel with Serbia in the early part of the twentieth century: how it began, and how it moved to its fateful conclusion. How did the duel end? What is significant is that the question is asked so rarely. During the last week of July 1914, Europe seems to have lost interest in the Austro-Serbian war. It had played its part. It had prepared the way. Then to some extent it disappeared from view.

The principal actors in the drama that unfolded in Berlin the last week in July were Germany's military leaders. Falkenhayn had told the Kaiser that matters were now out of his (the Kaiser's) hands, and the Kaiser seems, at least in part, to have accepted that. Yet at other times he acted and spoke as though he remained in charge. There had been no military coup d'état, yet the Kaiser—and the Chancellor—later in the week deferred to the views of the generals.

What had changed at the end of July was that the military were taking an active hand. The blank check had been the Kaiser's policy, though his officers had made no objection to it; and the advice to Austria as to how it should achieve its goals was formulated by the Chancellor, a civilian. Bethmann's plan had been for Austria to launch an invasion to crush Serbia so quickly that it would be achieved before the other European powers had time to interfere or even object. It was to be done before the powers were aware that it was starting to happen. It had been Bethmann's role to monitor Austria's performance. Austria had not performed. Now the top military leaders were proposing plans of their own.

Moltke always had believed that a war against Russia was inevitable—that it was a fated encounter between Germans and Slavs, and that time was on Russia's side, so a preventive war should be initiated by Germany as soon as possible. This was his doctrine now, in the July crisis, and seems to have been the doctrine of his fellow officers in general, as well as of the Great General Staff as a whole.

But the circumstances had to be favorable: Moltke had said this often, as had his colleagues.

What were the necessary circumstances?

In the Moroccan crisis of 1911—the Agadir affair—Germany had learned that the Hapsburgs would not support interests that were merely German. However, they would expect Germany to support them in defense of their own interests. It was, in that sense, a one-way alliance.

Only decades before, Prussia had fulfilled its objective of excluding

Austria from the rest of the German world. Now, within the convoluted ambiguities and ambivalences of the relationship between Berlin and Vienna—rivals bound together by mutual need—lay the explanation of unfolding events.

The Hapsburg alliance was vital to Germany's grand strategy. In the war that Moltke saw coming, he needed Austria-Hungary's armies to help defend against Russia in the initial weeks while Germany was preoccupied with France.

So chief among Moltke's requirements for the favorable circumstances for war were several that involved the Dual Monarchy. The dispute had to start as Austria's, not Germany's; otherwise Austria would not play. At first Austria had to make the running. Its quarrel had to be one that would provoke Russia. At first Germany would appear in the conflict only as Austria's protector. As a result, Russia would then have to attack Germany—or at least it had to appear to the German public that Russia had attacked.

Any German general in Berlin at the end of July could see that by sheer luck the stars were in the right position and that the constellations were unlikely to be so favorable ever again. Moltke was only one of those who said so.

So the generals in Berlin in the last week of July were agitating for war—not Austria's war, one aimed at Serbia, but Germany's war, aimed at Russia.

What seems to have mystified historians for decades, in attempting to answer all sorts of questions about war origins in 1914, is that there were *two* wars being proposed that summer, not one.

Moreover, the two wars were not entirely compatible with one another. It was something about which Moltke and Conrad were not completely candid with one another. Once hostilities commenced, it would become clear that Conrad needed all of his available troops in order to crush Serbia, while Moltke wanted all Conrad's armies to ward off Russia.

Each hoped that, when the time came, the other would give up his war. Conrad desired that Germany merely deter—not actually fight—Russia, while Conrad was destroying Serbia. Moltke insisted that Austria defer its own goals until Germany accomplished its own.

The German position became starkly clear on July 31 with mobilization. On that day Wilhelm cabled Franz Joseph a message to which attention rightly has been called by historian Fritz Fellner. Wilhelm told Franz Joseph: "In this hard struggle it is of the greatest importance that Austria directs her chief force against Russia and does not split it up by a simultaneous offensive against Serbia. . . . In this gigantic struggle on which we are embarking shoulder to shoulder, Serbia plays a quite subordinate role." It was not what the Hapsburg leaders wanted to hear, and, as will be seen presently, Conrad obeyed only reluctantly—and slowly. The message was: devote yourself to *our* war, because it is the important one, and postpone *your* war, which is unimportant, until we are in a position to turn our attention to minor matters.

If one underlines the distinction between the two wars, it helps to answer many of the questions that always have been asked about the July crisis. One of them, posed in various guises from the very outset, is why peoples all around the planet were fighting and dying because of something that happened to two people, Franz Ferdinand and Sophie, of whom most knew nothing.

The answer is: that was *not* why people on the far side of the world were fighting and dying. The local war between Austria and Serbia was connected with Franz Ferdinand and Sophie, but the Great War was not; the world war, which was not really the same conflict, was caused by the struggle for supremacy among the great European powers. The desire to be number one may have been a deplorable reason for starting a war, but it was neither surprising nor puzzling that it was what motivated the powers. Germany deliberately started a European war to keep from being overtaken by Russia.

There was a certain parallel between the origins of the two wars. The Austro-Serbian war supposedly was triggered by the murders in Sarajevo, even though the Austrian plot against Serbia was hatched two weeks earlier. Similarly, the German government made use of a pretext to start a world war, and that pretext was the possibility that Russia might interfere in the Austro-Serbian war. Thus pretext was piled upon pretext, and dust was thrown in the eyes of posterity. The two wars were intertwined, but—to repeat—they were different and distinct; and in the end, Germany made Austria discard its own war in favor of Germany's.

The German generals in July 1914 had taken advantage of their weeks of vacation to ponder their plans. They were not entirely isolated from events; they had made arrangements to be kept informed. They returned to Berlin calling for war. It was not for a war against Serbia. It was for the war against Russia for which the Serbian crisis gave them an excuse.

It should be noted that the Russians had done nothing yet when the German generals came back to Berlin July 23–27. The Russians had not intervened or interfered. They had undertaken only a minimal pre-mobilization (on July 26).

So what was driving up the temperature to fever pitch in Berlin was the prospect that the government could attack the Franco-Russian alliance in 1914 rather than later. The German generals had decided on war *before* Russia mobilized (July 31), so—as pointed out earlier—it was not (as is claimed so often) Russian mobilization that started the war. So far as one can tell, the question Moltke agonized over, seemingly changing his mind, was whether to seize Liège instantly, as he absolutely needed to do, or whether to wait for Russia to order mobilization and thus provide his government with its excuse for declaring war.

Once Russia obliged by ordering mobilization, the local and comparatively little Serbian war could be ignored and the world war of the Great Powers could start. Historians would write that the local Serbian war somehow had gotten out of control and had escalated into a global war. *But the one did not grow into the other. On the contrary, one had to be put aside in order to start the other.*

Two wars, not one; that is the key.

Sir Michael Howard, with his usual clarity, has explained what it is that has puzzled scholars of the First World War ever since: there was no logic to the German decision. Agreeing with Clausewitz that military plans have no inherent logic, Sir Michael writes: "There was certainly no logic in the decision by the German General Staff that *in order to support the Austrians in a conflict with Russia over Serbia*, Germany should attack France, who was not party to the quarrel, and do so by invading Belgium."

If you delete the italicized words—for we now see that Germany instigated the war against Russia on its own account, *not* Austria's—the puzzle is solved. And it shows that there *was* logic in the decisions of the German general staff. It was not to support the Austrians that the German leaders had maneuvered in July. It was just the reverse; it was to secure Austria's support for themselves in their own war. Germany's generals had to perform the trick of first getting Austria involved in a war and then getting it to change its enemy.

The wars were to some extent incompatible. One can see that, however, only if one first sees that there *were* two wars, not one.

CHAPTER 47: **WHAT WAS IT ABOUT?**

When we claim that something or another was what a war was "about," we can mean a number of different things, among them: why decision-makers said they were going to war; why they actually believed they were doing so; and what in the end proved to be the results of the conflict.

In the case of the Austro-Serbian war, Vienna claimed that it was going to war to seek justice for the Sarajevo slayings and to prevent similar crimes from occurring in the future. What the Austrian leaders really believed was somewhat different. They thought they were fighting to preserve the multinational character of their empire—in other words, to keep Austria-Hungary from disintegrating. As they saw it, Serbia, if given a respite of a few years from the Balkan wars, would threaten to take over the leadership of the southern Slavs within the Hapsburg Empire as it was constituted in 1914, as well as those without. So they were fighting for their empire's existence.

The case of Serbia was even simpler. The Serbs fought because they were attacked. If they lost, Austria planned to cut them up into pieces; Serbia would lose its existence as well as its independence.

The Austrians may well have been right in believing that, given a few years to rebuild, Serbia would have mounted a potent challenge to the Hapsburg Empire. Like its German ally, Austria in 1914 therefore was launching what it conceived of as a preventive war.

In the earlier years of his reign, the Kaiser had championed the claims of the navy. He had supported the program, advocated by Tirpitz, that pictured the rival empire Germany should challenge as Great Britain. If that program had succeeded, Germany—if Tirpitz was correct—would have been transformed from a dominant European power to a dominant world power.

But that was not the goal—or at least not the short-run goal—of the German government in 1914. Russia, not Britain, had become the enemy. The navy had been supplanted by the army; Tirpitz had in large part been eclipsed by Moltke and Falkenhayn. Those who now were dictating Germany's policy—the army generals—aimed at holding on to what Germany had got. They wanted to maintain their country's dominance on the European continent. They wanted to prevent a future challenge to that position by Russia, backed by France, by provoking a war immediately, while their chances of winning would be greater than in the future.

The army officers in Berlin who forced their war policy on the reluctant Kaiser were motivated by a fear of Russia's growing might. Their notion that a showdown between Teutons and Slavs was inevitable is not one that we would credit today. But their fear was real.

The men who led Germany in 1914 pursued what in their eyes was a defensive policy. It was conservative in the sense that they aimed at maintaining Germany's existing military mastery in Europe. The enemy—the challenger they would have to meet one day or another—was Russia. Like Austria, choosing to fight Serbia today rather than tomorrow, Germany—which is to say, Germany's military leaders—decided to fight Russia today rather than tomorrow.

What the war was about, in the view of Berlin's decision-makers at the end of July 1914, was which country would be master of Europe in the years to come: Germany or Russia?

• • •

During the war V. I. Lenin, the communist theorist and future Russian dictator, while still in Zurich, wrote that the war was about imperialism. Inspired by a British theorist, J. A. Hobson, Lenin claimed that capitalism had entered its final phase, in which the leading industrial countries could expand their economies only by acquiring colonial empires to use as captive markets. The 1914 war, as he saw it, was a war for empire.

Lenin was wrong. It was a war for control of continental Europe, not for empire in Asia or Africa. But what he wrote was plausible, and was widely believed, especially in the 1920s and 1930s. The evidence seemed to be persuasive.

When the world war was over, it could be seen that one of its results, in 1919, had been the dramatic expansion of the British Empire. England had taken German colonies in Africa. A British army of a million men was in occupation of the Middle East. Some who observed these results drew the conclusion that it had been an imperialist war, a war for imperial expansion all along. That was an illusion. In August 1914, Grey and Asquith, in bringing Britain into the war, harbored no desire to expand and pursued no strategy designed to further imperial expansion; and they did not preside over their country's entrance into the war in hope or expectation of acquiring more territory.

The same was true of Germany, although it expanded its ambitions as early as September 1914, as did other countries on both sides. They began by fighting to keep what they had. But once at war, which opened up all possibilities, they drew up wish lists, and then grew so attached to their desires that they were determined not to make peace without achieving them. The longer they fought, the more extravagant grew their war goals. So it was with Germany, and with France and England too.

As I have written elsewhere, it was not imperialism that caused the war; it was the war that produced a new wave of imperialism. What the belligerents asked at the peace conference bore little resemblance to what drove them to go to war in the first place.

We have seen why Austria and Germany went to war. What drove France and Russia to join in the fray can be covered in a sentence: Germany declared war on them, and they defended themselves. Of the Great Powers that stood together against Germany and Austria in August 1914, only Britain had been allowed the freedom to decide for itself whether to go in or to stay out.

One of the most extraordinary stories of the war's origins is that of how Britons, who were mostly against participating in the war as late as August 1 or 2, changed their minds and came close to becoming unanimous in favor of joining in by August 3. They were persuaded to change their minds by Sir Edward Grey. The issue on which he carried his case was Belgium.

Belgian neutrality had been guaranteed twice by the powers during the nineteenth century. There was no question that, as a guarantor, Britain was entitled to defend Belgium's neutrality if it chose to do so. What was less clear was whether Britain was *obligated* to intervene if its fellow signatories decided not to do so. There was a real question as to whether the guarantee by the European powers was joint or several.

Yet, for whatever reason, the cause of Belgium excited an emotional response among Britons of all sorts, politics, and persuasions. Some said that Britain's honor required it to keep its promise to protect Belgium. Some said that Germany, by violating a treaty obligation, had to be punished for not keeping *its* word. Others venerated neutrality and Belgium's dedication to defending it. Still others believed that England should keep big countries from trampling on the rights of small ones. Then there were those who viewed the neutrality of Belgium as a British vital interest, picturing the Channel ports in the hands of a potential enemy as a strategic threat to the British islands.

For large numbers of the British cabinet, Parliament, and the public, one or another of these aspects of the Belgian question—skillfully combined by Grey in his masterly speech to the Commons on August 3—brought about a change of mind. For Grey's audience, the martyrdom of Belgium was not the pretext; it was, in all honesty, the real reason for throwing England and its people into a life-or-death struggle. It was why Britain *said* it was going to war; and it was also why Britain *believed* it was going to war.

But Asquith and Grey, who led the country into war, did so not for the sake of a British ideal but for the sake of a British vital interest. There is reason to believe that had Belgian neutrality been violated by France rather than by Germany, Asquith and Grey would have looked the other way. But what Germany was doing threatened

Britain. By destroying France as a Power, Germany would destroy the balance of power in Europe, and would threaten to bring Britain's global supremacy to an end. By controlling the length of the French and Belgian Atlantic coast, including the Channel ports, Germany would render the British islands permanently vulnerable to attack, bombardment, or invasion. For Asquith and Grey, the war was about the balance of power and national security.

At one time it was common for historians to say (as Elie Halévy did, quoted earlier) that the Anglo-German duel in the First World War was about Germany's challenge to Britain's supremacy in the existing European system. England was depicted as fighting a defensive war to preserve the status quo; Germany, as a dynamic aggressor seeking to change the world.

Now that theory requires qualification. Both Germany and Britain were seeking in at least some respects to preserve the existing balance of power, as they perceived it to be. Germany could not afford to lose Austria either as an ally or as a Great Power; Britain could not afford to lose France either as an ally or as a Great Power. Germany fought to save Austria; Britain fought to save France. In the first instance, both sides went to war to retain what they had: their closest ally. In that sense it was—at the outset, though only at the outset—a defensive conflict on both sides.

It also was, in the case of the Prussian Junker caste in Germany, a defensive war in a larger sense. Moltke's officer corps was infused with a sense of pessimism that derived from an inability to see any way in which to preserve much longer its values, way of life, and dominant position—even within Germany.

We owe to Fritz Fischer the discovery that the German government prepared a grandiose program of war goals in September 1914: a grand design. It was expansionist and imperialist. But it was September's program, not July's. It was not what moved Falkenhayn and Moltke to act.

So it was, not only with the belligerents of 1914, but even of those who joined in the fighting later. What caused a country to enter the war was not always the same as what caused it to continue the war. They went to war for one set of reasons, but developed other reasons for battling their enemies as the conflict went on. Their differences with the other side widened, intensified, and shifted to new grounds. British entry into the conflict transformed a European war into a global war. America's entry into the war and into world affairs in 1917 changed balance-of-power equations. America's participation, together with the two Russian revolutions that year, brought ideological dimensions into the conflict that had not been there before, but that were to shape the rest of the twentieth century.

In the beginning, however, it was simply Great Powers fighting to stay where they were and to hold on to what they had.

CHAPTER 48: **WHO COULD HAVE PREVENTED IT?**

In the few days allowed to them, experienced and talented European statesmen in July 1914 scrambled to try to prevent war from breaking out. Why did they fail? Were they, as some say, simply not skillful enough? In the ninety years that have elapsed, speculation as to what could have been done has been practically endless. *Could* anything have been done?

The common assumption today is that everybody wants peace if it can be had on acceptable terms. What Europe did not understand at the time was that, exceptionally, it was not true of two governments in 1914. Vienna did not merely want to get its way with Serbia; it wanted to provoke a war with Serbia. Berlin did not want to get its way with Russia; it wanted to provoke a war with Russia. In each case it was war itself that the government wanted—or, put more precisely, it wanted to crush its adversary to an extent that only a successful war makes possible.

It takes at least two to keep the peace, but it takes only one to start a war. If a government is determined to bring on a war, no appeasement, no matter how extensive or imaginative, will restrain it. Europe, having failed to understand what happened to it in 1914, had to be taught that lesson all over again in the aftermath of Munich in 1938–39. Only countervailing power will stop a government bent on launching an invasion.

In the case of Austria's war, Vienna recognized that it could not get away with attacking Serbia unless Berlin offered protection. Given German cover, it was free to do what it liked. Of course Austria also needed to obtain (and did) the approval and support of Hungary. Thereafter nothing could stop Austria-Hungary's march toward war.

Europe's statesmen were in the dark about Austria's motives, and therefore were disoriented. They assumed that the Hapsburg Empire was what it pretended to be: a country with a grievance that it wanted remedied. In fact, it did not want its grievance remedied; it wanted a pretext. Austria did not seek justice, for that would have deprived it of an excuse for doing what it really wanted to do: go to war. It issued an ultimatum, not in order to bully Serbia into accepting it, but rather to force Serbia into rejecting it.

Of course the cumbersome machinery of the Austro-Hungarian government moved slowly. By early August, the Hapsburg armies had not initiated the hostilities that they should have concluded in July. But, at however snail-like a pace, the Dual Monarchy moved straight ahead toward its goal, never stopping, never deviating, never allowing itself to be distracted or turned aside. It was headed for the battlefield, and it would allow nothing to keep it from going there.

Could Britain or France or even Russia have done anything differently to stop the Austrian war on Serbia? Now we have the satisfaction of knowing that nothing they could have done would have kept Austria from attacking Serbia. Austria wanted war and could have been restrained only by Germany.

Herewith two counterfactuals: two might-have-beens. The first is that the German government might have followed the Kaiser's orders the week of July 27 and withdrawn support of the Dual

Monarchy unless it agreed to peace on German terms. The result might have been a dazzling diplomatic triumph for the German-speaking allies. Peace probably would have been secured on terms favorable to Austria and Serbia would have been severely punished.

A second counterfactual: Russia might have taken itself out of the conflict. This might have happened if Russia had been convinced of Serbian guilt in the Sarajevo affair. Russia could have made common cause with Austria against the regicides and terrorists, and given Vienna carte blanche, as Germany had done, to solve the problems as best it could, in its dealings with Serbia.

Had Russia done so, it would have deprived Germany's military leaders of the conditions and pretexts necessary to initiate their proposed war against Russia and France. A world war would at least have been postponed and at best prevented.

In the case of Germany's war, rather more stood in the way of those who wanted to initiate hostilities. The labor movement and the Social Democrats in Germany had to be won over, but that was accomplished by Bethmann during the turbulent last week of July. The complicated requirements of Germany's generals—the things that had to be done before they could start their war—had to do with Austria.

As seen earlier, Vienna had to be persuaded to commit its armies for one purpose, the Serbian venture, but then instead to use them in another venture: Germany's crusade against Russia, which Berlin was presenting at home as Russia's crusade against Germany.

All having been achieved, however, there was nothing to stop the German government from starting a war at the time most favorable to it—which turned out to be August 1, 1914. The strongest power on the Continent, with the most powerful army in the world, was doing what it deemed necessary to maintain its position. It is difficult to resist the conclusion that nothing could have stopped it.

A question asked throughout the twentieth century in one way or another was put this way by historian James Joll: why, since "War had been avoided in the immediately preceding crises—1908, 1911, 1913"—was it "not avoided in 1914?"

One answer is that in the previous crises none of the Great Powers had wanted to have a war. In 1914 two of them did. And one reason that Germany did not want to go to war in those previous crises was that it could not count on Austria—and Germany's generals were convinced that without Austrian troops holding back the Russians during the opening weeks of the war, they might not win.

CHAPTER 49: **WHO STARTED IT?**

Briefly and roughly stated, the answer is that the government of Austria-Hungary started its local war with Serbia, while Germany's military leaders started the worldwide war against France and Russia that became known as the First World War or the Great War.

Wars in the modern world tend to break out for a complex of reasons, and to involve a multitude of participants at various levels in the decision-making process. Impersonal forces can come into play, as can institutional pressures. Cultural predilections and affinities can shape events. The varied interests at work in a modern society often make domestic politics as much a focus of concern as international relations in determining whether and when countries go to war. Even so, accidents, blunders, misunderstandings, the characteristics of individuals, and other random factors continue to explain much of what actually happens.

The peculiarity of the First World War is that, even though it occurred in modern times, somewhat democratic and, to an extent, responsive to the voices of the public, its origins involved so few people: a handful in a handful of countries. It is not just that a tiny number of individuals made the decisions; it is startling that few people even knew that anything was happening or that decisions were there to be made or were being made. It was a crisis that arose and was played out in secret.

Of course, seen in broader perspective, powerful forces were at work over the course of decades and even centuries that created the world in which the Great War broke out: the explosion of the Industrial Revolution, the spread of nationalism, the rise of science, the triumph of imperialism, and the militarism of German society that was a product of how Germany was united in the 1860s and 1870s. But none of these mass movements and happenings explain the *immediate* outbreak of the war. None reveal why Europe did not put a match to the explosive material in the summer of 1913 but did so in the summer of 1914.

The people who lit the fuse were, of course, the products of their family backgrounds, of their societies, and of the historical circumstances in which they acted. Nor did they—nor could anybody— really speak for themselves alone. When Moltke, for example, spoke, he did so for the 650 members of the Great General Staff and, to some extent, for the officer corps as a whole. He spoke with the weight of his office; he was more than just an individual.

In suggesting that one or more individuals started the First World War, I am using words in their most everyday and ordinary sense. I mean that there were men who wanted to start a war, and who deliberately acted in such a way as to start one, and who succeeded, by what they did, in starting a war. So the detective in a murder mystery, summing up the evidence for the houseguests in the library, might point a finger accusingly and say: "There is the person who did it!" In the case of Germany we point to Moltke. He started the world war, and he did so deliberately.

In the case of the Austro-Serbian war, the obvious criminal was Gavrilo Princip. The teenage drifter and failed poet probably (though not certainly) conceived the Sarajevo murder plot, led it, and by his determination and persistence carried it through despite orders to abort, pleas to turn back, and changes of circumstance.

But Princip did not intend to inspire Austria to invade Serbia. Quite the contrary, under questioning by his captors he attempted to keep them from learning of any connection between the Serbs and himself. Moreover, the Austro-Hungarian foreign office was at work planning the destruction of Serbia even before Princip struck. The troubled and confused adolescent terrorist did indeed open the door to the Austrian invasion by killing the Archduke who had been blocking the way, but Princip did not know that; what he did, in that respect, was inadvert.

Kaiser Wilhelm, Chancellor Bethmann, Foreign Minister Jagow, and an assortment of their German military and civilian colleagues encouraged the Austrians to launch an attack on Serbia, and so were directly responsible for that war. In the case of the Kaiser, there was mitigation; when it looked as though there were a peaceful solution, he opted for it enthusiastically.

Austro-Hungarian Foreign Minister Count Leopold von Berchtold was the man most responsible for bringing about the Serbian war. Sometime during or after the Balkan wars he decided that his country could survive only if Serbia were crushed and altogether eliminated as a factor in politics. He seems to have believed that a merely diplomatic triumph would be insubstantial and might not last. Only victory in war would achieve his goal, and that could be accomplished only if Germany would keep Russia from interfering, while big Austria-Hungary crushed little Serbia.

As soon as Germany's blank check was received, Berchtold put himself to work starting his war. He was, like Princip, persistent and undiscouraged. He refused to be turned aside.

He would not be drawn into conversations or negotiations that might trap him into keeping the peace—even (and this confused other leaders) on favorable terms. The other players in European politics found the July crisis uniquely puzzling because they sensed they were missing something. What they were missing was the knowledge that Vienna did not want peace. They assumed that Berchtold hoped to secure his terms, which might well have been extreme. But he did not desire his terms or any terms; he preferred to fight a war. After the war (as his envoy Count Hoyos made clear in July 1914 in conversations in Berlin) he did not want (as the Kaiser wanted) a subservient Serbia; he wanted there to be no Serbia at all.

To the problem posed for his country by Serbia, he wanted, one might say, a final solution.

Berchtold operated under severe handicaps: the machinery of the Austro-Hungarian state moved with maddening slowness. He could not move swiftly enough to achieve the *fait accompli* that the Germans asked. Everything took time—time during which the powers might impose a peace. Since his armies could not move for weeks, he declared war anyway, doing nothing but using the "at war" status to fend off potential peacemakers.

Berchtold was surrounded by his foreign office staff, the firebrands inherited from Aehrenthal. They may have inspired him. The cabinet of Austro-Hungary—even Tisza, after holding out against him for a week—supported him. All shared his responsibility for the war. It need hardly be said that Conrad was Berchtold's full partner in starting the war.

Berchtold had one great asset in pursuing his goal. The foreign minister of any other Great Power would have been reined in by his allies. If Russia wanted to invade a neighbor, France—which financed Russia's military expansion—would keep St. Petersburg from doing so. When Germany meddled in Morocco in 1911, even Austria refused support and thereby helped stop Berlin. Only one country in Europe had an ally that would *not* restrain it—that would support it blindly. That was Austria, backed unconditionally by Germany, and against all odds that was the one country in Europe that was led by a man who was determined to start a war.

Why was Berchtold able to start a war? The answer is, because there was nobody to stop him. He was the only leader in Europe, we now know, whose ally gave him carte blanche. It should be noted, though, that he did not use it on his own. He declared war only when—and because—the German foreign minister, Jagow, told him to do so. So Jagow was one more person who started the Austro-Serbian war.

In the case of the preventive war against Russia and France, it had been contemplated by the leaders of the German army for a long time. It was a policy proposal that tended to surface whenever crises emerged. Moltke is the one usually quoted as advancing it, but he seems to have spoken for the officer corps as a whole. When the July crisis blew up, therefore, it looked to the German generals like the time to act rather than merely talk.

Falkenhayn and Moltke took the lead. They were the officers, supported by their military colleagues, who made the real decision for war in the summer of 1914. They thought they knew what they were doing. Moltke had predicted that the war would lead European civilization to ruin, but he felt the war to be inevitable. He believed that all he was deciding—all that he was in a position to decide—was when it would take place. And he did decide that.

Here again it confuses the issue to think in terms of one war rather than two. At the outset—at the time of the Outrage and the blank check—there was only the Serbian war initiative on the table: war was proposed by the Austrians. But it was the civilian government of Germany that crafted an actual plan of operations for Austria. And it was that civilian government—the Chancellor and his foreign office—that monitored Austria's performance.

So little progress had been made by the Dual Monarchy in initiating a war by the last week of July (according to Germany's generals)—or in arriving at a settlement (according to the Kaiser)—that neither side in Germany was willing to let the Chancellor, the foreign office, and the Austrians continue to be in charge of the operation.

Vienna had wanted to start and win a war, but as of the end of July had failed to do so. All it had created was what it—and the Kaiser and Bethmann—had wanted *not* to create: a war crisis, involving, to some extent, all the powers of Europe. But the German generals began to see that a war crisis was something they *did* want.

Such a war crisis, and such internationalization, created confusion. As spectators during July, Moltke, Falkenhayn, and Germany's other military leaders pondered the uses to which such confusion could be put. They had been willing to let Austria have its Serbian adventure, although it meant little to Germany; but now Austria had bungled it, and in doing so had involved itself perhaps inextricably, so Germany now could count on the Austro-Hungarian Empire's full support in launching a new war initiative of Germany's own—a war against the other powers of Europe.

The German government therefore was in the process of changing its policy from the weekend of July 25 onward. The Kaiser and the Chancellor, albeit with some misgivings, let Moltke and Falkenhayn have their way. In the confusion of a European war crisis, the German generals cleverly substituted one war for another. The world was deluded into believing, then and thereafter, that one grew out of the other, but it was not so; one had to be overridden in order to pursue the other.

On the part of Moltke and Falkenhayn, it was a supreme act of opportunism. They saw their opening and swiftly took advantage of it. It was as though they had seen a passenger airliner parked on a runway, fully fueled and ready to take off, boarded it and commandeered it, and at gunpoint forced the captain to divert from his scheduled destination to someplace in the opposite direction. Moltke and Falkenhayn had succeeded in an unprecedented act of political hijacking; they had taken over Berchtold's war against Serbia, and had forced it instead to take them to their own war against France and Russia.

CHAPTER 50: **COULD IT HAPPEN AGAIN?**

In the aftermath of the First World War—in the 1920s and 1930s—the survivors came to look upon that disastrous conflict as a European civil war. To have ignited it was condemned either as a ghastly mistake or as a dreadful crime. The overriding lesson of the catastrophe was deemed to be that humankind never must allow such a thing to happen again.

Of course it *did* happen again when, in 1939–45, the Allies—France, Britain, Russia, and the United States—continued the fight that had not been resolved in 1914–18. But then actual hostilities among the surviving powers—Britain, Russia, and the United States— did *not* develop when they failed to reach agreement on the peace terms that ought to have ended the two parts of the 1914–45 world war. They turned instead to a war that was "cold."

In managing the Cuban Missile Crisis of 1962, U.S. President John F. Kennedy was haunted by what he believed he had learned from reading about the origins of World War I in Barbara Tuchman's

The Guns of August. He felt that the war had been the result of an unintended chain reaction.

The Kennedy generation was educated in the interwar years, at a time when the leading American text, *The Origins of the World War* by Sidney B. Fay, taught that none of the Great Powers had wanted a war among themselves. They had been caught up in the Great War nonetheless, for which Austria-Hungary was more responsible than the other countries, although not even Vienna deliberately brought the war about. Similar views were popularized by Tuchman, whose book reached a mass audience.

Based on the evidence available in those pre-Fischer times, Fay's teachings seemed to be close to the truth, and even in Europe, leading scholars and politicians arrived at conclusions much like his.

In his war memoirs, former British Prime Minister David Lloyd George famously claimed that "the nations slithered over the brink into the boiling cauldron of war without a trace of apprehension or dismay." Raymond Aron, one of the greatest political thinkers of the twentieth century, saw in the story of July 1914 "the unleashing of the First World War which none of the principal actors consciously or directly wished for."

The lesson to be learned from the Great War, the world was told, is that governments must be careful not to lose control. They must not let confrontations inadvertently spill over into hostilities. They must not let small wars escalate into big wars. They must not let brushfires blaze into forest fires.

These are good lessons to learn, but it is not July 1914 that teaches them. It was no accident that Europe went to war at that time. It was the result of premeditated decisions by two governments. Once those two countries had invaded their neighbors, there was no way for the neighbors to keep the peace. That was true in World War II; at Pearl Harbor, Japan made the war-or-peace decision not merely for itself, but for the unwilling United States as well, by launching its attack. Nor had America any more choice in Europe in 1941; Hitler's Germany declared war on the United States, to which America was obliged to respond.

To repeat, it takes two or more to keep the peace, but only one to start a war. And that means that it *could* happen again. An aggressor can start a major war even today and even if other great powers desire to stay at peace—unless other nations are powerful enough to deter it.

At least one thing has changed greatly between then and now. In 1914 the coming of war was an almost complete surprise to the public. In the open world of today we would be likely to have at least some sort of advance warning. In turn, that would give peoples and parliaments at least a chance to make their views known. How much of a difference that might make is difficult to foretell.

CHAPTER 51: **SUMMING UP**

The international conflict in the summer of 1914 consisted of two wars, not one. Both were started deliberately. They were intertwined. They were started by rival empires that were bound together by mutual need. One war was launched by the Hapsburg Empire and the other by the German Empire. In each case the decision to launch a war was made by a few individuals at the top, whose peoples were unaware that such decisions were being considered, let alone made.

The wars were about power. Specifically, they were about relative ranking among the great European powers that at the time ruled most of the world. Both Germany and Austria believed themselves to be on the way down. Each started a war in order to stay where it was.

Austria's war on Serbia was, like so many terrible but small Balkan wars, one of history's minor episodes. It would have been soon forgotten had it not provided the German generals with the conditions they needed in order to start a war of their own: a European conflict, which grew into a global conflict. Although soldiers in the trenches for the four long years beginning in 1914 came to believe that the war was pointless, that was not so. It was about the most important issue in politics: who should rule the world.

The question was opened up in 1914 by the German war. In the decades that followed, new powers and forces arose to contest it. Whether Germany or Russia should control Europe, and whether Europe should continue to rule Africa and much of Asia, were issues that overlapped with rival ideologies: communism, fascism, Nazism, liberal democracy, and others. By the 1990s the question seemed finally to have been answered. Almost all the peoples in the world ruled themselves, rather than being ruled by foreigners; and most aspired to democracy, however defined.

The decision for war in 1914 was purposeful; and the war itself was not, as generations of historians have taught, meaningless. On the contrary, it was fought to decide the essential questions in international politics: who would achieve mastery in Europe, and therefore in the world, and under the banners of what faith.

EPILOGUE

CHAPTER 52: **AUSTRIA'S WAR**

From the beginning—which is to say, from mid-June, when Berchtold put his foreign office to work on a plan—Vienna's intent had been to crush Serbia without outside interference. To be able to focus all resources on the Serbian campaign was the Austrian dream. Vienna had declared war on Serbia July 28. Conrad von Hötzendorf, Austria's chief of staff, promptly sent half his army by railroad to the Serbian frontier, with the other half in reserve to back it up.

The Austrians learned almost at once that they and their German ally had been working at cross-purposes. Vienna had planned its invasion of Serbia in the belief that Berlin would take steps to keep Russia out of the war. Instead Germany deliberately was pulling Russia *into* the war.

Germany opted for war during the week of July 27 and made its move final on July 31. Mobilization was ordered that day, to be followed by a declaration of war on Russia the following day. Moltke and his colleagues in Berlin told Conrad to forgo a Serbian campaign for the time being and instead to send the bulk of his army to the Russian frontier, leaving only a skeleton force to defend against a possible Serbian attack. If Conrad complied—if he recalled troops to new positions before they had taken up the old ones—he risked bringing about administrative confusion.

The logistics of such a move were challenging. In any event Conrad did not want to do it. He had been scheming to bring about a Serbian war for so many years that it must have seemed unbearable to give it up at the last moment—just as he had gotten agreement for it—in order to help Germany first. He decided that his forces would remain in the Serbian campaign for a while but then some would be withdrawn on August 18 and reassigned to the Russian front.

Conrad wanted to cash Germany's blank check before Germany had a chance to withdraw it. He was trying to launch the invasion of Serbia in August that he was supposed to have initiated—and concluded—in July. In a letter to Moltke dated August 2, he explained that he was continuing to conduct his operations against Serbia in such a way as to keep Russia from entering the war.

One of the things that emerges from Conrad's various explanations is that he did not understand that Germany's policy and objectives had changed. On July 5–6 the Kaiser had hoped—and had been sure—that Europe would remain inactive on the sidelines while Austria succeeded in crushing Serbia. Germany's policy had been to persuade Russia, France, Britain, and the others to stay out. Now, animated by Moltke, Falkenhayn, and their colleagues, Berlin had reversed itself. Conrad was being told that Germany no longer was backing Austria's war and that Austria now had to back Germany's war.

Moltke and Conrad never had really coordinated their war plans fully. Since each proposed to use the other for his own purposes, the two army chiefs may have felt they could not afford to be too open with one another. In any event, they were paying the price for it in the opening months of the war, as each attempted to go his own way and to get his own way.

Conrad had wanted Russia deterred. He much preferred not to go to war with the Russians—or the French, or, later, the British, or, later still, the Americans. Germany's role, as Conrad saw it, was to keep Russia out of the fight—not to bring it into the conflict. The only country Conrad wanted to fight in the summer of 1914 was Serbia.*

But as pre-Sarajevo history demonstrated, Germany did not see Serbia as a danger. It felt no need to eliminate the Balkan kingdom. It was Conrad and his government that feared Serbia. Moltke feared Russia and its ally France. From Germany's point of view, the only use for the Serbian conflict was that it bound Austria to remain faithful to Germany in Germany's war against Russia and France. By August 1, 1914, that goal had been accomplished. From Moltke's point of view, the Serbian affair had served its purpose. But from Conrad's perspective it had not.

Hence Conrad played truant in the opening weeks of the two intertwined wars: he ordered his soldiers to ride the trains south instead of north. In doing so he stole for his country a fleeting chance to engage in its private duel with Serbia, one against one. His armies invaded Serbia. They brought the Serbians to battle. And—crushingly, overwhelmingly—the Austrians lost!

The Hapsburg armies never seemed to have recovered from their initial mislocations and dislocations. After attacking Serbia and being defeated, their private war was concluded, and they joined the wider conflict. They moved to the Russian front and were crushed there too.

By the beginning of December 1914 the Hapsburg Empire, according to John Keegan, no longer was a military great power; he tells us that it had lost 1,268,000 men out of 3,350,000 mobilized. Austria fought on, under German high commanders, in a struggle not so much to conquer as to survive.

Conrad was in despair. At the start of the war, awarded a medal, he had remarked: "If only I knew for what." As the failures mounted he confided to colleagues that if he lost the war it would "cost him the comfort of his beloved Gina." He was overcome by self-pity. All the blame, he reflected, would be "unloaded on to me. I will probably have to disappear from the scene like an outlaw. I have no home, no woman who will stand by my side in my final years."

---

*Conrad was bellicose, and in other circumstances would happily have waged war against such neighbors as Italy.

He remembered his sometime mentor, the Archduke Franz Ferdinand, who cared so much for his beloved Austrian army, and who,
year after year, had opposed the plans to fight Serbia and to estrange
Russia: the Archduke, whose murder had been exploited cynically by
Vienna in order to bring about the very war he so ardently opposed.
Franz Ferdinand's shadow loomed large over the world that summer.
What would he have thought? What would he have said? What
would he have done? Had the Archduke still been alive, Conrad had
to admit, he "would have had me shot."

CHAPTER 53: **GERMANY'S WAR**

B erchtold (especially in July) and Conrad (especially in August) were the active agents who led Austria into a war with Serbia. They did so with full support from the cabinet and the foreign office of the Dual Monarchy, and with at least the approval of the elderly emperor. There is no question that the two of them did it—and meant to do it. The only question in that regard is the extent to which Berchtold was influenced by his foreign office staff.

Berchtold frequently is named as the single person who also was most responsible for the wider war. That, as we can see now, is not true. The accusation confuses the two wars. What he wanted was the Serbian war, not the other one. He was willing to risk a wider conflict if he had to, but he did not desire it.

It was Moltke who wanted a war against Russia and France. He always had held back—or had been held back—from initiating such a war in past crises because the circumstances never had been quite right. Everything had to be in place: the Kaiser's authority had to be on the wane, Austrian participation had to be assured, and Russia had to look like the aggressor. Suddenly, toward the end of July 1914, all *did* fall into place. Moltke leaped at the chance; he saw that his hour had come, and he seized it. His artful substitution of his war for Berchtold's on Berlin's July agenda was a sort of confidence trick that kept generations afterwards in the dark as to who caused what. He had exchanged early July's policy for a late July policy, and one war for another.

He could not have done it had he not represented a force bigger than himself. He represented the Prussian Junker officer caste whose militarization of German life led to the war. Germany's militarist culture had been identified in 1914 as the cause of the coming war by, among others, Colonel House.

Germany declared war on Russia August 1. Its proposed timetable was the Moltke plan. The plan called for the German army to meet its rendezvous with destiny on French soil in six weeks. There and then it would bring France, Russia's ally, to battle. The battle would be decisive. It was intended to knock France out of the war, out of the Russian alliance, and out of the political history of Europe.

Six weeks after August 1 the German army did indeed meet its rendezvous with destiny on French soil. For friends of France and Britain, it was a heart-stoppingly close-run thing; the Germans almost won it. Instead France and Britain did. And the battle—the first battle of the Marne—was decisive. What it decided was that neither side could gain a quick victory or a real victory. Instead, the conflict was to become an endurance contest lasting four years, and ruining victor and vanquished alike. Nor were its results in 1918 conclusive, for the parties did not accept them as such.

The war between Germany, on one side, and Russia, France, Britain, and the United States, on the other, resumed in 1939–41; and it too failed to resolve the question of which power would be supreme on the Continent—and whether the United States and Britain would accept that supremacy. The conflict that Germany's military leaders initiated by declaring war on Russia August 1, 1914, did not come to an end until the last Russian soldier left German soil on August 31, 1994.

For nearly a century, debate has raged among participants and then among scholars about the decisive battle with which the Moltke plan concluded: the battle of the Marne in September 1914. On the German side, the question was whether it was Moltke or his young envoy Richard Hentsch who ordered the retreat and regroupment behind the Marne; and whether ordering the withdrawal was the correct decision or whether it snatched defeat from the jaws of victory. At the time thirty-three German generals were fired by the Kaiser. Shortly afterwards, Moltke, too, lost his job. Wilhelm was unforgiving.

Moltke obviously could not have foreseen the full hideousness of the long war of the twentieth century (the 1914 war that led to the 1939 war that led to the Cold War), nor the tens of millions who would die in it nor the multitude of consequences to which the war directly or indirectly would give rise. But he knew well enough who had started the war.

In June 1915, Moltke, who had been shifted to a job he regarded as of little importance, complained of this to his friend General (Baron) Colmar von der Goltz. "It is dreadful to be condemned to inactivity in this war," he wrote to his friend: *"this war which I prepared and initiated"* (emphasis added). It is an arresting thought that, to the extent that any individual did so, this modest, unexceptional, and indeed rather ordinary career army officer started the Great War, and thereby ushered in the twentieth century, with all of its horrors and wonders.

APPENDIX I: THE AUSTRIAN NOTE

Count Berchtold, Austrian minister for foreign affairs, to Count Mensdorff, Austrian ambassador in London. (Communicated by Count Mensdorff, July 24, 1914.) (Translation.) (From British documents in Public Record Office.)

The Austro-Hungarian Government felt compelled to address the following note to the Serbian Government on the 23rd July, through the medium of the Austro-Hungarian Minister at Belgrade:—

"On the 31st March, 1909, the Serbian Minister in Vienna, on the instructions of the Serbian Government, made the following declaration to the Imperial and Royal Government:—

"Serbia recognises that the *fait accompli* regarding Bosnia has not affected her rights, and consequently she will conform to the decisions that the Powers may take in conformity with article 25 of the Treaty of Berlin. In deference to the advice of the Great Powers, Serbia undertakes to renounce from now onwards the attitude of protest and opposition which she has adopted with regard to the annexation since last autumn. She undertakes, moreover, to modify the direction of her policy with regard to Austria-Hungary and to live in future on good neighbourly terms with the latter.

"The events of recent years, and in particular the painful events of the 28th June last, have shown the existence of a subversive movement wit the object of detaching a part of the territories of Austria-Hungary from the Monarchy. The movement, which had its birth under the eye of the Serbian Government, has gone so far as to make itself manifest on both sides of the Serbian frontier in the shape of acts of terrorism and a series of outrages and murders.

"Far from carrying out the formal undertakings contained in the declaration of the 31st March, 1909, the Royal Serbian Government has done nothing to repress these movements. It has permitted the criminal machinations of various societies and associations directed against the Monarchy, and has tolerated unrestrained language on the part of the press, the glorification of the perpetrators of outrages, and the participation of officers and functionaries in subversive agitation. It has permitted an unwholesome propaganda in public instruction, in short, it has permitted all manifestations of a nature to incite the Serbian population to hatred of the Monarchy and contempt of its institutions.

"This culpable tolerance of the Royal Serbian Government had not ceased at the moment when the events of the 28th June last proved its fatal consequences to the whole world.

"It results from the depositions and confessions of the criminal perpetrators of the outrage of the 28th June that the Serajevo assassinations were planned in Belgrade; that the arms and explosives with which the murderers were provided had been given to them by Serbian officers and functionaries belonging to the Narodna Odbrana; and finally, that the passage into Bosnia of the criminals and their arms was organised and effected by the chiefs of the Serbian frontier service.

"The above-mentioned results of the magisterial investigation do not permit the Austro-Hungarian Government to pursue any longer the attitude of expectant forbearance which they have maintained for years in the face of the machinations hatched in Belgrade, and thence propagated in the territories of the Monarchy. The results, on the contrary, impose on them the duty of putting an end to the intrigues which form a perpetual menace to the tranquillity of the Monarchy.

"To achieve this end the Imperial and Royal Government see themselves compelled to demand from the Royal Serbian Government a formal assurance that they condemn this dangerous propaganda against the Monarchy; in other words, the whole series of tendencies, the ultimate aim of which is to detach from the Monarchy territories belonging to it, and that they undertake to suppress by every means this criminal and terrorist propaganda.

"In order to give a formal character to this undertaking the Royal Serbian Government shall publish in the front page of their 'Official Journal' of the 26 July the following declaration:—

" 'The Royal Government of Serbia condemn the propaganda directed against Austria-Hungary—i.e., the general tendency of which the final aim is to detach from the Austro-Hungarian Monarchy territories belonging to it, and they sincerely deplore the fatal consequences of these criminal proceedings.

" 'The Royal Government regret that Serbian officers and functionaries participated in the above-mentioned propaganda and thus compromised the good neighbourly relations to which the Royal Government were solemnly pledged by their declaration of the 31st March 1909.

" 'The Royal Government, who disapprove and repudiate all idea of interfering or attempting to interfere with the destinies of the inhabitants of any part whatsoever of Austria-Hungary, consider it their duty formally to warn officers and functionaries, and the whole population of the kingdom, that henceforward they will proceed with the utmost rigour against persons who may be guilty of such machinations, which they will use all their efforts to anticipate and suppress.'

"This declaration shall simultaneously be communicated to the Royal army as an order of the day by his Majesty the King and shall be published in the 'Official Bulletin' of the Army.

"The Royal Serbian Government further undertake:

"1. To suppress any publication which incites to hatred and contempt to the Austro-Hungarian Monarchy and the general tendency of which is directed against its territorial integrity;

"2. To dissolve immediately the society styled Narodna Odbrana, to confiscate all its means of propaganda, and to proceed in the same manner against other societies and their branches in Serbia which engage in propaganda against the Austro-Hungarian Monarchy. The Royal Government shall take the necessary measures to prevent the societies dissolved from continuing their activity under another name and form;

"3. To eliminate without delay from public instruction in Serbia, both as regards the teaching body and also as regards the methods of instruction, everything that serves, or might serve, to foment the propaganda against Austria-Hungary;

"4. To remove from the military service, and from the administration in general, all officers and functionaries guilty of propaganda against the Austro-Hungarian Monarchy whose names and deeds the Austro-Hungarian Government reserve to themselves the right of communicating to the Royal Government;

"5. To accept the collaboration in Serbia of representatives of the Austro-Hungarian Government for the suppression of the subversive movement directed against the territorial integrity of the Monarchy;

"6. To take judicial proceedings against accessories to the plot of the 28th June who are on Serbian territory; delegates of the Austro-Hungarian Government will take part in the investigation relating thereto;

"7. To prevent by effective measures the co-operation of the Serbian authorities in the illicit traffic in arms and explosives across the frontier, to dismiss and punish severely the officials of the frontier service at Schabatz and Loznica guilty of having assisted the perpetrators of the Serajevo crime by facilitating their passage across the frontier;

"8. To prevent by effective measures the cooperation of the Serbian authorities in the illicit traffic in arms and explosives across the frontier, to dismiss and punish severely the officials of the frontier service at Schabatz and Loznica guilty of having assisted the perpetrators of the Serajevo [sic] crime by facilitating their passage across the frontier;

"9. To furnish the Imperial and Royal Government with explanations regarding the unjustifiable utterances of high Serbian officials, both in Serbia and abroad, who, notwithstanding their official position, have not hesitated since the crime of 28th June to express themselves in interviews in terms of hostility to the Austro-Hungarian Government; and, finally.

"10. To notify the Imperial and Royal Government without delay of the execution of the measures comprised under the preceding heads.

"The Austro-Hungarian Government expect the reply of the Royal Government at the latest by 6 o'clock on Saturday evening, the 25th July.

"A memorandum dealing with the results of the magisterial enquiry at Serajevo with regard to the official mentioned under heads (7) and (8) is attached to this note."

I have the honour to request your Excellency to bring the contents of this note to the knowledge of the Government to which you are accredited, accompanying your communication with the following observations:—

On the 31st March, 1909, the Royal Serbian Government addressed to Austria-Hungary the declaration of which the text is reproduced above.

On the very day after this declaration Serbia embarked on a policy of instilling revolutionary ideas into the Serb subjects of the Austro-Hungarian Monarchy, and so preparing for the separation of the Austro-Hungarian territory on the Serbian frontier.

Serbia became the centre of a criminal agitation.

No time was lost in the formation of societies and groups, whose objects, either avowed or secret, was the creation of disorders on Austro-Hungarian territory. These societies and groups count among their members generals and diplomatists, Government officials and judges—in short, men at the top of official and unofficial society in the kingdom.

Serbian journalism is almost entirely directed at the service of this propaganda, which is directed against Austria-Hungary, and not a day passes without the organs of the Serbian press stirring up their readers to hatred or contempt for the neighbouring Monarchy, or to outrages directed more or less openly against its security and integrity.

A large number of agents are employed in carrying on by every means the agitation against Austria-Hungary and corrupting the youth in the frontier provinces.

Since the recent Balkan crisis there has been a recrudescence of the spirit of conspiracy inherent in Serbian politicians, which has left such sanguinary imprints on the history of the kingdom; individuals belonging formerly to bands employed in Macedonia have come to place themselves at the disposal of the terrorist propaganda against Austria-Hungary.

In the presence of these doings, to which Austria-Hungary has been exposed for years, the Serbian Government have not thought it incumbent on them to take the slightest step. The Serbian Government have thus failed in the duty imposed on them by the solemn declaration of the 31st March, 1909, and acted in opposition to the will of Europe and the undertaking given to Austria-Hungary.

The patience of the Imperial and Royal Government in the face of the provocative attitude of Serbia was inspired by the territorial disinterestedness of the Austro-Hungarian Monarchy and the hope that the Serbian Government would end in spite of everything by appreciating Austria-Hungary's friendship at its true value. By observing a benevolent attitude toward the political interests of Serbia, the Imperial and Royal Government hoped that the kingdom would finally decide to follow an analogous line of conduct on its own side. In particular, Austria-Hungary expected a development of this kind in the political ideas of Serbia, when, after the events of 1912, the Imperial and Royal Government, by its disinterested and ungrudging attitude, made such a considerable aggrandisement of Serbia possible.

The benevolence which Austria-Hungary showed toward the neighbouring State had no restraining effect on the proceedings of the kingdom, which continued to tolerate on its territory a propaganda of which the fatal consequences were demonstrated to the whole world on the 28ᵗʰ June last, when the Heir Presumptive to the Monarchy and his illustrious consort fell victims to a plot hatched at Belgrade.

In the presence of this state of things the Imperial and Royal Government have felt compelled to take new and urgent steps at Belgrade with a view to inducing the Serbian Government to stop the incendiary movement that is threatening the security and integrity of the Austro-Hungarian Monarchy.

The Imperial and Royal Government are convinced that in taking this step they will find themselves in full agreement with the sentiments of all civilised nations, who cannot permit regicide to become a weapon that can be employed with impunity in political strife, and the peace of Europe to be continually disturbed by movements emanating from Belgrade.

In support of the above the Imperial and Royal Government hold at the disposal of the British Government a *dossier* elucidating the Serbian intrigues and the connection between these intrigues and the murder of the 28ᵗʰ June.

An identical communication has been addressed to the Imperial and Royal representatives accredited to the other signatory Powers.

You are authorised to leave a copy of this despatch in the hands of the Minister for Foreign Affairs.

Vienna, July 24, 1914

Annex

The criminal enquiry opened by the Court of Serajevo against Gavrilo Princip and his accessories in and before the act of assassination committed by them on the 28ᵗʰ June last has up to the present led to the following conclusions:—

1. The plot, having as its object the assassination of the Archduke Francis Ferdinand at the time of his visit to Serajevo, was formed at Belgrade by Gavrilo Princip, Nedeljiko Cabrinovic, one Milan Ciganovic, and Trifko Grabez, with the assistance of Commander Voija Tankosic.

2. The six bombs and the four Browning pistols and ammunition with which the guilty parties committed the act were delivered to Princip, Cabrinovic, and Grabez by the man Milan Ciganovic and Commander Voija Tankosic at Belgrade.

3. The bombs are hand-grenades coming from the arms depot of the Serbian army at Kragujevac.

4. In order to ensure the success of the act, Ciganovic taught Princip, Cabrinovic, and Grabez how to use the bombs, and gave lessons in firing Browning pistols to Princip and Grabez in a forest near the shooting ground at Top-schider.

5. To enable Princip, Cabrinovic, and Grabez to cross the frontier of Bosnia-Herzegovina and smuggle in their contraband of arms secretly, a secret system of transport was organised by Ciganovic.

By this arrangement the introduction into Bosnia-Herzegovina of criminals and their arms was effected by the officials controlling the frontiers and Chabac (Rade Popovic) and Loznica, as well as by the customs officer Rudivoj Grbic, of Loznica, with the assistance of various individuals.

APPENDIX 2: THE SERBIAN REPLY

Monday, July 27th

Reply of Serbian Government to Austro-Hungarian Note.—(Communicated by the Serbian Minister, July 27.) (Translation.) (From British documents in Public Record Office.)

The Royal Serbian Government have received the communication of the Imperial and Royal Government of the 10th instant, and are convinced that their reply will remove any misunderstanding which may threaten to impair the good neighbourly relations between the Austro-Hungarian Monarchy and the Kingdom of Serbia.

Conscious of the fact that the protests which were made both from the tribune of the national Skuptchina and in the declarations and actions of the responsible representatives of the State—protests which were cut short by the declarations made by the Serbian Government on the 18th March, 1909—have not been renewed on any occasion as regards the great neighbouring Monarchy, and that no attempt had been made since that time, either by the successive Royal Governments or by their organs, to change the political and legal state of affairs created in Bosnia and Herzegovina, the Royal Government draw attention to the fact that in this connection the Imperial and Royal Government have made no representation except one concerning a school book, and that on that occasion the Imperial and Royal Government received an entirely satisfactory explanation. Serbia had several times given proofs of her pacific and moderate policy during the Balkan crisis, and it is thanks to Serbia and to the sacrifice that she has made in the exclusive interest of European peace that that peace has been preserved. The Royal Government cannot be held responsible for manifestations of a private character, such as articles in the press and the peaceable work of societies—manifestations which take place in nearly all countries in the ordinary course of events, and which, as a general rule, escape official control. The Royal Government are all the less responsible, in view of the fact that at the time of the solution of a series of questions which arose between Serbia and Austria-Hungary, they gave proof of a great readiness to oblige, and thus succeeded in settling the majority of these questions to the advantage of the two neighbouring countries.

For these reasons the Royal Government have been pained and surprised at the statements, according to which members of the Kingdom of Serbia are supposed to have participated in the preparations for the crime committed at Serajevo; the Royal Government expected to be invited to collaborate in an investigation of all that concerns this crime, and they were ready, in order to prove the entire correctness of their attitude, to take measures against any persons concerning whom representations were made to them. Falling in, therefore, with the desire of the Imperial and Royal Government, they are prepared to hand over for trial any Serbian subject, without regard to his situation or rank, of whose complicity in the crime of Serajevo proofs are forthcoming, and more especially they undertake to cause to be published on the first page of the "Journal officiel," on the date of the 26th July, the following declaration:—

"The Royal Government of Serbia condemn all propaganda which may be directed against Austria-Hungary, that is to say, all such tendencies as aim at ultimately detaching from the Austro-Hungarian Monarchy territories which form part thereof, and they sincerely deplore the baneful consequences of these criminal movements. The Royal Government regret that, according to the communication from the Imperial and Royal Government, certain Serbian officers and officials should have taken part in the above-mentioned propaganda, and thus compromised the good neighbourly relations to which the Royal Serbian Government was solemnly engaged by the declaration of the 31st March, 1909, which declaration disapproves and repudiates all idea or attempt at interference with the destiny of the inhabitants of any part whatsoever of Austria-Hungary, and they consider it their duty to formally warn the officers, officials and entire population of the kingdom that henceforth they will take the most rigorous steps against all such persons as are guilty of such acts, to prevent and to repress which they will use their utmost endeavour."

This declaration will be brought to the knowledge of the Royal Army in an order of the day, in the name of His Majesty the King, by His Royal Highness the Crown Prince Alexander, and will be published in the next official army bulletin.

The Royal Government further undertake:—

To introduce at the first regular convocation of the Skuptchina a provision into the press law providing for the most severe punishment of incitement to hatred or contempt of the Austro-Hungarian Monarchy, and for taking action against any publication the general tendency of which is directed against the territorial integrity of Austria-Hungary. The Government engage at the approaching revision of the Constitution to cause an amendment to be introduced into article 22 of the Constitution of such a nature that such publication may be confiscated, a proceeding at present impossible under the categorical terms of article 22 of the Constitution.

The Government possess no proof, nor does the note of the Imperial and Royal Government furnish them with any, that the "Narodna Odbrana" and other similar societies have committed up to the present any criminal act of this nature through the proceedings of any of their members. Nevertheless, the Royal Government will accept the demand of the Imperial and Royal Government, and will dissolve the "Narodna Odbrana" Society and every other society which may be directing its efforts against Austria-Hungary.

The Royal Serbian Government undertake to remove without delay from their public educational establishments in Serbia all that serves or could serve to foment propaganda against Austria-Hungary, whenever the Imperial and Royal Government furnish them with facts and proofs of this propaganda.

The Royal Government also agree to remove from military service all such persons as the judicial enquiry may have proved to be guilty of acts directed against the integrity of the territory of the Austro-Hungarian Monarchy, and they expect the Imperial and Royal Government to communicate to them at a later date the names and the acts of these officers and officials for the purposes of the proceedings which are to be taken against them.

The Royal Government must confess that they do not clearly grasp the meaning or the scope of the demand made by the Imperial and Royal Government that Serbia shall undertake to accept the collaboration of the organs of the Imperial and Royal Government upon their territory, but they declare that they will admit such collaboration as agrees with the principle of international law, with criminal procedure, and with good neighbourly relations.

It goes without saying that the Royal Government consider it their duty to open an enquiry against all such persons as are, or eventually may be, implicated in the plot of the 15th June, and who happen to be within the territory of the kingdom. As regards the participation in this enquiry of Austro-Hungarian agents or authorities appointed for this purpose by the Imperial and Royal Government, the Royal Government cannot accept such an arrangement, as it would be a violation of the Constitution and of the law of criminal procedure; nevertheless, in concrete cases communications as to the results of the investigation in question might be given to the Austro-Hungarian agents.

The Royal Government proceeded, on the very evening of the delivery of this note, to arrest Commander Voislav Tankossitch. As regards Milan Ziganovitch, who is a subject of the Austro-Hungarian Monarchy and who up to the 15th June was employed (on probation) by the directorate of railways, it has not yet been possible to arrest him.

The Austro-Hungarian Government are requested to be so good as to supply as soon as possible, in the customary form, the pre-sumptive evidence of guilt, as well as the eventual proofs of guilt which have been collected up to the present, at the enquiry at Serajevo for the purposes of the later enquiry.

The Serbian Government will reinforce and extend the measures which have been taken for preventing the illicit traffic of arms and explosives across the frontier. It goes without saying that they will immediately order an enquiry and will severely punish the frontier officials on the Schabatz-Loznitza line who have failed in their duty and allowed the authors of the crime of Serajevo to pass.

The Royal Government will gladly give explanations of the remarks made by their officials whether in Serbia or abroad, in interviews after the crime which according to the statement of the Imperial and Royal Government were hostile toward the Monarchy, as soon as the Imperial and Royal Government have communicated to them the passages in question in these remarks, and as soon as they have shown that the remarks were actually made by the said officials, although the Royal Government will itself take steps to collect evidence and proofs.

The Royal Government will inform the Imperial and Royal Government of the execution of the measures comprised under the above heads, in so far as this has not already been done by the present note, as soon as each measure has been ordered and carried out.

If the Imperial and Royal Government are not satisfied with this reply, the Serbian Government, considering that it is not to the common interest to precipitate the solution of this question, are ready, as always, to accept a pacific understanding, either by referring this question to the decision of the International Tribunal or The Hague, or to the Great Powers which took part in the drawing up of the declaration made by the Serbian Government on the 18th (31st) March, 1909.

Belgrade, July 12 (25), 1914.

WHO WAS WHO

Some of Europe's Officials in 1914

ALEXANDER, Crown Prince
  Serbia: Regent
ASQUITH, Herbert
  Britain: Prime Minister
BENCKENDORFF, Count Alexander
  Russia: ambassador in London
BERCHTOLD, Count Leopold von
  Austria-Hungary: foreign minister
BERTIE, Sir Francis
  Britain: ambassador in Paris
BETHMANN HOLLWEG,
Theobald von
  Germany: Imperial Chancellor
  (prime minister)
BIENVENUE-MARTIN, Jean-Baptiste
  France: minister of justice
BUCHANAN, Sir George
  Britain: ambassador in St. Petersburg
CAMBON, Jules

France: ambassador in Berlin
CAMBON, Paul
  France: ambassador in London
CHURCHILL, Winston S.
  Britain: First Lord of the Admiralty
CONRAD VON HÖTZENDORF, Field
Marshal Franz
  Austria-Hungary: army chief of
  staff
CROWE, Sir Eyre
  Britain: Foreign Office official
FALKENHAYN, General Erich von
  Germany: minister of war
FLOTOW, Ludwig von
  Germany: ambassador in Rome
FORGACH, Count Johann
  Austria-Hungary: foreign ministry
  official
FRANZ FERDINAND, Archduke
  Austria-Hungary: heir apparent

FRANZ JOSEPH, Emperor of Austria
and King of Hungary: monarch

GEORGE V, King-Emperor
Britain: monarch

GIESL VON GIESLINGEN, Baron
Austria-Hungary: minister in
Belgrade

GOSCHEN, Sir Edward
Britain: ambassador in Berlin

GREY, Sir Edward
Britain: foreign secretary

HARTWIG, Nicolai de
Russia: minister in Belgrade

HOYOS, Count Alexander
Austria-Hungary: foreign ministry
chief of staff

IZVOLSKY, Alexander
Russia: ambassador in Paris (ex–
foreign minister)

JAGOW, Gottlieb von
Germany: foreign minister

LICHNOWSKY, Prince Karl von
Germany: ambassador in London

LLOYD GEORGE, David
Britain: Chancellor of the
Exchequer

LYNCKER, General Moritz von
Germany: chief of the Military
Cabinet

MACCHIO, Baron Karl von
Austria-Hungary: foreign ministry
official

MATSCHEKO, Franz von
Austria-Hungary: foreign ministry
official

MOLTKE, General Helmuth von
Germany: army chief of staff

MÜLLER, Admiral Alexander von
Germany: naval aide to Kaiser

NICHOLAS II, Czar
Russia: monarch

NICOLSON, Sir Arthur
Britain: head of Foreign Office

PALÉOLOGUE, Maurice
France: ambassador in St. Petersburg

PASIC, Nicola
Serbia: Prime Minister

POINCARÉ, Raymond
France: President

POTIOREK, General Oskar
Austria-Hungary: governor-general
of Bosnia-Herzegovina

POURTALÈS, Count Friedrich von
Germany: ambassador in St.
Petersburg

RUMBOLD, Sir Horace
Britain: embassy official in Berlin

SAN GIULIANO, Marchese Antonio di
Italy: foreign minister

SAZONOV, Sergei
Russia: foreign minister

SCHEBEKO, Nikolai
Russia: ambassador in Vienna

SCHOEN, Wilhelm von
Germany: ambassador in Paris

STUMM, Wilhelm von
Germany: foreign ministry official

STÜRGKH, Karl
Austria: Prime Minister

SVERBEJEV, Sergei
Russia: ambassador in Berlin

SZAPARY VON SZAPAR, Count
Friedrich
Austria-Hungary: ambassador in St.
Petersburg

SZÖGYÉNI-MARICH, Count Ladislaus
Austria-Hungary: ambassador in
Berlin

TIRPITZ, Admiral Alfred von
Germany: naval minister

TISZA, Count István
Hungary: Prime Minister

TSCHIRSCHKY, Count Heinrich von
Germany: ambassador in Vienna

VIVIANI, René
France: Prime Minister and
foreign minister

WILHELM II, Kaiser
Germany: monarch

ZIMMERMANN, Arthur
Germany: deputy foreign minister

NOTES

PROLOGUE

3   United Airlines Flight 826: based on newspaper accounts at the time.

5   mobilized about 65 million troops: *Encyclopaedia Britannica,* 15th ed., s.vv. "World Wars"

    80 percent of all males: Winter, Parker, and Habeck 2000:2

    20 million . . . perished: Herwig 1997:1

    21 million were wounded: *Encyclopaedia Britannica,* 15th ed., s.vv. "World Wars"

    20 million people died in the influenza pandemic: McNeill 1976:255

    "the greatest tragedy": quoted in *The Economist,* Dec. 31, 1999, p. 30.

6   Kennan wrote: Kennan 1979:3

    Stern . . . writes: Stern 1999:200

    in Winston Churchill's words: Gilbert 1975:355

7   As George Kennan observes: Kennan 1951:51

    " 'post–Cold War era' " . . . " 'post–World War I' era": Miller, Lynn-Jones, and Evera 1991:xi

8   "the war was many things": Lafore 1971:17

12   English observer: Lord Bryce, quoted in Fromkin 1995:58

13   "more summery": Zweig 1943:214

    "a sensible, law-abiding Englishman": Taylor 1965:1

13 André Siegfried: Braudel 1979:104
    John Maynard Keynes: Keynes 1920:11–12
    "much of the final quarter": Micklethwait and Wooldridge 2000:xviii
    "such as I suppose": Kennan 1951:9
14 "Age of Security": Zweig 1943:1
    "There is no doubt": Keiger 1983:133
    "exceptional calm": Ibid.

CHAPTER 3: NATIONS QUARREL

27 "The Press is awful": McLean 2001:98

CHAPTER 4: COUNTRIES ARM

28 "energy like that of the Cross": Adams 1918:383
29 "The plunge of civilization": Fussell 1975:8
31 Edward Grey claimed: Stevenson 1996:1
    "All sides are preparing": Ibid.:203
32 "Slav East": Gunther E. Rothenberg, "Moltke, Schlieffen, and the Doctrine of
    Strategic Envelopment," Paret 1986:306
35 "never achieved the final, perfected form": Daniel Moran, "Alfred von Schlief-
    fen," Cowley and Parker 1996:415
37 "the Kaiser's friend . . . a tall dashing military figure": Mombauer 2001:55
    "the same lottery": Ibid.:54, 56
    "his constant companion": Ibid.:51

CHAPTER 5: ZARATHUSTRA PROPHESIES

40 "Men's minds seem to have been on edge": Taylor 1956:121
41 "No triumph of peace is quite so great": Morris 1979:569
    "the basic principle behind all the events": Strachan 2001:68

CHAPTER 6: DIPLOMATS ALIGN

44 "In the seventeenth and eighteenth centuries": Morgenthau 1978:248
    "He is nothing but a boy": McLean 2001:16
45 "He's raving mad!": Ibid.:44
    "mischievous and unstraight-forward": Ibid.:79

CHAPTER 9: EXPLOSIVE GERMANY

54 "the salient feature": Berghahn 1993:172
55 "We shall . . . receive an increase": Joll 1992:56
56 "to suppress internal revolutions": Berghahn 1993:28
    "one nation is found to have gained": Halévy 1930:6

57   "*90 per cent* of the Reich budget": Berghahn 1993:88
58   John Röhl: Clark 2000:19
      "headstretching machine": Ibid.:20
59   "I am the sole master": Ibid.:123
      "it cannot be done": Ibid.:125
60   "From the mid-1890s onwards": Berghahn 1993:16
62   Fritz Fischer tells us: Fischer 1975:28

CHAPTER 10: MACEDONIA—OUT OF CONTROL

67   "The most difficult, complicated . . . problem": Shaw and Shaw 1977 II:207–208

CHAPTER 11: AUSTRIA—FIRST OFF THE MARK

72   "fearful stupidity": Bridge 1990:228
      "deeply offended": Albertini 1952 I:228
      "Our problem could be stated": Ibid.:230
74   "out of the internal and external difficulties": Berghahn 1993:93
      "will not come so soon": Ibid.:91
75   "Moltke had changed the treaty of 1879": Craig 1978:323

CHAPTER 12: FRANCE AND GERMANY MAKE THEIR PLAY

78   "If it comes to a war": Joll 1992:58
      called in foreign debts: Gooch and Temperley 1926:205
79   "the Fleet might be attacked": W. Churchill 1923:48
81   "The most significant military consequence of the second Moroccan crisis":
      Herrmann 1996:172

CHAPTER 13: ITALY GRASPS; THEN THE BALKANS DO TOO

84   "Nobody took the slightest notice": Varé 1938:70
85   Sazonov told the Serbian ambassador: Albertini 1952 I:486

CHAPTER 14: THE SLAVIC TIDE

88   "flung out of Europe": Röhl 1994:167
      to intervene to "keep the peace": Clark 2000:189
      should form a "ring": Ibid.:190
      "get on with it": Ibid.
      "Afterwards there will be time to talk": Ibid.
      "at the right time for us!": Ibid.
      not to "hinder the Bulgars": Ibid.
      "United States of the Balkans": Ibid.
      "I see absolutely no danger": Ibid.

88 He denied that the terms of the Triple Alliance: Ibid.
89 "existential struggle": Ibid.
    "have spoken in detail": Röhl 1994:168
    "under no circumstances": Ibid.:191
    "comprehensible to the German people": Ibid.
    "the position which I wanted": Ibid.
    Germany would back Austria "in all circumstances": Ibid.
90 "both Italy and England are on our side": Ibid.:170
    "for whatever reason": Ibid.
    "the consequences . . . incalculable": Ibid.:173
91 "idiocy . . . eternally into our enemy": Ibid.
92 Wilhelm told the Swiss minister: Ibid.:176
    "an even more galvanizing effect": Herrmann 1996:177
93 hard to find a rallying cry: Stevenson 1996:264

CHAPTER 15: EUROPE GOES TO THE BRINK

95 "an historic process": Albertini 1952 I:488
97 "swaddling clothes": Kautsky 1924:53
    "Against us": Ibid.
    "early war": Ibid.:54
    "Twaddle!": Ibid.

CHAPTER 16: MORE BALKAN TREMORS

100 "Two important people are against it": Geiss 1967:48
102 "Conrad first proposed preventive war": Strachan 2001:69
103 "When starting a world war": Geiss 1967:43

CHAPTER 17: AN AMERICAN TRIES TO STOP IT

104 "a slender, middle-aged man": Smith 1940:51
105 "the President had given very little thought": Ibid.:102
106 "House sees nobody": Ibid.:2
    "Even at sea": House Papers, 1914 Diary, May 23
    "Teutonic nations": Wall 1989:909
    "Why should these": Ibid.
    "It lies today": Ibid.:924
107 "tended to confirm": Link 1979:108–109
108 "as against the Oriental": House Papers, 1914 Diary, June 1
    House "spoke of the community": Ibid.
109 "I am glad to tell you": Link 1979:139
    German emperor had "seemed pleased": Ibid.:140
    "one feeling in common": Ibid.

09   "principals should get together": House Papers, 1914 Diary, June 24
     "in a fair way": Ibid.: June 1
     "my work in Germany": Ibid.: June 12
     "everything cluttered up with social affairs": Link 1979:190
     House . . . warned Grey: House Papers, 1914 Diary, June 27
10   "Neither England, Germany": Ibid.
     "the undeveloped countries": Ibid.: June 24
     "House had just come from Berlin": Grey 1925 I:323

CHAPTER 18: THE LAST WALTZ

14   Franz Ferdinand . . . "came to enjoy influence": Williamson 1991:21

CHAPTER 19: IN THE LAND OF THE ASSASSINS

20   Zeman . . . population pressures: Evans 1990:32
     "the poorest part of a poor province": Ibid.:23
22   "to make trouble for Pasic": Albertini 1952 II:63

CHAPTER 20: THE RUSSIAN CONNECTION

30   "used the Serb cause as a weapon": Albertini 1952 II:117
     "a party to the Black Hand": Thomson 1964:47
31   to have "that foolish Ferdinand" killed: Wilson 1995:85

CHAPTER 21: THE TERRORISTS STRIKE

32   The rest of the procession . . . depending upon whose account: Remak 1959;
     Morton 1989
34   "Of the other conspirators": Taylor 1964:72

CHAPTER 22: EUROPE YAWNS

38   "international illuminati": Mann 1983:18
     "it is a great worry less": Morton 1989:267
     "a certain easing of mood": Ibid.
39   "the death . . . came as a relief": Albertini 1952 II:115
     "a dispensation of Providence": Ibid.:216
41   "hardly mentioned": Keiger 2002:164
     "It has been curious to study": Zeman 1971:2
     "mine I displayed": Keiger 2002:102
43   Poincaré jested: Ibid.:160
     "the event almost failed to make any impression": Zeman 1971:2
     "no particular shock or dismay": Zweig 1943:216

CHAPTER 23: DISPOSING OF THE BODIES

144   "the whole officer corps": Albertini 1952 II:117
       "his full insignia": Ibid.

CHAPTER 24: ROUNDING UP THE SUSPECTS

146   Princip, "exhausted by his beating": Albertini 1952 II:42–43
       "people took me for a weakling": Dedijer 1966:197
147   Potiorek was able to cable: Albertini 1952 II:43
148   failed to forward or communicate it: Williamson 1991:193
       "nothing to indicate": Marshall 1964:25
       "very depressed": Kautsky 1924:63–64
       "He must have known it!": Ibid.
       "press are blaming Serbia": Great Britain 1915:10
       "both assassins are Austrian": Ibid.:11
       "put an end . . . to the anti-Serbian campaign": Ibid.:12
149   "Now or never!": Kautsky 1924:61
       "no sign of consternation": Great Britain 1915:9–10
       Gagarin was struck: Lieven 1983:140

CHAPTER 25: GERMANY SIGNS A BLANK CHECK

154   "Who authorized him": Kautsky 1924:61
155   "reckoning" with Serbia: Albertini 1952 II:125
156   time "to annihilate Serbia": Geiss 1967:66
       "Austria must beat the Serbs": Berghahn 1993:200
157   "a factor of political power": Kautsky 1924:69
158   authoritative work: Berghahn 1993
       "Germany . . . had surrendered": Williamson 1991:197
159   "the situation would be cleared up": Berghahn 1993:199
       "the Austrian government will demand": Ibid.
       Falkenhayn . . . not convinced: Geiss 1967:72
160   "Russians . . . will not join in": Ibid.:71
       Russia "was not . . . prepared": Clark 2000:203
       France . . . lacked heavy artillery: Geiss 1967:71

CHAPTER 26: THE GREAT DECEPTION

163   "childish!": Geiss 1967:90
164   Capelle recalled: Kautsky 1924:47
       Zenker: Ibid.:49
       "I shall not give in": Fischer 1975:478
165   "stiff but not impossible": Berghahn 1993:204
166   "thoroughly confident": Geiss 1967:105

166   telegram of congratulations: Kautsky 1924:95, 97
       "Too bad": Geiss 1967:114
167   "Austrian words": Albertini 1952 II:277

CHAPTER 28: THE SECRET IS KEPT

170   "Italian diplomats could not even arrange": Bosworth 1983:121
171   Williamson, who relates this story: Williamson 1991:201
       "Austro-Hungarian government are in no mood": Albertini 1952 II:184
       "Austria was capable of taking an irrevocable step": Ibid.
       "only a very small circle of men": Berghahn 1993:197

CHAPTER 29: THE *FAIT* IS NOT *ACCOMPLI*

175   "unacceptable to the dignity": Albertini 1952 II:184–85
176   "a larger measure of sovereign independence": *Encyclopaedia Britannica*, 11th ed.,
       s.v. "Bavaria"
       Schoen explained: Geiss 1967:127–30
177   "one expects a localization": Berghahn 1993:209
       "*practically excluded*": Kautsky 1924:113
       "a stagnant mood": Ibid.:126
       "the demands were really of such a nature": Ibid.:141
       In the words of . . . Morton: Morton 2001:298
178   On a motion from Berchtold: Geiss 1967:139
       "Berlin was beginning to get nervous": Ibid.
179   "should remain localized": Ibid.:142
       "he knew nothing about it": Ibid.:154
180   Rumbold . . . Eyre Crowe: Geiss 1967:159; Albertini 1952 II:212
       Bullitt: Fromkin 1995:98
       Moltke . . . asked . . . to provoke a world war soon: Röhl 1973:29
181   "everything that exists upside down": Berghahn 1993:201
       "a leap in the dark": Ibid.
       "paralyzed": Ibid.
       "The future belongs to Russia": Ibid.:201–202
182   As Grey writes: Grey 1925 I:283–90
       The Chancellor brooded: Berghahn 1993:209
183   Grey "believed that a peaceful solution": Kautsky 1924:144–45
       "an exceptional tranquility": W. Churchill 1923:178
       "The strange calm of the European situation": Ibid.:181
184   "the cry of Civil War": Hyde 1953:370
       King George . . . "*emotionné*": Brock and Brock 1985:122

CHAPTER 30: PRESENTING AN ULTIMATUM

185   "a kind of indictment": Albertini 1952 II:280
       Austria was preparing: Ibid.:282

187 the oft-quoted lines: W. Churchill 1923:193
188 "a real Armageddon": Brock and Brock 1985:122–23
     "Europe is trembling": R. Churchill 1969:1987–88
     "a document . . . so formidable": Great Britain 1915:30–31
     Lichnowsky reported: Kautsky 1924:184–85
189 "did not aim at a territorial gain": Albertini 1952 II:378
190 "Then it is war": Ibid.
     "You are setting fire to Europe": Ibid.:291
191 "Russia is rapidly becoming": Evans and Strandmann 1990:76
     "saw their position": Ibid.:77
     "ten states": Ibid.
     "242,000 were on strike": Ibid.
192 "enough for all": Massie 1996:186
193 "in strict confidence": Kautsky 1924:180
     "unable to counsel Vienna": Ibid.
     Berchtold an "Ass!": Ibid.:182
194 Hayne tells us: Hayne 1993:294–95
     "an . . . internal affair": Geiss 1967:180

CHAPTER 31: SERBIA MORE OR LESS ACCEPTS

195 A "pretty strong note": Görlitz 1961:5
     "to express his despair": Albertini 1952 II:348
196 Ballin . . . "disappointment" . . . "joy": Fischer 1975:464–65
197 "demands could bring about": Geiss 1967:200–201; Albertini 1952 II:372
198 "Bravo! One would not have believed it": Kautsky 1924:186
     "neither London . . . wants war": Evans and Strandmann 1990:102

CHAPTER 32: SHOWDOWN IN BERLIN

201 reports of the Saxon and Bavarian: Berghahn 1993:212
202 "the almost complete destruction of Moltke's papers 'precludes formal connec-
     tion' ": Mombauer 2001:186
     "would be pleased if war were to come": Ibid.:187
     "an opportunity rather than a threat": Ibid.
203 Russia's mobilization . . . smaller scale: Ibid.:200
204 As Conrad saw it . . . Austria would crush Serbia: W. Churchill 1931:120–26
     "the most modern in Europe": Keegan 1999:77–78

CHAPTER 33: JULY 26

206 "official hours . . . twelve to six": Steiner 1969:12
207 "War is thought imminent": Albertini 1952 II:390
     "Russia cannot allow Austria": Ibid.
     "Russia is trying to drag us": Brock and Brock 1985:125–26

208   "he thought there would be peace": Riddell 1986:84
       "Only a calendar of events": Steiner 1977:219
       "a European forum": Albertini 1952 II:404
209   "Berlin is playing with us": Geiss 1967:235
210   In Conrad's account: Ibid.:227
       He "urgently entreated" Germany: Kautsky 1924:220–21
211   Moltke . . . "very dissatisfied": Mombauer 2001:197

CHAPTER 34: JULY 27

212   "You have cooked the broth": Bülow 1931 III:184
213   Bethmann explained ". . . it is not possible for us to refuse": Fischer 1967:70
       "If Germany candidly told Sir E. Grey": Geiss 1967:236
215   The press lord . . . among those present: Riddell 1986:85
       "war . . . by no means impossible": R. Churchill 1969:1988
216   The small war . . . to a big one: Geiss 1967:239
       "Our entire future relations with England": Ibid.:240
       "it would never again be possible": Ibid.:241
       "war is inevitable": Albertini 1952 II:416
       "allow Russia to put herself in the wrong": Berghahn 1993:216
       "Austro-Hungarian note was so drawn up": Great Britain 1915:74

CHAPTER 35: JULY 28

217   "It has now been decided to fight": Herwig 1997:26
218   "singularly favorable situation": Berghahn 1993:212
       "every cause for war has vanished": Geiss 1967:256
       "never have ordered a mobilization": Clark 2000:208
       "Nevertheless, the piece of paper": Geiss 1967:256
       The Austrians were to be told . . . no longer: Clark 2000:208–209
219   "Perhaps the most striking thing": Ibid.:209
       "The Kaiser absolutely wants peace": Mombauer 2001:199
       "made confused speeches": Clark 2000:208
       "no longer had control": Herwig 1997:26
       House . . . "military oligarchy" . . . "determined on war": Ensor 1936:484
220   Serbian troops had opened fire: Albertini 1952 II:460–61
       "chiefly to frustrate . . . intervention": Kautsky 1924:243
221   "the frivolous provocation": Berghahn 1993:216
222   "upon a preparatory precautionary basis": R. Churchill 1967:692
       "everything tends towards catastrophe": Ibid.:694
       "It looks ominous": Brock and Brock 1985:161

CHAPTER 36: JULY 29

224   "Germany was likewise obliged to mobilize": Albertini 1952 II:499
       "war which will annihilate the civilization": Ibid.:488–89

224   Chancellor . . . "had collapsed": Ibid.:495
225   "in order to keep England neutral": Ibid.:498
       To his ambassador in Austria: Albertini 1952 III:1
226   "In order to prevent general catastrophe": Ibid.:2
       "Who rules in Berlin?": Mombauer 2001:205
       In diplomatic language: Albertini 1952 II:513–14
       "We have been trying to accomplish this": Kautsky 1924:319–22
       "unless Austria is willing": Ibid.:313
227   "England *alone*": Ibid.:319–22
       "It is one of the ironies of the case": Brock and Brock 1985:132
       "as darkness fell": W. Churchill 1923:212

                          CHAPTER 37: JULY 30

229   Stengers has shown: Wilson 1995:125
230   "all too late": Kautsky 1924:368
       "It will hardly be possible . . . Russia's shoulders": Ibid.:372
       "the incontrovertible suspicion": Ibid.
       "behind my back": Albertini 1952 III:2
231   "I have got to mobilize as well!": Ibid.:3
       could "remain mobile behind their frontier": Lieven 1983:146
       "Right, that is it": Kautsky 1924:375; Cimbala 1996:389
232   "Russia does not intend to wage war": Berghahn 1993:217
       "War must not be declared on Russia": Ibid.
       "His changes of mood": Mombauer 2001:205
       "Irresponsibility and weakness": Albertini 1952 III:34
233   "expectant and excited women": Bonham-Carter 1965:305
       Viviani cabled: Wilson 1995:127
       "in the precautionary measures": Albertini 1952 II:604
       "the prospect very black today": Brock and Brock 1985:136

                          CHAPTER 38: JULY 31

234   Jules Cambon . . . cabled: Hayne 1993:293
       Williamson suggests: Williamson 1991:207 *n.*122
235   "the peace of Europe . . . maintained": Albertini 1952 III:37
       "I thank you . . . for your mediation": Ibid.:56
       "extraordinarily near to war": Ibid.:62
       "There is still hope": Gilbert 1975:21
236   "keep out at almost all costs": Brock and Brock 1985:138
       " 'We shall all be ruined' ": Riddell 1986:85
       "very strong" . . . against intervention: Gilbert 1971:21
       Churchill told Smith: Ibid.:22

CHAPTER 39: AUGUST 1

37 "Ll. George—all for peace": Brock and Brock 1985:140
"It is our whole future": R. Churchill 1969:701
38 "I am most profoundly anxious": Ibid.
"these measures do not mean war": Massie 1996:258
39 "Nobody today can have a notion": Mombauer 2001:206
" 'Then we simply deploy' ": Albertini 1952 III:172
40 "my heart would break": Ibid.:176
"there must be some misunderstanding": Ibid.:177
41 "War declared by Germany on Russia": Beaverbrook 1960:29
42 "one of my strangest experiences": Brock and Brock 1985:140
"I run to the War Ministry": Evans and Strandmann 1990:120
"The mood is brilliant": Ibid.

CHAPTER 40: AUGUST 2

44 We have no obligation: Brock and Brock 1985:146
suggestions "of a military-political nature": Geiss 1967:179 ff.
45 France and Russia already had commenced: Kautsky 1924:496
"a war of aggression": Ibid.:501
"the Grand Duchy is being occupied": Ibid.:482
"attack by the French": Ibid.:483
46 "The question as to whether": Ibid.
Britain was bound to come to its aid: Albertini 1952 III:410

CHAPTER 41: AUGUST 3

47 German forces had done so too: Kautsky 1924:527
"not a single French soldier": Ibid.
"with almost Austrian crassness": Brock and Brock 1985:148
48 according to Barbara Tuchman: Tuchman 1963:139
"Grey made a most remarkable speech": Jenkins 1966:329
Violet Asquith asked: Bonham-Carter 1965:312

CHAPTER 42: AUGUST 4

50 As A. J. P. Taylor tells us: Taylor 1965:2–3
"a panic in Berlin": Evans and Strandmann 1990:116
Moltke told Tirpitz: Ibid.

CHAPTER 43: SHREDDING THE EVIDENCE

51 suppression or destruction of evidence: Herwig 1997 and the Herwig chapter in
Winter/Parker/Habeck 2000 are followed in this chapter.
53 Röhl . . . "discovered in a chest": Röhl 1973:17

CHAPTER 46: THE KEY TO WHAT HAPPENED

273   Fellner . . . "In this hard struggle": Wilson 1995:22
274   "There was certainly no logic": Howard 2002:28

CHAPTER 48: WHO COULD HAVE PREVENTED IT?

284   why, since "War had been avoided": Joll 1992:234

CHAPTER 50: COULD IT HAPPEN AGAIN?

293   "the nations slithered": Mombauer 2002:95
       "the unleashing of the First World War": Aron 1990:275

CHAPTER 52: AUSTRIA'S WAR

301   no longer was a military great power: Keegan 1999:170
       it had lost 1,268,000 men: Ibid.
       "If only I knew for what": Herwig 1997:91
       "cost him . . . Gina": Ibid.:92
       "I have no home": Ibid.:96
302   "would have had me shot": Ibid.:94

CHAPTER 53: GERMANY'S WAR

305   *this war which I prepared*": Mombauer 2001:281

BIBLIOGRAPHY

Adams, Henry. 1918. *The Education of Henry Adams: An Autobiography.* Boston: Houghton Mifflin.

Albertini, Luigi. 1952. *The Origins of the War of 1914.* Translated and edited by Isabella M. Massey. 3 vols. Oxford: Oxford University Press.

Aron, Raymond. 1990. *Memoirs: Fifty Years of Political Reflection.* New York: Holmes & Meier.

Bartlett, C. J. 1994. *The Global Conflict: The International Rivalry of the Great Powers, 1880–1990,* 2nd ed. London: Longman.

Beaverbrook, Lord. 1960. *Politicians and the War, 1914–1916.* London: Oldbourne.

Beckett, Ian F. W. 2001. *The Great War: 1914–1918.* Harlow, Eng.: Longman.

Berghahn, V. R. 1993. *Germany and the Approach of War in 1914,* 2nd ed. New York: St. Martin's.

Bonham-Carter, Violet. 1965. *Winston Churchill as I Knew Him.* London: Eyre & Spottiswoode and Collins.

Bosworth, Richard. 1983. *Italy and the Approach of the First World War.* London: Macmillan.

Braudel, Fernand. 1979. *Afterthoughts on Material Civilization and Capitalism.* Translated by Patricia Ranum. Baltimore: Johns Hopkins paperback.

Bridge, F. R. 1990. *The Habsburg Monarchy Among the Great Powers, 1815–1918.* New York: Berg.

Brock, Michael, and Eleanor Brock. 1985. *H. H. Asquith: Letters to Venetia Stanley.* Oxford and New York: Oxford University Press.

Bülow, Prince Bernhard von. 1931. *Memoirs.* 3 vols. Boston: Little, Brown.

Cawood, Ian, and David McKinnon Bell. 2001. *The First World War.* London: Routledge.

Churchill, Randolph S. 1967. *Winston S. Churchill: Young Statesman—1901–1914.* Boston: Houghton Mifflin.

———. 1969. *Winston S. Churchill. Companion*, Volume II, Part 3, *1911–1914.* Boston: Houghton Mifflin.

Churchill, Winston S. 1923. *The World Crisis: 1911–1914.* London: Thornton Butterworth.

———. 1931. *The World Crisis: The Eastern Front.* London: Thornton Butterworth.

Cimbala, Stephen J. 1996. "Steering Through Rapids: Russian Mobilization and World War I," *Journal of Slavic Military Studies* 9:376–98.

Clark, Christopher M. 2000. *Kaiser Wilhelm II.* Harlaw, Essex, Eng.: Longman.

Cowley, Robert, and Geoffrey Parker, eds. 1996. *The Reader's Companion to Military History.* Boston: Houghton Mifflin.

Craig, Gordon A. 1978. *Germany: 1866–1945.* New York: Oxford University Press.

Dangerfield, George. 1961. *The Strange Death of Liberal England.* New York: Capricorn.

Dedijer, Vladimir. 1964. "Sarajevo Fifty Years After," *Foreign Affairs* 42, no. 4 (July 1964).

———. 1966. *The Road to Sarajevo.* New York: Simon & Schuster.

Earle, Edward Mead, ed. 1943. *Makers of Modern Strategy: Military Thought from Machiavelli to Hitler.* Princeton: Princeton University Press.

Eksteins, Modris. 2000. *Rites of Spring: The Great War and the Birth of the Modern Age.* London: Papermac.

Ensor, R. C. K. 1936. *England: 1870–1914.* Oxford: Oxford University Press.

Evans, R. J. W., and Hartmut Pogge von Strandmann, eds. 1990. *The Coming of the First World War.* Oxford: Clarendon.

Ferguson, Niall. 1998. *The Pity of War.* New York: Basic Books.

Fischer, Fritz. 1967. *Germany's Aims in the First World War.* New York: Norton.

———. 1975. *War of Illusions: German Policies from 1911 to 1914.* London: Chatto & Windus.

Foley, Robert T. 2003. *Alfred Von Schlieffen's Military Writings.* London: Cass.

Fromkin, David. 1995. *In the Time of the Americans: FDR, Truman, Eisenhower, Marshall, MacArthur—The Generation That Changed America's Role in the World.* New York: Knopf.

Fussell, Paul. 1975. *The Great War and Modern Memory.* New York: Oxford University Press.

Geiss, Imanuel, ed. 1967. *July 1914—The Outbreak of the First World War: Selected Documents.* New York: Scribner's.

Gilbert, Martin. 1971. *Winston S. Churchill: The Challenge of War.* Boston: Houghton Mifflin.

————. 1975. *Winston S. Churchill: The Stricken World*. Boston: Houghton Mifflin.

Glenny, Misha. 1999. *The Balkans, 1804–1999: Nationalism, War and the Great Powers*. London: Granta.

Gooch, G. P., and Harold Temperley, eds. 1926. *British Documents on the Origins of the War*, vol. 11. London: Controller of Her Britannic Majesty's Stationery Office.

Gooch, John. 1989. *Army, State and Society in Italy, 1870–1915*. New York: St. Martin's.

Görlitz, Walter, ed. 1961. *The Kaiser and His Court*. New York: Harcourt, Brace & World.

Great Britain. 1915. Abridged edition 1919. *War 1914: Punishing the Serbs*. London: Stationery Office.

Grey, Viscount of Fallodon. 1925. *Twenty-Five Years*. 2 vols. London: Hodder and Stoughton.

Halévy, Elie. 1930. *The World Crisis of 1914–1918: An Interpretation*. Oxford: Oxford University Press.

Hayne, M. B. 1993. *The French Foreign Office and the Origins of the First World War: 1898–1914*. Oxford: Clarendon Press.

Herrmann, David G. 1996. *The Arming of Europe and the Making of the First World War*. Princeton: Princeton University Press.

Herwig, Holger H. 1997. *The First World War: Germany and Austria-Hungary, 1914–1918*. London: Arnold.

House, Edward M. Papers. New Haven: Yale University Library.

Howard, Michael. 2001. "The Great War: Mystery or Error?" *The National Interest* 64 (Summer 2001).

————. 2002. *The First World War*. Oxford: Oxford University Press.

Hughes, Michael. 2000. *Diplomacy Before the Russian Revolution: Britain, Russia and the Old Diplomacy, 1894–1917*. New York: St. Martin's.

Hunt, Barry, and Adrian Preston, eds. 1977. *War Aims and Strategic Policy in the Great War*. London: Croom Helm.

Hyde, H. Montgomery. 1953. *Carson*. London: Heinemann.

Jannen, William, Jr. 1997. *The Lions of July: Prelude to War, 1914*. Novato, Calif.: Presidio.

Jarausch, Konrad H. 1973. *The Enigmatic Chancellor*. New Haven: Yale University Press.

Jenkins, Roy. 1966. *Asquith: Portrait of a Man and an Era*. New York: Dutton.

Joll, James. 1979. "Politics and the Freedom to Choose," in Alan Ryan, ed., *The Idea of Freedom: Essays in Honour of Isaiah Berlin*. New York: Oxford University Press.

————. 1992. *The Origins of the First World War*, 2nd ed. Harlow, Essex, Eng.: Longman.

Kautsky, Karl. 1924. *Outbreak of the World War: German Documents Collected by Karl Kautsky*. Translated by the Carnegie Endowment for International Peace. New York: Oxford University Press.

Keegan, John. 1999. *The First World War*. New York: Knopf.

Keiger, J. F. V. 1983. *France and the Origins of the First World War*. London: Macmillan.

————. 2002. *Raymond Poincaré*. Cambridge, Eng.: Cambridge University Press paperback.

Kennan, George F. 1951. *American Diplomacy: 1900–1950*. New York: Mentor.

———. 1979. *The Decline of Bismarck's European Order*. Princeton: Princeton University Press.

Kennedy, Paul M. 1980. *The Rise of the Anglo-German Antagonism*. London: Allen & Unwin.

———, ed. 1985. *The War Plans of the Great Powers*. Boston: Allen & Unwin paperback.

Keynes, John Maynard. 1920. *The Economic Consequences of the Peace*. New York: Harcourt, Brace and Howe.

Lafore, Laurence. 1971. *The Long Fuse: An Interpretation of the Origins of World War I*, 2nd ed. New York: HarperCollins.

Lieven, Dominic. 1983. *Russia and the Origins of the First World War*. London: Macmillan.

———. 2000. *Empire: The Russian Empire and Its Rivals*. London: Murray.

Link, Arthur S., ed. 1979. *The Papers of Woodrow Wilson*, vol. 30. Princeton: Princeton University Press.

Ludwig, Emil. 1929. *July '14*. New York: Putnam.

MacKenzie, David. 1989. *Apis: The Congenial Conspirator: The Life of Colonel Dragutin T. Dimitrijevic*. New York: Columbia University Press.

———. 1995. *The "Black Hand" on Trial: Salonika, 1917*. New York: Columbia University Press.

———. 1998. *The Exoneration of the "Black Hand": 1917–1953*. New York: Columbia University Press.

McLean, Roderick R. 2001. *Royalty and Diplomacy in Europe, 1890–1914*. Cambridge, Eng.: Cambridge University Press.

McNeill, William H. 1976. *Plagues and Peoples*. Garden City, N.Y.: Anchor/Doubleday.

Mann, Thomas. 1983. *Reflections of a Nonpolitical Man*. Translated by Walter D. Morris. New York: Ungar.

Marder, Arthur J. 1961. *From the Dreadnought to Scapa Flow: The Royal Navy in the Fisher Era, 1904–1914*. London: Oxford University Press.

Marshall, S. L. A. 1964. *The American Heritage History of World War I*. New York: Simon & Schuster.

Martel, Gordon. 1996. *The Origins of the First World War*, 2nd ed. London and New York: Longman.

Massie, Robert K. 1991. *Dreadnought: Britain, Germany, and the Coming of the Great War*. New York: Random House.

———. 1996. *Nicholas and Alexandra*. London: Indigo.

Micklethwait, John, and Adrian Wooldridge. 2000. *A Future Perfect: The Essentials of Globalization*. New York: Crown.

Miller, Steven E., Sean M. Lynn-Jones, and Stephen Van Evera, eds. 1991. *Military Strategy and the Origins of the First World War*. Princeton: Princeton University Press.

Mombauer, Annika. 2001. *Helmuth Von Moltke and the Origins of the First World War*. Cambridge, Eng.: Cambridge University Press.

———. 2002. *The Origins of the First World War: Controversies and Consensus.* Harlow, Eng.: Longman.

Morgenthau, Hans J. 1978. *Politics Among Nations: The Struggle for Power and Peace,* 5th ed. rev. New York: Knopf.

Morris, Edmund. 1979. *The Rise of Theodore Roosevelt.* New York: Coward, McCann & Geoghegan.

Morton, Frederic. 1989. *Thunder at Twilight: Vienna 1913/1914.* New York: Scribner's. Paperback edition 2001. Cambridge, Mass.: Da Capo.

Nicolson, Colin. 2001. *The First World War: Europe 1914–1918.* Harlow, Eng.: Longman.

Paret, Peter. 1986. *Makers of Modern Strategy: From Machiavelli to the Nuclear Age.* Princeton: Princeton University Press.

Ponting, Clive. 2002. *Thirteen Days: The Road to the First World War.* London: Chatto & Windus.

Porch, Douglas. 1986. *The Conquest of Morocco.* New York: Fromm.

Prior, Robin, and Trevor Wilson. 2001. *The First World War.* London: Cassell paperback.

Remak, Joachim. 1959. *Sarajevo.* New York: Criterion.

Riddell, Sir George. 1986. *The Riddell Diaries, 1908–1923.* London: Athlone.

Robbins, Keith. 1993. *The First World War.* Oxford and New York: Oxford University Press paperback.

Röhl, John C. G. 1994. *The Kaiser and His Court: Wilhelm II and the Government of Germany.* Cambridge, Eng.: Cambridge University Press.

———. 1998. *Young Wilhelm.* Cambridge, Eng.: Cambridge University Press.

———, ed. 1973. *1914: Delusion or Design.* New York: St. Martin's.

Schorske, Carl E. 1980. *Fin-de-Siècle Vienna: Politics and Culture.* New York: Knopf.

Seaman, L. C. B. 1955. *From Vienna to Versailles.* London: Methuen.

Shaw, Stanford J., and Ezel Kurel Shaw. 1977. *History of the Ottoman Empire and Modern Turkey.* Vol. 2, *Reform, Revolution, and Republic: The Rise of Modern Turkey, 1808–1975.* Cambridge, Eng.: Cambridge University Press.

Smith, Arthur D. Howden. 1940. *Mr. House of Texas.* New York and London: Funk & Wagnalls.

Steiner, Zara S. 1969. *The Foreign Office and Foreign Policy, 1898–1914.* Cambridge, Eng.: Cambridge University Press.

———. 1977. *Britain and the Origins of the First World War.* London: Macmillan.

Stern, Fritz. 1999. *Einstein's German World.* Princeton: Princeton University Press. Penguin paperback edition, 2001.

Stevenson, David. 1991. *The First World War and International Politics.* Oxford: Oxford University Press.

———. 1996. *Armaments and the Coming of War: Europe 1904–1914.* Oxford: Oxford University Press.

———. 1997. *The Outbreak of the First World War: 1914 in Perspective.* New York: St. Martin's.

Strachan, Hew. 2001. *The First World War.* Vol. 1, *To Arms.* Oxford: Oxford University Press.

Taylor, A. J. P. 1948. *The Habsburg Monarchy: 1809–1918*. London: Hamish Hamilton.
———. 1950. *From Napoleon to Stalin*. London: Hamish Hamilton.
———. 1954. *The Struggle for Mastery in Europe: 1848–1918*. Oxford: Oxford University Press.
———. 1956. *Englishmen and Others*. London: Hamish Hamilton.
———. 1963. *The First World War: An Illustrated History*. London: Hamish Hamilton.
———. 1964. *Politics in Wartime and Other Essays*. London: Hamish Hamilton.
———. 1965. *English History: 1914–1945*. Oxford: Oxford University Press.
———. 1966. *From Sarajevo to Potsdam*. New York: Harcourt, Brace & World.
Thomson, George Malcolm. 1964. *The Twelve Days: 24 July to 4 August 1914*. New York: Putnam.
Tuchman, Barbara W. 1963. *The Guns of August*. New York: Dell.
———. 1966. *The Proud Tower: A Portrait of the World Before the War, 1890–1914*. New York: Macmillan. Papermac paperback, 1980.
Turner, L. C. F. 1970. *Origins of the First World War*. New York: Norton.
United Kingdom. 1999. *War 1914: Punishing the Serbs*. London: The Stationery Office.
Varé, Daniele. 1938. *Laughing Diplomat*. London: John Murray.
Wall, Joseph Frazier. 1989. *Andrew Carnegie*. Pittsburgh: University of Pittsburgh Press.
Weber, Eugen. 1986. *France: Fin de Siècle*. Cambridge, Mass.: Harvard University Press.
Williamson, Samuel R., Jr. 1991. *Austria-Hungary and the Origins of the First World War*. London: Macmillan.
Wilson, Keith, ed. 1995. *Decisions for War, 1914*. London: UCL.
Winter, Jay, Geoffrey Parker, and Mary R. Habeck, eds. 2000. *The Great War and the Twentieth Century*. New Haven: Yale University Press.
Wohl, Robert. 1979. *The Generation of 1914*. Cambridge, Mass.: Harvard University Press.
Wolff, Theodor. 1936. *The Eve of 1914*. New York: Knopf.
Zeman, Z. A. B. 1971. *The Gentlemen Negotiators: A Diplomatic History of the First World War*. New York: Macmillan.
Zuber, Terence. 2003. *Inventing the Schlieffen Plan: German War Planning, 1871–1914*. Oxford: Oxford University Press.
Zweig, Stefan. 1943. *The World of Yesterday*. New York: Viking.

ACKNOWLEDGMENTS

In 1999, or thereabouts, Joy de Menil, to whom I had been introduced briefly at a party, sent me a note favorably comparing my descriptions of the July crisis of 1914—in earlier writings—with accounts by other historians that had just appeared. The thought stayed with me when I had lunch soon afterwards with Ashbel Green, my editor at Knopf. I asked Ash what sort of book he wanted me to write for him next. He said he hoped for a work dealing with European history in a narrow time frame. The idea came immediately to mind: the thirty-seven days from the assassination of Archduke Franz Ferdinand until the outbreak of the First World War. So many brilliant new monographs had been researched and written by scholars in recent decades that I felt sure that if I put them together a new picture of the July crisis might well emerge.

As I started doing my reading for the book, I was struck by how many preconceived ideas had to be discarded. From such persuasive writings as those quoted in the text by John Maynard Keynes and A. J. P. Taylor, I had taken away the notion that prewar Europe lived in idyllic and peaceful times. Instead it was a torn, conflicted world caught up in the grip of an arms race that one might well have called suicidal. I searched for a metaphor and found it in commercial aviation: on the one hand, forces in the air that threaten destruction but at first, because they are invisible, remain unnoticed by the passengers; on the other, the contrast between passengers oblivious to danger, and captains and cabin crews keenly aware of it. I remembered reading news accounts of a particular flight that might illustrate my point. Elie Montazeri, a former student of mine, generously volunteered to do the necessary research, and conducted it expertly. To Joy, to Ash, and to Elie, many thanks for getting me started.

I wanted facilities in which to work undisturbed during the summers, when academic holidays free us to write. I am grateful to Richard Herland and Martine Callandrey for providing me with everything I needed in this respect: for, indeed, creating a one-person writers' colony for me at their home in Cap d'Antibes, France, summer after summer. My thanks, too, to Gwenyth E. Todd for her extraordinary generosity in supplying me with a peaceful place to work during August 2003, and to Robert Baker for having arranged it, and much more.

Carol Shookhoff managed to read my longhand and convert my manuscript into something publishable. She has my admiration as well as my thanks. I am grateful, too, to Dr. Ilya Zaslowsky for researches in the Russian archives on my behalf.

For close readings of the finished manuscript, thoughtful suggestions, and challenging criticisms on practically every page, I am immensely grateful to Timothy Dickinson, to Professor Emeritus Alain Silvera of Bryn Mawr College, and to Dr. Annika Mombauer of The Open University in Great Britain. Even more than usually is the case, I must stress that these readers bear no responsibility for the preceding text or for the opinions expressed in it.

My warm and constant thanks to Ash Green, best of editors, and to his ever helpful assistant Luba Ostashevsky. My thanks, too, to the wonder-working Carol Janeway; may she always be on my team.

As always I am grateful to my agent Suzanne Gluck, the best there is or, I think, ever will be. My thanks to her, and to her able and cheerful assistants, first Emily Nurkin and now Christine Price, who aid and assist with unobtrusive efficiency.

My thanks, too, to Robert and Jeanne-Mary Sigmon for locating books and photos in Britain that I needed.

Lunches on Sundays with Professor Ralph Buultjens, with their stimulating conversations, provided me with new perspectives, for which I am thankful.

Finally, my thanks, as always, to James Chace, my lifelong literary advisor. In a sense, all my works are dedicated to him.

DF
Antigny-le-Chateau (Cote d'Or), France
August 27, 2003

INDEX

David Fromkin is Frederick S. Pardee Professor, University Professor, and Professor of History at Boston University. He is the author of In the Time of the Americans, *a History Book Club selection, and the national best-seller* A Peace to End All Peace, *which was a finalist for both the National Book Critics Circle Award and the Pulitzer Prize, and was singled out by the* New York Times Book Review *as an Editors' Choice, one of the thirteen Best Books of the Year. He lives in New York City.*

A NOTE ON THE TYPE

This book was set in Janson, a typeface long thought to have been made by the Dutchman Anton Janson, who was a practicing typefounder in Leipzig during the years 1668–1687. However, it has been conclusively demonstrated that these types are actually the work of Nicholas Kis (1650–1702), a Hungarian, who most probably learned his trade from the master Dutch typefounder Dirk Voskens. The type is an excellent example of the influential and sturdy Dutch types that prevailed in England up to the time William Caslon (1692–1766) developed his own incomparable designs from them.

COMPOSED BY
North Market Street Graphics, Lancaster, Pennsylvania

PRINTED AND BOUND BY
Berryville Graphics, Berryville, Virginia

MAP BY
David Lindroth

DESIGNED BY
Iris Weinstein